A1

# CULTURAL POLITICS

**Writing Ireland:** colonialism, nationalism and culture
*David Cairns and Shaun Richards*

lscape

© Steve Bell 1989 — AFTER CLAUDE LORRAIN

# Reading landscape

## country – city – capital

*edited by* Simon Pugh

MANCHESTER UNIVERSITY PRESS
MANCHESTER and NEW YORK

distributed exclusively in the USA and Canada by ST. MARTIN'S PRESS

Published by Manchester University Press
Oxford Road, Manchester M13 9PL, UK
and Room 400, 175 Fifth Avenue,
New York, NY 10010, USA

Distributed exclusively in the USA and Canada
by St. Martin's Press, Inc.
175 Fifth Avenue, New York, NY 10010, USA

British Library cataloguing in publication data
Reading landscape : country, city, capital. – (Cultural
   politics).
   1. Landscape. Aesthetics
   I. Pugh, Simon    II. Series
   719'.01

Library of Congress cataloging in publication data
Reading landscape : country, city, capital / edited by Simon Pugh.
      p.  cm. – (Cultural politics)
   ISBN 0-7190-2979-1. – ISBN 0-7190-3189-3 (pbk.)
   1. Pastoral art.  2.  Ut pictura poesis (Aesthetics)
   3. Picturesque, The.  4. Nature (Aesthetics)  5. Politics and
   culture.  I. Pugh, Simon.  II. Series.
   N8205.R4    1990
   701–dc20              89-12742

   ISBN 0 7190 2979 1 hardback
         0 7190 3189 3 paperback

Photoset in Linotron Joanna
by Northern Phototypesetting Company, Bolton

Printed in Great Britain
by Bell and Bain Ltd, Glasgow

# Contents

# Illustrations

# Notes on the contributors

John Barrell is Professor of English at the University of Sussex. He is the author of The idea of landscape and the sense of place 1730–1840: an approach to the poetry of John Clare (1972), The dark side of the landscape: the rural poor in English painting 1730–1840 (1980) and The political theory of painting from Reynolds to Hazlitt (1980).

Stephen Bann is Professor of Modern Cultural Studies at the University of Kent and the author of The Clothing of Clio: a study of the representation of history in nineteenth-century Britain and France (1984) and The true vine (1989). He has contributed articles on Bernard Lassus and Ian Hamilton Finlay to the Journal of Garden History.

Ann Bermingham is an Associate Professor of Art History at the University of California, Irvine. She is author of Landscape and ideology: the English rustic tradition, 1740–1860 (1986).

Stephen Daniels is Lecturer in Geography at the University of Nottingham. He is the co-editor (with Denis Cosgrove) of The iconography of landscape (1988) and of Landscape, image, text to be published by Polity Press in 1990.

Nicholas Green is Lecturer in Art and Cultural History at the University of East Anglia. He is author of The spectacle of nature. Landscape and bourgeois culture in nineteenth-century France (1990).

Fred Inglis is Reader in Arts Education at the University of Warwick. He is author of The management of ignorance (1985) and Popular culture and political power (1989).

John Murdoch is Assistant Director (Collections) at the Victoria and Albert Museum. He organised the exhibition The discovery of the Lake District at the Victoria and Albert Museum in 1984, and is the author of The English miniature (1981) and The Lake District: a sort of national property (1986).

Marcia Pointon is Professor of History of Art at the University of Sussex. She is author of William Dyce, R.A. 1806–64: a critical biography (1979), The Bonington Circle – English Watercolour and Anglo-French Landscape, 1790–1855 (1985), Bonington, Francia and Wyld (1985), Mulready (1986) and she is the editor of the collection of essays, Pre-Raphaelites re-viewed (1989).

Simon Pugh is Director of Cultural Studies at Central St Martin's College of Art and Design (The London Institute). He is author of Garden–Nature–Language (1988).

John Roberts is an art critic and author of Postmodernism, politics and art to be published by Manchester University Press in 1990.

David Solkin is Lecturer in History of Art at the Courtauld Institute. He was the curator of the exhibition Richard Wilson, the landscape of reaction at the Tate Gallery in London (1982).

John Taylor is Lecturer in Photographic History at Wolverhampton Polytechnic. He is editor of Ten. 8 International Photography Magazine and author of War/photography – photographic realism in the press (1990).

# Acknowledgements

I would like to express my gratitude to the following: Joy Williams, Bodley Head Ltd and Jonathan Cape Ltd for permission to reprint Raymond Williams's 'Between country and city'; *Turner Studies* for permission to reprint Stephen Daniels's 'The implications of industry: Turner and Leeds'; and Neil McWilliam, editor of *Art History*, the Association of Art Historians and Basil Blackwell Ltd for permission to reprint David Solkin's 'The battle of the Ciceros: Richard Wilson and the politics of landscape in the age of John Wilkes' (first version), Ann Bermingham's 'Reading Constable' and the part of Marcia Pointon's 'Aesthetic and commodity: an examination of the function of the verbal in Turner's artistic practice' that appeared previously under the title 'Turner: language and letter'. In addition, the following kindly gave permission to reproduce works: the Society of Antiquaries of London for 'East Prospect of Leeds, 1720'; Wadsworth Atheneum, Hartford (The Ella Gallup Sumner and Mary Catlin Sumner Collection) for Claude Lorrain's *St George and the Dragon*; and Yale Center for British Art, Paul Mellon Collection, for J. M. W. Turner's *Leeds*.

S.P.

Dedication
To Raymond Williams
August 1921 to January 1988, in memoriam

# Introduction: Stepping out into the open
## Simon Pugh

'Landscape' and its setting, the countryside and the rural, are in the news: the 'greening of capitalism', the 'little Englandism' heritage industry and one of the moral panics of the late 1980s, rural violence (itself a contradictory phrase), are three examples. Landscape in recent years, as Raphael Samuel argues, has stood as a surrogate for more politicised notions of nationhood (a displaced expression of sentiments of attachment which are denied expression elsewhere) and as a source of spiritual strength, a 'moral therapy'.[1] 'Landscape' signifies a seductive mixture of peace and solitude with security and visual pleasure. Yet despite the discrediting, by writers like Raymond Williams and Peter Laslett, of the prevalent model 'rural = gemeinschaft = good' (humanity-leisure-individual-the weekend) versus 'urban = gesellschaft = bad' (materialism-work-society-the week) in, for example, the work of German sociologist Ferdinand Tonnies a hundred years ago, the rural world and its landscape idyll still connote peace, health, utopia, community, as well as 'organic' food and 'getting away from it all' (both the 'little place in the country' and the country house). If it could be argued that the reframing of the functions of landscape is especially prevalent during the passage from one economic order to another (Venice at the beginning of the sixteenth century, Holland in the seventeenth, Britain in the eighteenth, France in the nineteenth), the ideological uses of landscape now in the 1980s should give pause for thought. In examining the relationship between landscape and the country, the city and capital, this collection of essays scrutinises historical aspects of landscape from the mid-eighteenth century when landscape, its design and its mode of representation, were part of the ideological setting for the passage from rural to metropolitan capitalism. If the 'city' is now 'capital', this mode of production developed its particular characteristic effects first in the English rural economy (phrases like 'the bull market', 'industrial village' and 'business park' indicate the persistence of rural imagery). Such effects (increase of production, the re-ordering of the physical world, human displacement, destruction of the environment) were first evident in rural eighteenth-century Britain and subsequently extended not only to the cities but also to colonies and then the whole world. The design of landscape and the mode of its representation became signifiers of the way that the country-side and its workers are controlled and how power is structured and made evident. In Britain, representations of the beautiful in nature, initially signifying a critique of absolutism and a celebration of the 'natu-ralness' of English constitutional law, quickly lost this critical edge once it became apparent that bourgeois emancipation led not to a less but a more reified empirical world.

That landscape imagery is contested political terrain has been well explored in the work of writers like Raymond Williams and John Barrell In his essay on Richard Wilson, David Solkin shows how landscape painting was used to define moral ground around the scandal of Wilkes and liberty. Wilson's argument, adumbrated in his 1770 *Cicero and his friends*, proposes that patrician power is one with the order of nature. An idealised landscape becomes a moral lesson legitimating political authority. The rhetoric of landscape is also a field for the civil definitions of 'the public' and 'the private' and of class differentiation. The 'public' panorama, as John Barrell shows, connotes the 'notion of a wider society', abstract reasoning, classification, and surveys not individual occupations but their relations. The 'private', occluded view is 'narrow', conceals the distance, and sees objects in and for themselves as objects of 'consumption and possession', without understanding their relation. The ways of seeing landscape, from a high point able to view land and sea, town and country (surveying the plan), or imprisoned within a few acres at the bottom of a hill (caught in the maze), become a metaphor for those who organise and 'comprehend' (with Kantian 'disinterest') and those who are 'comprehended', for those who understand society and those who are its 'objects'. Stephen Bann describes this distinction as being either 'well in' or on the outside looking in. A correct taste in landscape and a commanding view of the scene establishes 'position' and the right to generalise. This, of course, 'coincides' with ownership of heritable property in land and the possession of a sufficient 'eminence' to look down on the world.

This serious moral ground sets the scene for much of the discussion of landscape that was to follow. How landscape is 'read' illustrates the primary role that discourses of landscape play in the field of cultural contestation. This collection of essays proposes that landscape and its representations are a 'text' and are, as such, 'readable' like any other cultural form. This readability can take many forms. It can be argued that the discourse of 'landscape' and the 'rural' was first negotiated through verbal modes of representation (literature, agricultural writing, 'natural history'), through the work of Theocritus, Virgil, Pliny and Columella, and that our experience of landscape, instanced in the example from the seventeenth-century writer Norgate cited by Gombrich,[2] is determined by descriptive language which modifies, even constitutes ways of seeing landscape. The verbal interpellates the visual. Ann Bermingham and Marcia Pointon both delineate the dependence of the visual on the verbal in the practice of Constable and Turner respectively. Turner employs many 'languages': of poetry, belles-lettres, technology, the market economy. His writing, and writings on him, disclose apparent contradictions between 'the assumed specialness of the work of art and the work as product of a set of economic circumstances' (Pointon). These 'languages' question the specificity of the visual, the hegemony of painting as the landscape mode and the visual as the primary property of pictures at a time when a plurality of landscape modes from dioramas and the postcard to the rural cottage and the country jaunt begin to compete as 'historically pertinent visual structures' (Green). The development of the Lake District villa is, as John Murdoch shows, a case in point. In the nineteenth-century city, landscape imagery is not the 'mediated reflex' that reflects interest in landscape and the rural but, according to Nicholas Green, the very 'vocabulary' that constructs that interest. This 'interest' opens up the parameters of what landscape imagery is, a spectacle of nature within the city, a pleasure to compete with other commodities for sale, display and consumption in the arcades and shops of the metropolis. Landscape imagery is marketed on an increasingly popular level. John Taylor argues that early landscape photography was caught between the landscape as amenity (and hence as a commodity) and its 'cockneyfication' (Henry James) and a class-based language of 'dignity', 'propriety', and 'comeliness' which (especially through SCAPA) sought to conserve and preserve the landscape from 'the lower orders'. An Edenic landscape can be saved 'in pictures' and the countryside both celebrated and avoided as a talisman of national life. The work of photographers like H. P. Robinson perpetuates the traditional idea of the countryside as a labour-free Arcadia, peopled with 'folk', descendants of Dresden china, Petit Trianon shepherdesses and progenitors of the Volksgemeinschaft of the Third Reich. In a way that anticipates the 1980s, photographs of the English countryside reinforce nationhood: 'the farmhouse in the hollow, the sheepfold on the hill have rendered their share in the making of England, and in the building up of that race whose sons are emulating on the battlefield the deeds of their forefathers . . .' says the text accompanying 125 photographs of The English countryside published by Batsford in 1915. In the 1980s, the mood of this 'little Englandism' reappears as a revenge against modernism and a return to traditional ways. In the 1980s Garden Festivals, as John Roberts shows, the pursuit of leisure and heritage proposes to reverse industrial and urban decline.

But the response to landscape is also one of the most direct forms of what Adorno calls 'aesthetic immanence'. The critic deconstructing landscape imagery must also be prepared to countenance that rich vein of aesthetic experience which accords (for example, in Proust) the appreciation of a hawthorn hedge the status of a 'primal phenomenon of aesthetic behaviour' (Adorno). Even *Kulturlandschaft* (culturescape, heritage), with its promotion of phoney togetherness and authenticity especially prevalent in advertising, Adorno argues, could in a state of freedom from nationalism be reappropriated along with the historical past. When reviewing the 1859 Salon, Baudelaire ignores the landscape paintings with this admission:

I long for the return of the dioramas whose enormous, crude magic subjects me to the spell of a useful illusion. I prefer looking at the backdrop paintings of the stage where I find my favourite dreams treated with consummate skill and tragic concision. Those things, so completely false, are for that reason much closer to the truth, whereas the majority of our landscape painters are liars, precisely because they fail to lie.

If the experience of landscape-as-nature in the city is an illusion, what Walter Benjamin calls Baudelaire's 'magic of distance' judges reality with 'tragic concision' as the recognition of a subtle, seductive but necessary counterfeit. This cannot be dismissed as just false consciousness, any more than the activities of the suburban 'gnome' gardener or the modern-day *habitants–paysagistes* who transform 'small open spaces available to them in ways which completely bypassed conventional good taste' (Bann). As Fred Inglis points out, the 'incidents' of landscape can evoke feelings of 'deep familiarity' because of the poignancy, the 'certain intensity of longing and anticipation'. Such images may be kitsch, ersatz art, but they can still be a powerful invocation of a non-repressive condition that may never have existed but which still seems to be exemplified best in natural beauty or 'landscape'. This can stimulate 'an experience of disinterested observation [that] gives birth to a happiness instantly recognisable as your own' (John Berger, quoted by Inglis).

Landscape is popular culture because it 'provides the images of non-consuming, unself-regarding beauty out of which most people make their best thoughts and feelings' (Inglis). Yet natural beauty is still a myth transposed into imagination and redeemed. Adorno argues that

the song of birds is judged beautiful by nearly everybody. No sensitive person of European background, for example, fails to be moved by the song of a robin after a shower of rain. All the same, there is something frightening lurking in the song of birds, which is not really a song but merely a response to natural necessity . . . The ambivalence of natural beauty can be traced back to the ambivalence of myth.[3]

The ambiguities behind the construction of 'natural beauty' and the atavism that determines its transposition account for the intense power of the experience and images of landscape both to evoke 'best feelings' and yet also to provide adequate means for a seductive and manipulative control.

These essays, dedicated to Raymond Williams who died early in 1988 when this collection was first conceived, chart the complex relationship of country and city which determines any examination of landscape imagery and which was first systematically explored in his book, The country and the city, of 1973 (his 'return' to the theme, written in 1984, is the first essay in the collection). Images of country and city are ways of responding to social development. The image of a lost rural world that most landscape representations speak to is, Williams argues, in direct contradiction to any effective shape of the future in which work on the land will become more rather than less central. It is this extraordinary displacement in space and time upon past and/or distant lands that emphasises both the deformations that industrial capitalism is capable of and the 'persistence and historicity' of that displacement. Images of country and city express key aspects of our experience and of the periodic crises we face: 'deconstructing' these images does not dispel them as false consciousness because the central problematic remains. Raymond Williams argues that capitalism, as a mode of production, is the fundamental rationale behind the history of the country and the city (the social relations and means of production) and the last model of this history, imperialism, has also altered the world. Empire was the country-side writ large: an idyllic retreat, an escape and an opportunity to make a fortune. What the West has done is to translate the imagery and impose the crises on the world as a whole. What Williams calls 'the real history of city and country' is a history also of the extension of a dominant model of capitalist development to all regions of the world, but that history also provides the challenge and the resistance to that model from the Russian *mir* and the Indian village to the Chinese Cultural Revolution and the 'killing fields' of Pol Pot's Cambodia. 'Improvement', that euphemism employed to describe both the beautification and the 'industrialisation' of the eighteenth-century countryside, now proposes universal industrialisation as the only way to advance the 'undeveloped'. In the post-industrial world, all 'country', becomes 'city'. The archetypal site of modernity today may no longer be the metropolis with its shanty-towns and *barriadas* but the desert.[4] As Estragon says in Beckett's *Waiting for Godot*, 'Recognise [the place]! What is there to recognise? All my lousy life I've crawled about in mud! And you talk to me about scenery!'

## Notes

1 See 'Existing to be English' in his forthcoming 'History Workshop' book on patriotism to be published by Routledge during 1989. These quotations come from an extract published in *New Statesman and Society* (21 October 1989), pp. 27–30.
2 See 'The Renaissance theory of art and the rise of landscape', in *Norm and form* (Phaidon, London and New York, 1966), p. 116.
3 This quote, and the other references to Adorno, come from ch. 4, 'The beauty of nature', in his *Aesthetic theory*, trans. C. Lenhardt (Routledge & Kegan Paul, London, 1984).
4 Dick Hebdige asks this question in his article 'Banalarama, or can pop save us all?', in *New Statesman and Society* (9 December 1988), pp. 29–32.

# 2

# Between country and city
## Raymond Williams

I wrote The Country and the city in the late 1960s and early 1970s. Looking at it again, the other day, I was surprised to find how many things had happened, in both country and city, in those few intervening years. It is true that the main tendencies I had identified seemed strongly confirmed. I do not mean only that there has been an intensifying crisis in the cities, and especially in the inner cities, though that record of a mounting pressure on housing and services, of financial emergencies and in some extreme cases of actual riots and burning, is evidently grave. Nor do I mean only that there have been some important changes in the country districts: the further rapid development of agribusiness and high-input arable farming; the rapid relative increase in the importance of the agricultural sector in the national economy, especially since joining the European Community; and the continuing growth of country settlement and rural work of new kinds. But my central case in The Country and the city was that these two apparently opposite and separate projections – country and city – were in fact indissolubly linked, within the general and crisis-ridden development of a capitalist economy, which had itself produced this division in its modern forms. With the increasing development of a more fully organised agrarian capitalism, ever more closely linked with the general money market, this is clearly even more true now than then.

Yet this was always the underlying social, economic and historical analysis. What I was more immediately concerned with was the set of human responses, in everyday attitudes and activities but also in art and writing and ideas, to these always practical facts and developments. Here again I found much to confirm what I had argued. There was a continuing flood of sentimental and selectively nostalgic versions of country life. Identification of the values of rural society with the very different values of certain dominant and privileged mansions seemed even more strong; indeed these mansions were now often defined, flatly, as 'our heritage'. I say 'mansions' rather than 'country houses' because that ordinary term is part of a very revealing ideological confusion. These places of the landed aristocracy but now much more of the rich of all kinds, including notably the leaders of City finance and of urban industry, are 'country houses' in necessary relation to their 'town houses' or apartments. The real country houses are those of the people who find their diverse livelihoods in the country. The presumptive 'country house' is, by contrast, the formal expression of the double base – in city and country alike – of a class based on linked property, profit and money. A more modest and economically different version of a comparable double base is the 'country cottage' of those who mainly earn their livelihood in salaried employment and professional fees in the cities. There is a wide variation of scale, in both kinds, but it is always necessary to distinguish 'the country' as a place of first livelihood – interlinked, as it always must be, with the most general movements of the economy as a whole – and 'the country' as a place of rest, withdrawal, alternative enjoyment and consumption, for those whose first livelihood is elsewhere.

Yet while that distinction is clear and firm, there is no simple corresponding distinction in attitudes to 'the country' or in the 'country' images that we make and exchange. There are, it is true, some obvious general differences, notably in accounts of rural work, which vary according to how often and on what terms – above all, for whom – it is done. But in the increasing interaction of 'country' and 'city' several interesting changes in more general attitudes seem now to be happening, some of them in complex ways. It is these I will now try to define, at least provisionally, as a contribution to an ever more widely-based argument.

The first and most obvious change, which has been developing for many years but is now at a critical stage, relates precisely to the rapid increase in agribusiness, and specifically to the practices of high-input arable farming and new forms of intensive animal and poultry rearing. In a historical perspective these new methods and techniques are evidently the result of the application of industrial methods to traditional farming practices. They are thus a prime case of the interaction of 'country' and 'city' within a single industrial–capitalist economy, just as the closely associated changes in land ownership, agricultural finance and modes of capitalisation are elements of the operation of a single money market. It is then not surprising that there should be some familiar but also some unfamiliar kinds of opposition to them. In cities, in arable areas, but perhaps even more in country towns and villages, there is intense and often angry opposition to such effects as straw-burning and crop-spray drift, which have markedly increased. In a more general way there is strongly organised opposition to conditions of intensive animal and poultry rearing which are seen as cruel.

This overlaps in one direction with intense opposition to most forms of the exploitation and even use of animals, and of course with strong objections to older forms of country sport such as hunting. But it overlaps in another direction with a much more general ecological case. Straw-burning is seen as not only polluting but typically wasteful. Crop-spraying, even when there is no drift, is seen as in at least some instances a characteristic example of profitable production taking priority over both public health and the natural environment as a whole. Selective breeding of some plants and animals is seen as diminishing the necessary genetic range, and this is related to the underlying dependence of these varieties on heavy use of imported fertilisers and feedstuffs, itself necessarily connected, not only in the long but even in the short run, with the facts of finite natural resources, renewable and non-renewable, and their now biased distribution in favour of the old rich economies. Thus there are several new kinds of antagonism between what are no longer simple 'country' and 'city' positions, but between and across changing versions of both.

This already complex situation is made even more complex by the fact, unlooked-for even a generation ago, that agriculture is now the most successful sector of a generally failing economy. The time is past when a powerful and influential contrast could be made between busy and thriving industrial areas and a depressed and neglected agriculture. Moreover, and greatly to the long-term advantage of the whole society, the proportion of food raised within the country has increased remarkably, and could be still further increased, with important effects on the viability – and in extreme cases the survival chances – of this heavily populated island. It is common to reply to criticism of the new methods and techniques with the facts of this genuine advantage. What is then replayed within agriculture is the old argument, from the nineteenth century onwards, between the advantages of increased production and the full social, human and natural effects of its processes.

But this has been, from the beginning, a much more difficult argument than it is usually made to seem. The producers, in majority, deploy their powerful statistics of supply and demand, and dismiss most objections as sentimental or at best marginal. This is clearly expressed in that ideological term 'by-product', which is an attempt to separate out the often unwanted but usually predictable and even necessary results of a whole productive process, keeping only the favourable outputs as real 'products'. On the other side, many objectors to these processes are indeed only objecting to the inconvenience of any production, if it happens to blow their way. There is a long tradition of *rentier* objection to physical productive processes of all kinds, though its profits are regularly taken and used to finance other styles of life. There is some continuation of these attitudes among many who are not strictly *rentiers* (people living on incomes from invested money and property) but who, finding their own livelihood elsewhere, are intolerant of other people at work, especially in those country areas which they have chosen for withdrawal and rest. While the argument is confined to exchanges between these two large groups – statistical producers and *rentiers*/weekenders – there is plenty of heat but little light. The real arguments are at once more discriminating and more general.

Thus it is not reasonable, in my view, to pick out a few obviously damaging agricultural applications of science and technology and suppose oneself to have proved some general case. Every particular technique and method needs specific assessment. I am myself persuaded that very-high-input arable farming, with its expensive reliance on heavy fertiliser, energy and pesticide applications, and with its necessary relation to varieties selected for these conditions, leading to some consequent neglect of other possible (including new) varieties, is unsustainable in the long term, given probable developments in both world economics and world ecology. I am similarly persuaded that intensive animal and poultry breeding on imported feedstuffs or on the deliberate surpluses of high-input grain production is wrong both in terms of world food needs – where the surpluses of meat, grain and dairy products in the old rich countries coexist with widespread basic starvation in the growing populations of the poor majority of the world – and in terms of any sustainable economy in our own land. But there are shadings to put on even these conclusions, and in other cases there are significant and valuable real gains, especially in scientific agriculture, as from improved grasses and improved breeds of sheep – which I have been watching fairly closely.

Underlying all these problems of intensive production there is an increasing actual pressure of a financial rather than an economic kind. The huge involvement of agriculture in high-interest debt and credit is usually a truer cause of the most frantic attempts to increase production at any environmental cost than the causes more often assigned, of merely cruel or greedy exploitation. This is not to say that there is no cruelty, no greed, but these can be better distinguished when this much more general pressure is defined and traced to its sources in a specific kind of money-market economy. Moreover this is something that could be changed, with the provision of longer-term and lower-interest credits for more generally agreed kinds and levels of production: reforms which would have to carry with them the acceptance of realistic prices for food, realistic interest on savings, and some dietary changes – especially in sugar, meat and dairy products – if a general and long-term policy were to have a chance of holding.

Why do most of us not now think in these ways? The superficial divisions of country and city – and specifically, now, of 'agriculture' and 'the rest' – push in to prevent us. This latter division, between 'agriculture' and 'the rest', is especially significant and interesting. For what has happened, at one level, is a misleading simple identification of 'the country' with agriculture. This is better than identifying it with 'country houses', but it is still misleading. A rural economy has never been solely an agricultural economy. Indeed it is only as a consequence of the Industrial Revolution that the idea (though never the full practice) of rural economy and society has been limited to agriculture. It is obvious that food production will always be central in any rural economy, as indeed in any stable whole economy. But this does not mean that a more complex and diverse economy and society cannot or should not develop beyond this base. All rural economies and societies of the past have been more than agricultural; they have included, because that was their natural place, a wide diversity of crafts and trades. The unbalanced development of cities and industrial towns, through the periods of centralisation of state power, concentration of the money market, and large-scale factory production, drained the rural economy of much of its work and, with that, its relative autonomy.

Yet all these developments are now moving, or are capable of being moved, the other way. There is a powerful demand for the decentralisation of state power. There are early opportunities for altering the conditions of the money market, in the now critical circumstances of local government finance and development capital: a range of possible initiatives for more local resource audits, financing and control. Meanwhile there is a firm trend away from factory processes requiring the physical concentration of large numbers of workers, and towards smaller and more specialised workplaces, which with the advantages of new energy and communications technologies can be more diversely sited, including in country areas.

At such a time it is especially necessary to broaden the arguments about rural economy and society from the simple specialisation to agriculture. Beyond even the environmental and resource effects of high-input farming is the effect of the reduction of human work on the land, through mechanisation and automation, with damaging results not only for rural employment prospects of the traditional kind, but for the cities which are no longer the thriving centres to which displaced workers can go. It is here that the structure of modern capitalist agriculture has complex and even contradictory effects. The revitalising effects of a profitable agriculture are real, in many areas, but its political base in the whole society is uncertain and even precarious, given the present scale of subsidies and arranged markets. If it is at the same time, as in the arable areas, actually reducing the broader rural economy and society, it will soon find that it has few friends. It could be overwhelmed at any time by a shallow urban consumerism, pushing its way back, however shortsightedly, into a global free market. Hatred for the Common Agricultural Policy is already intense, and its political outcome – reduction or cancellation – could be disastrous for our rural economy. Yet if profitable production and market criteria are the only norms, as in capitalist agriculture itself, there is no principled way of resisting their global extension. The only sustainable objective of a Common Agricultural Policy is – as some French ministers have correctly stated – the maintenance of a viable rural economy *and* society. If capitalist agriculture is concerned only with itself, and not with rural society as a whole, in a necessary and changing balance with urban and metropolitan society, it has little long-term future and virtually no political defences.

This has several effects on our ways of thinking about the future of rural economies. First, it is necessary to oppose the current drive to get rid of what are called 'small inefficient producers'. This drive is powered by an unholy combination of large agrarian capitalists and the urban Left. It is one of the miseries, indeed crimes, of agrarian capitalism, throughout its history, that it has reduced the spread and diversity of landholding and repeatedly made so many of its neighbours redundant. The cruel fact about contemporary redundancy, by comparison with earlier periods in which the cruelties were of a different kind, is that there is now almost literally nowhere to go: not the old Empire; not the new lands; not the expanding factory towns.

Yet in these new conditions the number of farms in Britain has declined from a pre-1914 figure of 400,000 to some 200,000 at the time of writing. The pressure to reduce this number yet further comes from a whole range of political and economic bodies which disagree about almost everything else. The identification of efficiency is almost wholly in capitalist terms, as return on capital. Real returns on land use need to be quite differently assessed, not only by extension from the immediate operation to the true full costs in the economy as a whole, but also by extension to an accounting of the full social costs, including the costs of maintaining growing numbers of the displaced and unemployed and the usually overlooked costs of the crisis of the cities to which so many of them gravitate.

This is a worldwide phenomenon, much more serious in many other countries than in Britain, but its shape is already discernible here. What is called environmentalism resists pollution and the destruction of habitats by high-input large-scale farming. Ecology, in its usual forms, resists in terms of the unbalanced and often reckless use of non-renewable resources. Agrarian capitalism answers both with its own version of the priorities of profitable production. What is then necessary is a new kind of political ecology, based in but surpassing these earlier cases, which can trace the processes to the economic and social structures which developed and are strengthened by them, and which can reasonably propose alternative kinds of economic and social organisation.

Thus efficiency must never be reduced to a momentary criterion, or to a simple criterion by gross commodities. Efficiency is the production of a stable economy, an equitable society and a fertile world. Every local measurement is important but the full accounting has to be in these broad terms. Ironically, in all such real accounting, the maintenance and development of rural economies and rural settlements comes out as a high priority. All those who are really committed to them have a central interest in such wider accounting, and in resisting the kinds of calculation, derived from urbanism and industrialism, which have become specific to capitalist agriculture and especially to money-market agribusiness.

Among its many other uses, this perspective helps us to understand a growing contemporary tendency which still awaits its full analysis. There has been a good deal of scattered comment on the movement of a new kind of people into country areas: not just the retired and the commuters, which is an older phenomenon, but a wide range of active people in a diversity of occupations. Some of this has been disparagingly described as the descent of the drop-outs, and there have indeed been many odd encounters between these new arrivals and an older rural population. Yet it seems in reality to be a very mixed phenomenon.

Some of course have 'dropped into' forms of farming and smallholding, including some experimental forms. But others are simply taking advantage of independence of location for their particular kinds of work, finding the physical country a major attraction and able, in part, to settle in it because of the relative depopulation caused by earlier phases of industry and agriculture. If we look at this tendency in terms of a whole rural society, rather than of a rural economy limited to agriculture, the judgement seems to alter.

I noted down recently the first occupations of my neighbours within five miles of my house in the Black Mountains. This wasn't a proper statistical survey, just a series of informed impressions. The largest single group of the economically active are of course farmers; most of them sheep-farmers. Just beyond these are the growing number of small contractors: hedge-cutters, tree-fellers, shearers, earth-movers, and (travelling because little grain is grown there) harvesters. Then there are the carriers, of animals and of straw. There are butchers and in one case a sausage-and-pie maker in a new small factory unit. There is the usual range of trades: jobbing builders, electricians, plumbers, plasterers, carpenters. There are the council roadmen. There is a septic tank emptier. Then there are the doctor, the teachers, the school bus drivers, the parson, the police, the publicans, the shopkeepers, the postmen, the garage and petrol station people. All these already show the actual diversity of a working rural society.

But it is the rest of the list that shows the change: weavers and knitters; potters; cabinet-makers; pine-furniture makers; booksellers; book illustrator; antique-clock restorer; antique dealers; painter and gallery owner; writers; sculptor; restaurateurs; glass engraver; stained-class maker. The majority of all these are comparatively recent immigrants, but consider how much they are, taken as a whole, restoring a genuine fabric of rural society. There are some problems of integration and settlement, but at least in the pastoral areas, with their natural beauty, there is some real movement towards a more diverse and more balanced society. For look also at the move from the other direction. Several of the sheep-farmers double as pony-trekking providers, a rapidly increasing activity. There has been an equally rapid development of farmhouse bed-and-breakfasts, holiday cottage letting and, along quite another line, of farm shops and of growing pick-your-own fruit and vegetables (including potatoes). There is even the beginning of a system of shares in breeding sheep. Some of this is directly related to the attraction of such districts to tourists. Some, again, is part of that pattern of part-time country living which can have depressing effects when many houses and cottages are shut up for the winter. But, taking it all in all, this movement has very interesting implications for the future of a balanced rural society.

It is important to look at some continuities and changes in images of the country in the context of this kind of development. They tell a strange, mixed story. On the one hand there is a continuation of the false or weak pastoral and landscape images, as can be seen in some of the painting and writing and in some pottery. On the other hand the weavers and knitters and furniture-makers are working with the grain of the actual rural economy, and bringing to it qualities of design and, even in reproductions, of workmanship which had been thought to have been exiled to the towns. It is the same with country knowledge and lore. There is a distinct strain of the merely quaint and also of the highly irrational and unhistorical, including the ley-line, medical–magic and supernatural tendencies. In the Black Mountains this seems perverse, since the real history and prehistory are so very much more interesting and surprising. Yet the only real local anger I have seen was against a few isolated cases of cannabis-growing and a more organised camp to cele- brate the 'liberty cap' fungi: pitched, as it happened, on a neolithic site.

Yet it would be false to make this odd tendency the dominant element. On the contrary the major element is undoubtedly the recovery, explor- ation and propagation of kinds of natural knowledge, some strength- ened by modern learning and science, which were in part drained out of the surviving rural population in the period of urban and industrial dominance. For every cranky or overstated case, as at times with some of the descriptions of medical herbs, there are twenty cases of genuine practical knowledge, interacting with the best of the surviving rural economy: in the wholefoods, the honeys, the culinary herbs, the fuels, the jams and cordials. As this floods into print and into shops it can be seen as mere fashion, but in general it is a healthy practical recovery of the skills and resources of the land. Moreover it is reaching back into the cities and suburbs, providing a different and better base for urban atti- tudes to the country.

Necessarily, however, these are marginal uses and forms of production. The commitment to an industrial and then imperial social order has occurred in much more than the head. It is now literally on the ground and in the air, not only in its massive physical and social embo- diments but above all in its crowded population, which has for at least a century gone beyond the possibilities of any acceptable model of natural subsistence. Thus there are deep current contradictions. First, between the true necessities of production as such, industrial and agricultural, and the inherited and monetarily imposed patterns of production which obscure but then make others unreasonably deny these absolute necessities. Second, between the country areas as necessary places of production, in either mode, and the inherited and culturally imposed patterns of rural enjoyment, placing access to the 'unspoiled' as primary, in the long dream of a simple Rural England which could export, to the colonies, a large part of its rural working population. There are good ways forward beyond each of these contradictions, but much of the cultural and intellectual argument is still held, confusingly, within them.

I have, for example, watched the problem of access in two very different areas: one Eastern arable; one Western pastoral. The three fields behind the house in which I was living when I wrote The Country and the city have been cleared into one, and the old ponds drained. A council signpost still indicates a footpath that used to run beside a hawthorn hedge but is now across the middle of the large field. If you have the nerve or indifference to walk across growing corn you can still always use it, but country-bred, I found I could only walk it in autumn and winter: the respect for crops is still too strong, though I saw clearly enough what had happened. Then in the Black Mountains I admired the arrangements for access to the open tops, with so many miles of attractive hill-walking: the car parks, the picnic sites, the signposts. Yet I have watched, only this summer, a car arrive at the edge of a mountain full of grazing sheep, and three large dogs immediately released and of course chasing and terrifying them. A young farmer neighbour told me that much of his cut winter firewood had been stolen from a stack by his gate, but that he had only lost his temper when the newly-made timber gate had also been stolen. There are also more frequent reports of the theft and butchering of sheep and cattle. In the actual country community you can leave anything open around the place, without the least chance of theft or damage by your neighbours.

Again, once or twice a year, a notice is put through our doors that there is to be an overnight car 'rally' by an urban club: no rally but a timed race in the dark along the narrow twisting lanes where all year it is necessary to reverse or manoeuvre if another vehicle is met. There are procedures for objection and complaint, but the cool advice to keep animals off the roads, as if they were dogs on Guy Fawkes night, is a voice from another world. It is intolerable, I believe, that offences and indifferences of this kind are unnoticed or underplayed within a general position which has its own strong examples: of the destruction of habitats and earthworks, including many that have been listed; of resistance and obstruction on real rights of way; and of organised prejudice against National Parks and even some minimal planning regulations.

None of these complex matters can be resolved within the simplifying images of a polarised 'country' and 'city'. I would take the naming of 'wilderness' – a cultural import from the United States – as an example. It is indeed important that some 'wild' places should be kept open and within the forms of natural growth. The acid blanket-peat uplands are those I know best and most value. Yet these, as I have seen them over many years, are entirely compatible with extensive sheep-farming. Some of them would be more inaccessible without it. When I see the amount of hedging and ditching that goes on in our valley I know what would happen if, for their own reasons, the sheep-farmers were not doing or paying for it. There is not much wilderness in this anciently worked island, and most of it is a man-made facsimile of the real thing, but we might find there was too much for most tastes of this kind of tending stopped. When I see the amount of work on urban parks and gardens publicly paid for as a matter of course, I wonder at the common urban blindness to all this work that actually produces and preserves much of the 'nature' that visitors come to see. If there were not farmers of these uplands, with the hill-sheep subsidy and guaranteed prices, there would have to be paid wardens if much accessible country were to be left. Indeed I have often thought that some direct part-time payment of that kind would be the fairest kind of settlement on rights of way and important sites.

On the other hand I know that there are sharp and perhaps absolute differences, in these matters, between the pastoral and the arable areas, and especially the arable areas in their current phase of high-input mechanised farming. The linkage between grain surpluses and intensive livestock feeding, in those areas, has to be contrasted with the natural benefits of sensible grassland improvement for pastoral livestock-rearing of a radically different kind. It is a matter, always, for specific judgement, as when I find myself a friend of bracken above a thousand feet and an enemy below that contour. Yet when I once mentioned grassland improvement as an investment priority, to an eminent socialist friend, he looked at me as if he thought I had gone mad.

The deepest problems we have now to understand and resolve are in these real relations of nature and livelihood. I argued in *Towards 2000* that the central change we have to make is in the received and dominant concept of the earth and its life forms as a raw material for generalised production. That change means, necessarily, ending large-scale capitalist farming, with its linked processes of high land costs, high interest-bearing capitalisation, high-input cash-crop production. But in the equally necessary perspective of what I called in *The Country and the city* an apparently unmediated nature – the living world of rivers and mountains, of trees and flowers and animals and birds – it is important to avoid a crude contrast between 'nature' and 'production', and to seek the practical terms of the idea which should supersede both: the idea of 'livelihood', within, and yet active within, a better understood physical world and all truly necessary physical processes.

Both industrial and agrarian capitalism have overridden this idea of livelihood, putting generalised production and profit above it. Yet the dominant tendencies in socialism have mainly shared the same emphases, altering only the distribution of profit. The most hopeful social and political movement of our time is the very different and now emergent 'green socialism', within which ecology and economics can become, as they should be, a single science and source of values, leading on to a new politics of equitable livelihood. There is still very much to be done, in clarifying and extending this movement and in defining it, practically and specifically, in the many diverse places, requiring diverse solutions and resolutions, where it must take root and grow. But here, at least, it is a sense of direction, born in the experiences between city and country and looking to move beyond both to a new social and natural order.

## Note

First published in Richard Mabey, ed., with Susan Clifford and Angela King, *Second nature* (Jonathan Cape, London, 1984), pp. 209–19.

# 3

# The public prospect and the private view: the politics of taste in eighteenth-century Britain
## John Barrell

## I

I want to offer a comment on some ideas about landscape that are commonly found among writers on art, on literature, and on various other subjects in the second half of the eighteenth and in the early years of the nineteenth centuries in Britain. The main point of my doing this is to show how a correct taste, here especially for landscape and landscape art, was used in this period as a means of legitimating political authority, particularly but not exclusively within the terms of the discourse of civic humanism. If we interrogate writers from the polite culture of this period on the question of what legitimates this claim, one answer we repeatedly discover, though it may take very different forms, is that political authority is rightly exercised by those capable of thinking in general terms; which usually means those capable of producing abstract ideas – decomplex ideas – out of the raw data of experience. The inability to do this was usually represented as in part the result of a lack of education, a lack which characterised women and the vulgar; and because women are generally represented in the period as incapable of generalising to any important degree, I shall be in this essay very careful *not* to use a vocabularly purged of sexist reference: when I speak of what men thought, of Man in general, of the spectator as 'he', I am doing so with forethought, and in order to emphasise the point that, in the matter of political authority, legitimated as I have described, women were almost entirely out of the question, and the issue to be determined was which men could pass the test of taste.

To develop the ability to think accurately in abstract terms required more, however, than an appropriate education: one further condition in particular is necessary: a man must occupy a place in the social order where he has no need to devote his life to supporting himself and his dependents, or at least (in some versions of the argument) of supporting them by mechanical labour. For if he does have such a need, three things will follow: first, he will be obliged to follow one, determinate occupation, and will discover an interest in promoting the interests of that occupation, and of his own success in it: and his concern with what is good for himself, or for one interest-group, will prevent him from arriving at an understanding of what is good for man in general, for human nature, for the public interest. Second, the experience that falls in the way of such a man – expecially if he follows, not a liberal profession, but a mechanical art – will be too narrow to serve as the basis of ideas general enough to be represented as true for all mankind, or even for all the members of a state. Third, because mechanical arts are concerned with things, with material objects, they will not offer an opportunity for the exercise of a generalising and abstracting rationality: the successful exercise of the mechanical arts requires that material objects be regarded as concrete particulars, and not in terms of the abstract or formal relations among them. The man of independent means, on the other hand, who does not labour to increase them, will be released from private interest and from the occlusions of a narrowed and partial experience of the world, and from an experience of the world as material. He will be able to grasp the public interest, and so will be fit to participate in government.

Of this ability, a taste in landscape provides one of various tests. And let me begin my account of that test by saying that it turns on the social and political function of the distinction between panoramic, and ideal landscape, on the one hand, and, on the other, actual portraits of views, and representations of enclosed, occluded landscapes, with no great depth of field. I had better explain that I am using the word 'panoramic', here, simply as a shorthand for the kind of extensive prospect we find typically in a landscape by Claude. But I had better offer some more explanations, because I am aware that I am making a bipartite distinction between a considerable range of kinds of landscapes, some of which – the topographical panorama, the ideal composition of a woodland glade – exhibit characteristics which seem to belong to the different halves of the distinction.

Let me explain the distinction more clearly. It is between landscapes which seek to exhibit substantial, representative forms of nature arranged in a wide extent of land, and views which, even if panoramic, exhibit the accidental forms of nature, and even if ideal, exhibit their

ideal forms within a restricted terrain. That such a distinction is crucial to
an understanding of the various kinds of landscape art is, I think,
obvious enough; and it is well known that in eighteenth-century England
these different kinds of landscape were often – if not always – assumed to
be the productions of, and designed for the entertainment of, two
different spheres of life, and even of two different classes of people –
what and who they were will be considered shortly. It does seem to me
however that we continually overlook the importance of the distinction
to the eighteenth century; and that it has been possible to do so for a long
time is suggested, for example, by a passage from Hazlitt's essays on
Reynolds, published in the *Champion* in 1814, in which he comments on
what he calls Reynolds's 'learned riddle', whether accidents in nature
should be introduced in landscape painting. Accidents in nature, as there
is probably no need to explain, are *untypical* natural phenomena: sometimes they are regarded as phenomena rare enough to be the result of a
complex conjunction of natural causes: storms and rainbows are
accidents. More generally, however, accidents are anything in the prospect of nature which suggests that the prospect is being observed at one
particular moment rather than another, and which calls attention to that
fact: when the light, for example, strikes objects in such a way as to
suggest that it will strike them differently a second later; when the form of
a tree is such that it seems to be ruffled by a blast of wind of such or such a
particular force, blowing from such or such a direction. Anything, in
short, is an accident, which suggests a view of nature as other than
abstract, typical, a permanent phenomenon, but particularly untypical
effects of light, or untypical forms of objects. The debate about whether
accidents in nature should be admitted into landscape was not
originated by Reynolds: it was a familiar topic among writers on painting
committed to an aesthetic of illusion, as Reynolds of course was not. For,
of course, a landscape full of accidents is likely to deceive our eyes more
successfully, but in doing so it would attach us to images of nature less
elevating than those represented in entirely ideal landscapes. But, as shall
be seen, Reynolds's 'learned riddle', posed in his fourth discourse, was
about much more than this.

Of that riddle, Hazlitt writes:

We should never have seen that fine landscape of his [Rubens] in the Louvre, with
a rainbow on one side, the whole face of nature refreshed after the shower, and
some shepherds under a group of trees piping to their heedless flock, if instead of
painting what he saw and what he felt to be fine, he had set himself to solve the
learned riddle proposed by Sir Joshua, whether *accidents in nature* should be

introduced in landscape, since Claude has rejected them. It is well that genius gets the start of criticism, for if these two great landscape painters, not being privileged to consult their own taste and inclinations, had been compelled to wait till the rules of criticism had decided the preference between their different styles, instead of having both, we should have had neither. The folly of all such comparisons consists in supposing that we are reduced to a single alternative in our choice of excellence, and the true answer to the question. Which do you like best, Rubens's landscapes or Claude's? is the one which was given on another occasion – both.[1]

Hazlitt, characteristically, cuts a knot that Reynolds had attempted to untie; and it seems likely that he does so, not because he is unaware of the importance to eighteenth-century art of the distinction I have referred to, but because he is hostile to the political basis of a division between kinds of landscape, which could also be a division between the kinds of viewer appropriate to each. But either way, Hazlitt suppresses a distinction important to Reynolds, and succeeds in obscuring its importance to us. In this paper I want to re-tie the knot that Hazlitt has cut.

That Hazlitt's response to Reynolds's 'learned riddle' is the result not of a failure to understand the point of the riddle, but of a refusal to accept the assumptions on which it is based, is suggested by that fact that three years later Coleridge, who was not at all antagonistic to the notion that the political republic, and the republic of taste, were constituted on a distinction between two kinds of persons with greater and lesser intellectual capacities, was still able to represent that distinction in terms of a distinction between kinds of landscape. Coleridge describes an allegoric vision, in which a company of men are approached by a woman, tall beyond the stature of mortals, and dressed in white, who announces that her name is Religion.

The more numerous part of our company, affrighted by the very sound, and sore from recent impostures or sorceries, hurried onwards and examined no further. A few of us, struck by the manifest opposition of her form and manners to those of the living Idol, whom we had so recently abjured [SUPERSTITION], agreed to follow her, though with cautious circumspection. She led us to an eminence in the midst of the valley, from the top of which we could command the whole plain, and observe the relations of the different parts, of each to the other, and of all to each. She then gave us an optic glass which assisted without contradicting our natural vision, and enabled us to see far beyond the limits of the Valley of Life: though our eye even thus assisted permitted us only to behold a light and a glory, but what, we could not descry, save only that it was, and that it was most glorious.[2]

Then 'with the rapid transition of a dream', Coleridge finds himself again with the more numerous party, who have come to 'the base of a lofty and

almost perpendicular rock', which shuts out the view; the 'only perfor-
ation' in the precipice is 'a vast and dusky cave', at the mouth of which sits
the figure of Sensuality.

The distinction between a viewpoint from which a vast and panoramic
prospect is visible, and low, sunken situations from which only the
nearest objects are visible, only in close-up, is a repeated motif of Coleridge's poems. In 'Reflections on Having Left a Place of Retirement', for
example, composed in 1795, the year also of the composition of the first
version of the Allegoric Vision, Coleridge compares the low and humble
position of his cottage with the view available by climbing from that low
dell up the stony mount nearby: 'the whole World', he writes, 'seem'd
imag'd' in the 'vast circumference' of the horizon: the images in that
extensive prospect seem representative and substantial, so that the prospect becomes a microcosm of the world. One theme of 'This Lime-Tree
Bower My Prison' (1797) is to consider how objects within the occluded
prospect of the bower may be seen, as can the objects in the 'wide
landscape' described earlier in the poem, in terms of the relations of
things, rather than as things in themselves. In 'Fears in Solitude' (1798),
the 'burst of prospect' seen from the hill 'seems like society', in opposition to the 'silent dell' in which Coleridge has considered his fears, in
solitude, and in opposition also to his own 'lowly cottage'. There are
numerous poems based on the same pattern of opposition, and the
meaning of each component – panorama, and occluded view – is
complex, and changes from poem to poem. It is possible, however, to
abstract and collocate a number of the significances attached to each image:
and to notice that, among the meanings attached to the panoramic view
may be the notion of a wider society, and the notion of the ability to grasp
objects in the form of their relations to each other; among the meanings
attached to the occluded view, from a low viewpoint, are seclusion, of
course, and privacy as something opposed to the social in its more
extended sense, and also sensuality, which for Coleridge (and also for
numerous writers, including Reynolds, before him) was particularly
characterised by a tendency to see objects not in terms of their relations,
or their common relation to a general, and representative term, but in
and for themselves, as objects of consumption and possession.

## II

Let me focus first on the opposition between different landscapes as
appealing to two different classes of people, and therefore between the

ability to grasp things in terms of their relations – of 'the different parts of each to the other, and of all to each' – and the inability to do so, which leaves us focusing, myopically, on the objects themselves, on, as Coleridge puts it elsewhere, 'an immense heap of little things',[3] the world as perceived by the sensual eye unilluminated by imagination, or the ideal. For a version of that opposition is of course crucial also to Reynolds's theory of art, and in particular to the doctrine of the central form, which is arrived at by the ability to abstract substance from accident, 'to get above all singular forms, local customs, particularities, and details of every kind'.[4] True taste, for Reynolds, is the ability to form and to recognise representative general ideas, by referring all the objects of a class to the essential character by which a class is constituted; the lack of true taste is the inability to perform this operation, so that we take pleasure not in the ideal representation of objects in terms of their generic classes, but in the unpurged, accidental forms of objects, minutely delineated. For the Coleridge of 1817 that distinction is grounded, of course, in an idealist philosophy: to grasp the relations among objects is to grasp them in terms of the idea which is at once the ground of their existence and the end for which they exist. For Reynolds, and for almost all writers in the eighteenth century in England, the distinction is founded on a distinction between those who can, and those who cannot form general ideas, normally by the processes of abstraction; between those who can compose details into a whole, or compose a whole by the elimination of detail, and, on the other hand, the ignorant who, as Reynolds explains, 'cannot comprehend a whole, nor even what it means'.

The critic Thomas Tickell, or it may be Richard Steele, makes the same distinction in the context of pastoral poetry in an unsigned essay of 1713:

Men, who by long study and experience have reduced their ideas to certain classes, and consider the general nature of things abstracted from particulars, express their thoughts after a more concise, lively, surprising manner. Those who have little experience, or cannot abstract, deliver their sentiments in plain descriptions, by circumstances, and those observations which either strike the senses, or are the first motions of the mind.[5]

For that reason, he argues, the shepherds of pastoral 'are not allowed to make deep reflections', and for that reason too, one of the main pleasures that sophisticated readers take in pastoral is that it exhibits a state of mind which is delightfully simple in itself, at the same time as it promotes the delightful reflection that we are emancipated from its bondage, from the tyranny of external impressions which we cannot control and organise. That is also a reason why pastoral is the lowest of the genres of poetry – because it imitates the motions of the minds of the least rational, the most ignorant, members of society.

Thus, if pastoral or landscape art – however lowly its position in the hierarchy of genres – is to be of value, is to be an object worth the attention of men who can abstract, then it must be defended either as Tickell has defended it – so that the pleasure we take in the genre derives from the contrast between the perception of those who are merely in the landscape, and those who are outside it, and observe it – or it must be defended as an art capable of *calling forth* the ability to abstract substance from accident, the general from the particular.

James Harris defends it in this second way. In his *Philogical Inquiries*, he considers the cause of the pleasure we derive from natural beauty. 'The vulgar', he notes, 'look no further than to the scenes of culture, because all their views merely terminate in utility.' They are 'merged in sense from their earlier infancy, never once dreaming anything to be worthy of pursuit, but what either pampers their appetite, or fills their purse'; they 'imagine nothing to be real, but what may be touched or tasted'. These dwellers in the cave of sensuality thus 'only remark, that it is fine barley; that it is rich clover; as an ox or an ass, if they could speak, would inform us. But the liberal have nobler views; and though they give to culture its due praise, they can be delighted with natural beauties, where culture was never known.'

But what are the pleasures that the liberal find in natural beauty, which are unknown to the vulgar, the ox and the ass? Harris makes a poor job of explaining what they are – he mostly attempts, simply, to prove that they exist, by adducing those classical authorities who have affirmed their existence. But he *exemplifies* those pleasures with precision; for example, when he writes, 'the great elements of this species of beauty are water, wood, and uneven ground; to which may be added a fourth, that is to say, lawn'.[6] That is the pleasure: the enjoyment of the ability to abstract from the labyrinth of nature, from the infinite varieties of accidental and circumstantial appearances, the general classes of natural beauty whose combinations please only when, on analysis, they can be resolved again into their components. It is the same pleasure that William Gilpin experienced when he announced that 'few views, at least few good views, consist of more than a foreground & two distances': the pleasure, that is, of abstracting the essential from its confusing particulars, and reducing those particulars to order.[7]

As Harris makes clear, the pleasures of nature are different, according to whether we are among the company of the liberal, or the vulgar; and it is worth reminding ourselves that in the eighteenth century the word liberal still has its primary meaning: it is the adjective that describes the free man, and the liberal arts are still remembered to be the arts which are worthy of the attention of free men. Free men are opposed to the vulgar or – for the terms are in most contexts virtually indistinguishable – the servile. In the civic humanist theory of art that Harris and Reynolds are heirs to, the word servile most usually occurs as the qualifier of 'imitation': the 'mere' imitation of everyday nature, unabstracted, with all its accidental deformities and details upon its head, is 'servile' imitation, unworthy of the attention of a free man. The imitation of the ideal; of nature, in Opie's phrase, 'as meaning the general principles of things rather than the things themselves';[8] of the object as freed from the tyranny of sense or need, and represented thus not as a thing, but as idea, and so as incapable of being possessed – this is what makes an art a liberal art. It is such an idea of imitation that is the basis of the hostility evinced by Reynolds, for example, against the notion that it is the job of an artist to deceive the eye, to make us believe that a painted object is really there, could be touched as well as seen.

The kind of landscape that can most fully offer this pleasure is panoramic and it is so for various reasons, some of which I shall consider in a moment, but for now it will be enough to point out that the panoramic landscape offers a wide range and variety of objects to abstract from: it is like the 'wide experience' which is, according to Tickell, denied to the shepherd, which is not only a more sure basis for accurate generalisation, because it minimises the distorting effect of extreme departures from generic form, but is also capable of offering the most gratifying test of our ability to reduce it to classes and structures. As Fuseli explains, it offers 'characteristic groups' of 'rich congenial objects'. The groups are characteristic, not individual; they are rich, for there is a profusion of them; they are congenial, because organised into reciprocity by the abstracting power of the mind. On the other hand, argues Fuseli, those who imitate the landscape of the Dutch school are worthy of admiration only as they 'learn to give an air of choice to necessity'[9] – by which he means, that imitations of Dutch landscape remain merely servile imitations so long as the eye is determined in what it represents by necessity, by the mere fact of an object's being there; or is determined by that servile and sensual vassalage to objects as capable of being possessed, which is never far from characterisations of Dutch art as, par excellence, the art of a commercial nation. The more such art rises above the determination of necessity, and learns to represent landscape in terms of a will free from the tyranny of sense, the more it becomes free itself, a liberal art.

By the time Fuseli was appealing to the distinction that I have drawn, it had become so familiar and so general that the distinction between the learned and the ignorant – the polite and the vulgar, the liberal and the servile – was repeatedly and regularly represented in terms of the ability of the former group to apprehend the structure and extent of panoramic landscape. This, for example, is the rhetorician George Campbell, describing the progress of knowledge:

in all sciences, we rise from the individual to the species, from the species to the genus, and thence to the most extensive orders and classes [and] arrive . . . at the knowledge of general truths . . . In this progress we are like people, who, from a low and confined bottom, where the view is confined to a few acres, gradually ascend a lofty peak or promontory. The prospect is perpetually enlarging at every moment, and when we reach the summit, the boundless horizon, comprehending all the variety of sea and land, hill and valley, town and country, arable and desert, lies under the eyes at once.[10]

Notice how Campbell, like Harris, though his list is longer, is concerned to produce from his eminence an account of all the classes of objects the landscape contains: the knowledge he arrives at is a general knowledge, in that it is all there is – the whole world imaged in the circumference of the horizon – and it is general knowledge, too, in that all the various objects of sight and knowledge are named by singular nouns, and so reduced to their various classes; when we see the sea and land, hill and valley, town and country, arable and desert, we see all there is to see. It will follow, of course, that those who remain imprisoned within their few acres at the bottom of the eminence will have nothing like the same range of objects to examine, and will have no possibility, therefore, of deriving accurate, general classes from them. They will remain, indeed, as objects in the landscape: they will not be observers, but observed. The point is well exemplified by Aaron Hill, writing to congratulate Pope on his poetry and to apologise for earlier attacks upon him: "'Tis a noble triumph you now exercise, by the Superiority of your Nature; and while I see you looking down upon the Distance of my Frailty, I am forc'd to own a Glory, which I envy you; and am quite asham'd of the poor Figure I am making, in the bottom of the Prospect.'[11] Those who can comprehend the order of society and nature are the observers of a prospect, in which others are merely objects. Some comprehend, others are comprehended; some are fit to survey the extensive panorama, some are confined within one or other of the micro-prospects which, to the comprehensive observer, are parts of a wider landscape, but which, to those confined within them, are all they see.

It is appropriate that Hill should be addressing Pope, who was shortly to be the author of a poem, the *Essay on man*, which attempts to describe the 'scene of man' as a prospect, which can be observed, and comprehended categorically, from some single viewpoint; and it is appropriate too that Pope, at the opening of his poem, should have identified that point of view as the station occupied by the independent landed gentleman:

> Awake, my ST. JOHN! leave all meaner things
> To low ambition and the pride of Kings.
> Let us (since Life can little more supply
> Than just to look about us and to die)
> Expatiate free o'er all this scene of Man;
> A mighty maze! but not without plan . . .
> Together let us beat this ample field,
> Try what the open, what the covert yield;
> The latent tracts, the giddy heights explore
> Of all who blindly creep, or sightless soar;
> Eye Nature's walks, shoot Folly as it flies,
> And catch the Manners living as they rise . . .[12]

In its migration from renaissance Italy to seventeenth- and eighteenth-century Britain, a crucial mutation had occurred in the discourse of civic humanism, a mutation whose origin is identified in the writings of James Harrington, but which was soon eagerly adopted by the range of eighteenth-century spokesmen, including Bolingbroke, Thomson, and Pope himself, for the ideals of those groups which we lump together under the title of the country party, and whose writings are, more than those of any other grouping in early and mid eighteenth-century Britain, concerned with the definition and defence of public virtue. When Florentine republican theory was transplanted to Britain, the ability of the disinterested citizen to grasp the true interests of society had come to be identified as a function of his ownership of landed property.

This was the result of a number of considerations: of the fact that the franchise, the title of citizenship, was attached to a property qualification; of the fact that a substantial landed property produced a sufficient unearned income for its owner to have the time, the leisure, to devote himself to political life; of the fact that he was therefore a member of no profession, and thus could be assumed to favour no particular occupational interest; but most particularly, of the fact that landed property was fixed property, and therefore its survival was involved (it was believed) in the ability of the state itself to survive the corruptions of accident. The owner of fixed property, even when conscious (according to some theorists) of consulting only his own interests, would also necessarily be consulting the true, the permanent interests of the country in which his family had a permanent stake. Whether, therefore, his independence and his leisure actually enabled him to see the public interest, or whether he was conscious only of consulting his own, made little difference: inasmuch as his own interests were those of the public at large, he was, to all intents and purposes, disinterested in a way that others, more dependent for their income on the fluctuating value of moveable property, and thus of property which, like *argent liquide*, circulated instead of remaining rooted in one spot, could not be. It is then as a man of landed property that St John Bolingbroke (and with him, by association, Pope) can 'expatiate free o'er all this scene of man' – can grasp the 'plan', the design of the wide prospect, which remains simply a 'maze' to those who, situated in one partial position or another, 'latent tract' or 'giddy height', can only 'blindly creep' or 'sightless soar'. And it is thoroughly appropriate that, as Bolingbroke and Pope range freely over the landscape, they do so as sportsmen: they 'beat' the field, and 'catch' the Manners', they thus put up. Only the lords of manors, or those possessed of an annual income or £100 or more from a freehold estate, were permitted to shoot game.

## III

Let me expand at this point on my introductory remarks on the relation between the ability to generalise, a correct taste in landscape, and the claim to be capable of exercising political authority. In so far as the representation of panoramic prospects serves as an instantiation of the ability of the man of 'liberal mind' to abstract the general from the particular, it was also understood to be an instantiation of his ability to abstract the true interests of humanity, the public interest, from the labyrinth of private interests which were imagined to be represented by mere unorganised detail. It was precisely the ability of the liberal mind of the free citizen to do this which constituted his claim to be a citizen, a free man, or, as he was often described (though the phrase has a range of meanings) a 'public man'. A citizen, a public man in this sense, had long been distinguished in republican political theory by the fact that this ability was a function of his reason; whereas private men, men who were not citizens, who were servile, who were mechanics, had been understood, from Aristotle onwards, to have no ability to understand reason, or to follow anything but their own immediate instincts. That is why Harris can compare them with oxen and asses. And because the civic humanist aesthetic of which such men as Harris, Campbell, Reynolds and Fuseli are the inheritors, is based in the language of republican political theory, their own implied definition of who is properly a citizen of the republic of taste is based on the same distinction. The power to abstract, as metaphorised everywhere in the power to comprehend and organise an extensive prospect, is a testimony of the ability to prefer and to promote an art which itself promotes the public interest, as opposed to ministering to the private appetites and interests of particular men.

The relation between these various concerns is clear, for example, in Reynolds's preface to his 'Ironic discourse', a work dedicated to pointing out the congruence of the principles of politics and art. According to Reynolds:

A hundred thousand near-sighted men, that see only what is just before them, make no equivalent to one man whose view extends to the whole horizon around him, though we may safely acknowledge at the same time that like the real near-sighted men they see and comprehend as distinctly what is within the focus of their sight as accurately (I will allow sometimes more accurately) than the others. Though a man may see his way in the management of his own affairs, within his own little circle, with the greatest acuteness and sagacity, such habits give him no pretensions to set up for a politician.[13]

— or, of course, as a man of taste; for the function of both is to grasp the relation of particular to general which is the same thing as the relation of private to public; and the function of both is to promote, whether in art or politics, the public over the private interests. It was exactly the inability to do this that, in his *Reflections on the revolution in France*, Burke had claimed to be necessarily a characteristic of the revolutionary assemblies – composed as they were of tailors and carpenters, men accustomed to considering their own interests as in competition with those of others;[14] and that Reynolds, Blake and Fuseli point out in the Dutch and Venetians, the tradesmen, the mechanics of the republic of taste, not its free gentlemen–citizens. And the binary by which 'gentlemen' are opposed not only by 'mechanics' but by 'tradesmen', together with the civic notion that it is particularly or exclusively the independent owner of a substantial freehold in land who is capable of exercising political authority, often though not always produces an account of the man of liberal taste as one who is not simply a gentleman, but a landed

gentleman; and that connection between the public man, the disinterested citizen, the freeholder, and the man of taste, remains available,
though it is increasingly challenged, well into the next century. It is
evident in the work of Pope, Thomson, and Richard Wilson, and is more
than merely vestigial in the writings of Burke, Wordsworth and
Coleridge.

Sometimes however, by some writers, the ability to comprehend the
structure of relations within a panoramic prospect is attributed to a rather
wider group of potential spectators than we have so far encountered,
though this may not always involve attributing a comprehension of the
public interest in its widest sense. In *The wealth of nations*, Adam Smith
encounters the problem that within a complex, commercial society,
there may be no viewing-position from which the organisation of society
or the public good can possibly be grasped: if the philosopher is as much
implicated in the division of labour, is as much defined by
the propensity to truck and barter, and so as much blinded by his own
interests as is any other man, then he has as little access as anyone else to
that general view which would seem to legitimate a claim to a general
social knowledge. He is reduced to inventing a fictitious and disembo-
died social spectator, the 'philosophic eye', whose viewpoint and whose
breadth and depth of vision no individual can be imagined as possessing,
unless, as Rameau's nephew puts it, he can 'perch on the epicycle of
Mercury'.[15] But in *The theory of moral sentiments*, where the public interest is
conceived of more often in narrower terms – the propensity to place the
interests of another before our own, private interests – the viewing-
position necessary to make that choice is imagined as accessible to
everyone, and it is precisely a viewing-position, from which the interests
of ourselves and of another are visible as if within a landscape. Consider
this passage, for example, where Smith seems to be reworking an argument from Berkeley on Passive Obedience:

In my present situation an immense landscape of lawns, and woods, and distant
mountain, seems to do no more than cover the little window which I write by,
and to be out of all proportion less than the chamber in which I am sitting. I can
form a just comparison between those great objects and the little objects around
me, in no other way, than by transporting myself, at least in fancy, to a different
situation, from which I can survey both at nearly equal distances, and thereby
form some judgment of their real proportions. Habit and experience have taught
me to do this easily and so readily, that I am scarce sensible that I do it; and a man
must be, in some measure, acquainted with the philosophy of vision, before he
can be thoroughly convinced, how little those distant objects would appear to the
eye, if the imagination, from a knowledge of their real magnitudes, did not swell

and dilate them.

In the same manner, to the selfish and original passions of human nature, the loss or gain of a very small interest of our own, appears to be of vastly more importance, excites a much more passionate joy or sorrow, a much more ardent desire or aversion, than the greatest concern of another with whom we have no particular connection. His interests, as long as they are surveyed from this station, can never be put into the balance with our own, can never restrain us from doing whatever may tend to promote our own, how ruinous soever to him. Before we can make any proper comparison of those opposite interests, we must change our position. We must view them, neither from our own place, not yet from his, neither with our own eyes nor yet with his, but from the place and with the eyes of a third person, who has no particular connection with either, and who judges impartially between us.[16]

The third person who occupies the position from which the relation of one person's interest and another's can be apprehended is a version of the fictional character whom Smith terms (among other things) the 'impartial spectator', the imagined arbiter among different interests. And he is outside the landscape, and not as we are in our private capacities, within it, unable to grasp its structure of relations. But unlike most of the other passages I have referred to, Smith seems to suggest that if anyone can attain the viewing-position of this spectator of the moral landscape, we all can. The corollary of that concession, however, is that the extensive prospect cannot be used as an image of a wider society than the one in which most of us make our private determinations on moral questions.

Or consider this record of a spoken observation by Reynolds, on the nature of happiness:

It is not the man who looks around him from the top of a high mountain at a beautiful prospect on the first moment of opening his eyes, who has the true enjoyment of that noble sight: it is he who ascends the mountain from a miry meadow, or a ploughed field, or a barren waste; and who works his way up to it step by step; – it is he, my lords, who enjoys the beauties that suddenly blaze upon him. They cause an expansion of ideas in harmony with the expansion of the view. He glories in its glory; and the mind opens to conscious exaltation; such as the man who was born and bred upon that commanding height . . . can never know; can have no idea of; at least, not till he come near some precipice, in a boisterous wind, that hurls him from the top to the bottom, and gives him some taste of what he had possessed, by its loss; and some pleasure in its recovery, by the pain and difficulty of scrambling back to it.[17]

We can read this passage simply as a more than usually eloquent rehearsal of a moral commonplace, that a happiness achieved after suffering and effort is a good deal more worth having than a happiness which, because its possessor has never known suffering, is the less grateful to him on that account. But if we read it, as surely it invites to be read, in the context of the assumed connection between an ability to comprehend the order of society, and the ownership of heritable property in land, it becomes an impassioned outburst, the more impassioned because this account of how a 'noble sight' may truly be enjoyed is addressed to a noble company, 'my lords', who claim to enjoy it simply because 'born and bred on that commanding height', from which they seem to observe and command the view below. In order to distinguish between the kind of enjoyment that they derive from the prospect, and the kind enjoyed by those who have to toil up to that eminence, Reynolds suggests that to the 'lords' the prospect is not really a metaphor at all: they may presume that the 'expansion of the view' produces a similar 'expansion' of their 'ideas', but it does not; and if to them the prospect has any metaphorical application, it is simply as a figure for the 'eminence' they enjoy as a result of the nature and quantity of their inherited fortunes. The figure achieves its full significance only – as the geography of the passage suggests – for whoever can appropriately be represented as a labourer, who 'works his way up' to the eminence 'from a miry meadow, or a ploughed field, or a barren waste'. The passage suggests that the image of the panoramic landscape could be appropriated from the 'lords' whose political authority it has been used to justify; but it suggests too that a struggle to appropriate the viewing position usually attributed to the landed aristocracy can simply result, whoever comes out on top, the lords or a meritocratic bourgeoisie, in a continuation of the division of society into the observers and the observed, the rulers and the ruled.

## IV

Let me now collect up the various characteristics we have so far seen attributed to the two kinds of landscape that I distinguished at the start of this essay. On the one hand is the ideal, panoramic prospect, the anologue of the social and the universal, which is surveyed, organised, and understood by disinterested public men, who regard the objects in the landscape always as representative ideas, intended to categorise rather than deceptively to imitate their originals in nature, and so who study, not the objects themselves – not for example the individuals in a society, or their individual occupations – but their relations. They are enabled to do this by their ability to abstract, and by their ability to comprehend and classify the totality of human experience.[18]

On the other hand is the occluded landscape, which has so far been treated as representing the 'confined views' of the private man, whose experience is too narrow to permit him to abstract. Such landscapes conceal the general view by concealing the distance: and Fuseli, appropriately, uses an image derived from such landscapes to figure, more generally, the detrimental effect which a profusion of detail has on the 'breadth' of composition he admires: 'the discrepance', he writes, 'of obtruding parts in the works of the infant Florentine, Venetian, and German schools distracts our eye like the numberless breakers of a shallow river, or as the brambles and creepers that entangle the paths of a wood, and instead of showing us our road, perplex us only with themselves'.[19] The characteristic imagery of occluded landscapes – a cottage, for example, embosomed in trees which permit the distance to appear only as spots or slices of light, is emblematic of a situation in life from which no wider prospect is visible.

On this other hand, also, is topographical landscape, which did not represent objects as classified and comprehended. Topographical landscape seems to become more despised – in the theory, though not in the practice of landscape-painting – as the century grows older; not just because of the hostility of the academy, or of that hostility taken as something internal to a theory of art disjoined from social and political change. Towards the end of the century it had become increasingly clear that landed property was not as fixed as it had by some been claimed to be earlier in the century: it was involved in an economy of credit, and was not in itself a guarantee of disinterestedness, except perhaps in so far as it permitted its owners the leisure necessary for a career in public life. The hostility to topographical landscape thus comes to be based not only in its un-idealised, un-intellectual character, but on the connection, also, between sensuality as the failure to abstract from the data of sensation, and sensuality as a desire to possess objects which could only be redeemed, as objects worthy the attention of a free man, by elevating them into representative types which could not be possessed. Thus for James Barry, who described the property market in late eighteenth-century England as anything but stable, more like 'a game of chance',[20] topographical landscape was simply a portrait of our possessions, or of land as inviting possession; and for Fuseli, such landscapes may 'delight the owner of the acres they enclose', but delight and interest him therefore only in his private capacity.[21]

That last point suggests a distinction between two kinds of landscapes

I have been considering that is more complex than the one I have largely been making so far, by which the different landscapes appeal to different classes of people, to citizens and to the rest. For they can also be understood as appealing to two different spheres of life of the citizen: the public sphere, where he is enjoined to consult only the public interest, and the private sphere, where he is temporarily rèleased from his obligations as a citizen. This distinction has already been suggested, perhaps, by my remarks on Coleridge's conversation-poems. The distinction made in these terms is not a simple one, and in attempting to understand why it is not, we can approach an understanding of Reynolds's learned riddle, with which Hazlitt expressed such impatience; and we can approach, also, an understanding of Hazlitt's impatience. For if ideal panoramic landscape is constructed as public, in opposition to various different kinds of landscapes constructed as private, the fact remains that, within the terms of the doctrine of the hierarchy of genres, landscape-art, of whatever kind, is constructed as private, in opposition to the public art of history-painting.

Reynolds, for example, makes it quite clear – as who does not? – that one function (perhaps it is no longer for him the main function) of history paintings in the grand style, is that their subject 'ought to be either some eminent instance of heroick action, or heroick suffering. There must be something either in the action, or in the object, in which men are universally concerned, and which powerfully strikes upon the publick sympathy.'[22] We should always remember, when we encounter the term 'public' in civic humanist criticism, that it is never a simple shorthand for the audience, or for anyone. It is the audience, it is everyone, only in their public character: history painting must appeal to whatever concerns us universally; with what concerns us as universal men, as men considered in the light of what is common to all of them, their substantial nature, and not what is of concern to their private and accidental identities. Landscape painting, on the other hand, is, as Reynolds and Barry suggest, concerned with the representation of quietness and repose, with what were understood to be private feelings, and with what were described as private virtues: the only virtues open to be exhibited by those who were not public men, but open to them, also, when in retirement, or for some other reason not acting upon the public stage. It is this function of landscape-painting that justifies its existence, but which, in doing so, depresses it to the lower reaches of the hierarchy of genres, as it similarly depresses pastoral poetry below the epic and the tragic. It may be, as Barry points out, that in a society threatened by the forces of corruption, the private virtues are the only secure values left, and that landscape will come to seem preferable even to the subject-matter which history-painting exhibits, in an age without public heroes;[23] but in such an age, it is equally true that the public virtues of history-painting are more urgently in demand, or should be, and the supremacy of the genre, as the only genre capable of effecting a reform of public life, must be more urgently insisted upon.

It is at the interface of these two classifications of ideal panoramic landscape that Reynolds's learned riddle is engendered. According to one system of classification, the representation of such landscapes is an instantiation of the political capability of the public man, perhaps especially of value in an age in which the sphere of action of such a man was steadily being confined, as I have argued elsewhere,[24] to the *comprehension* of the social order, rather than its reformation; to the vindication of social structure as ordained by providence, or by the market, rather than to the creation of a social order other than that created by commerce, by the forces of private interest. On the other hand, according to the system of classification of the hierarchy of genres, landscape art is the instantiation of private virtues, often as a muted criticism of the values of that parody of a truly public, civic life which is the actuality of affairs in courts and cities. How then should landscape be represented? If as a public genre, it is essential that it should eliminate accident, and should exhibit ideas, as George Campbell puts it, 'not in their private, but, as it were, in their representative capacity'.[25] If on the other hand it is a private genre, it seems that the representation of accident is appropriate to it: and that Reynolds, for all his seeming decision in his fourth discourse in favour of Claude's landscape, purged of accident over the accidental forms of Rubens, is nevertheless impressed by the argument from the privacy of the genre, is clear by the terms in which he poses his riddle. He does not ask, as Hazlitt suggests, simply whether the landscape-painter should 'introduce' the accidents of nature. His terms are far more specific than that. He asks whether 'landscape painting has a right to *aspire so far* as to reject what the painters call Accidents of Nature' (my emphasis).[26] His meaning is, that an artist who, like Claude, does so reject them, may be aspiring above his station, and presuming to give to a private genre the universal and public status of history-painting. To answer, no, it shouldn't thus 'aspire', is to deny the power of images of panoramic landscape to instantiate the intellectual abilities and talents of public men, of the disinterested citizens of the republic of taste and of the political republic alike. To answer, yes it should, risks threatening the public status of history-painting, by encroaching upon it, and by suggesting, perhaps too openly, that public virtue is now indeed rather a matter of seeing than of doing. The riddle could not be solved, and though in his fourth discourse Reynolds appears to decide, as Hazlitt suggests, in favour of Claude, in his later discourses he shows considerable approval of the representation of the accidental forms of nature by the happy accidents of technique. This is a concession he makes only to landscape-painters, and only to them on the understanding that they work in a private genre, one addressed to our privacy, in which we may therefore take pleasure in the accidental forms of nature unidealised into generic form.

## V

We can sum up the problem which generates Reynolds's 'learned riddle' in some such way as this: for Reynolds, though history-painting is still unchallengeably at the top of the hierarchy of genres, its position there is no longer easily justifiable in terms of a *rhetorical* aesthetic, and an aesthetic of illusion, by which it deceives us into a sympathy with its actors which can move us to desire to perform the acts of public virtue which they perform. Reynolds justifies its pre-eminence, instead, as a genre which casts the spectator in the role, less of potential agent than of observer, the observer of common humanity, represented by general forms. As far as landscape-painting is concerned, then, as long as it is considered as a private genre – as occluded landscapes always, but as ideal landscapes only sometimes are – it is still imagined to be governed by a rhetorical aesthetic: it moves us to delight in, and to wish for, tranquillity and repose; and, as such, it can be enjoyed by all, for it is a law constitutive of a rhetorical aesthetic that *all* can feel the effects of art, even if all cannot determine the principles on which those effects are produced.

But when ideal panoramic landscape is treated as a public genre – as I hope I have shown it continually but not invariably was, in Britain in the period I have been considering – it was not accorded that status by means of a rhetorical, but of what may be called a philosophical aesthetic: the best landscape-painters, and those best equipped to appreciate them, are those few who can successfully reduce concrete particulars to abstract categories, the signs of which are less natural and more arbitrary than those employed in occluded landscapes, and are absolutely not intended to deceive the eye. If landscape can appeal to its audience in this way, however, and no longer simply rhetorically, then there are good reasons why it should be treated, as for rather different reasons Ruskin would treat it, as a genre as important, and as public, as history-painting; for it is now the aim of both to enable the exercise of that broad and comprehensive vision and that ability to abstract representative from actual nature that are now more clearly the qualifications for citizenship than a disposition to perform acts of public virtue. In short, it is by Reynolds's philosophical aesthetic that landscape has a claim to be regarded as a genre with a public function, which it does not have in terms of a rhetorical aesthetic.

Why then should Hazlitt, who is unlikely to have been unaware of the implications of the riddle, choose to ignore them? One reason is that he clearly considers it one of his tasks as a writer to abolish the distinctions between public and private – in politics, as a distinction between who can and who cannot participate in government; in painting, as a distinction between one kind of picture that appeals to us as citizens, another that appeals to us as private individuals. If Hazlitt succeeds in collapsing this distinction in his writings on art, it is largely by denying that painting has any public function at all, and by treating it as an art which offers private satisfactions to private individuals. But still his impatience with the distinction is a political impatience, in so far as it is related in particular to a distaste for the habit of addressing the politer part of that audience as 'the public', whether they acted as a public or simply as the acquisitive purchasers of pictures as private property. Anything that perpetuated this flattery, and the political division on which it was based, was an object of his attack; and he was especially hostile to the notional connection between the ownership of landed property and the claim to political disinterestedness.

For these reasons, I cannot help admiring Hazlitt for treating Reynolds's 'learned riddle' as a knot to be cut; but nor can I help regretting that he could do so, as it seems to me, only by denying the connection between art and politics, or rather between art and the public sphere, which had given such explanatory power to the writings of Reynolds, Barry, Blake and Fuseli, and had insisted on the interdependency of the republic of taste and the political republic, which Hazlitt was determined to dissolve.[27]

## Notes

First published in J. C. Eade, ed., *Projecting the landscape* (Canberra, 1987).
  1  Hazlitt, 'On genius and originality', *The Champion*, 4 December 1814, reprinted in Robert R.

Wark, ed., *Sir Joshua Reynolds: discourses on art*, 2nd edn (New Haven, Conn, and London, 1975), p. 324.

2  S. T.. Coleridge, *Lay sermons* (1817), ed. R. J. White (London, 1972), p. 136.

3  *Collected letters of S. T. Coleridge*, ed. E. L. Griggs (Oxford and New York, 1956–71), vol. 1, p. 349.

4  *Discourses*, p. 44.

5  *The Guardian*, no. 23 (7 April 1713).

6  Harris, *Philological inquiries* (1780–81), and *Hermes* (1751), in *The works of James Harris* (Oxford, 1841), pp. 218, 525–6.

7  Gilpin to William Mason, quoted in C. P. Barbier, *William Gilpin* (Oxford, 1963), p. 50.

8  John Opie, *Lectures on painting* (London, 1809), p. 13.

9  *The life and writings of Henry Fuseli*, ed. John Knowles (London, 1831), vol. 2, pp. 217–18.

10  G. Campbell, *The philosophy of rhetoric* (London, 1776), vol. 1, p. 5.

11  A. Hill, 'Preface to Mr Pope' (Preface to *The Creation*, 1720), Augustan Reprint· Society, Series 4, no. 2 (Ann Arbor, Mich., 1949), p. 1.

12  Alexander Pope, *An essay on man*, Epistle 1 (1733), ll. 1–6, 9–14; my remarks on Pope in this essay are adapted from my *English literature in history, 1730–1780: an equal, wide survey* (London, 1983), pp. 35–6.

13  Reynolds, 'Preface' to the 'Ironical discourse' in Frederick W. Hilles, ed., *Portraits by Sir Joshua Reynolds* (London, 1952), p. 129.

14  Edmund Burke, *Works* (London, 1815), vol. 5, p. 104.

15  D. Diderot, *Le Neveu de Rameau*, ed. Jean Fabre (Geneva, 1963), p. 103. The phrase is borrowed from Montaigne: see n. 312, p. 236.

16  A. Smith, *The theory of moral sentiments* (1759), ed. D. D. Raphael and A. L. MacFie (Oxford, 1976), p. 135. Raphael and MacFie suggests a source for this passage in Berkeley's *New theory of vision*, Sec 54; to me it seems closer to his *Discourse of passive obedience*, Sec 28:

> if we have a mind to take a fair prospect of the order and general well-being, which the inflexible laws of nature and morality derive on the world, we must, if I may so say, go out of it and imagine ourselves to be distant spectators of all that is transacted and contained in it; otherwise we are sure to be deceived by the too near view of the little present interest of ourselves, our friends, or our country.

17  Spoken observation of Reynolds, recorded in Madame D'Arblay, *Memoirs of Dr Burney* (London, 1832), vol. 2, pp. 281–2; quoted in Lawrence Lipking. *The ordering of the arts in eighteenth-century England* (Princeton, 1970), pp. 204–5.

18  I can make this point more clearly to those who have read David Solkin's essay, 'The battle of the Ciceros: Richard Wilson and the politics of landscape in the age of John Wilkes', reprinted elsewhere in this volume, in which Solkin discusses Wilson's *Cicero and his two friends at his villa an Arpinum, 1770*. Solkin's brilliant account of the painting might be strengthened by pointing out that the image of Cicero as the guardian of the public interest is further defined by his being represented in an ideal, extensive prospect, and not in the kind of occluded landscape depicted, for example, in Wilson's *Solitude* of eight years earlier.

19  Fuseli, vol. 2, p. 251.

20  J. Barry, *An inquiry into the real and imaginary obstructions to the acquisition of the arts in England* (London, 1775), p. 207.

21  Fuseli, vol. 2, p. 217.

22  *Discourses*, p. 57.

23  *Ibid.*, p. 70; Barry, *Works* (London, 1809), vol. 2, p. 405.

24  Barrell, *Survey*, 'Introduction'.

25  Campbell, vol. 2, p. 104.

26  *Discourses*, p. 70.

27  This essay has been developed from a paper given at the conference 'Landscape and the Arts', held at the Humanities Research Centre of the Australian National University at Canberra in July 1984. It was first published in garbled form in J. C. Eade, ed., *Projecting the landscape* (Canberra, 1987). When it was submitted for publication, it was imagined that it

would be published before my recent book, *The political theory of painting from Reynolds to Hazlitt: 'the body of the public'*, (London and New Haven, Conn., Yale University Press, 1986). A number of passages in that book are repeated from this essay. The first chapter of the book contains a more detailed account of the 'rhetorical' and the 'philosophical' aesthetic, and of Reynolds's thinking about the principles and place of landscape painting.

# 4

# The battle of the Ciceros:
## Richard Wilson and the politics of landscape in the age of John Wilkes
### David H. Solkin

The Royal Academy exhibition of 1770 contained one of Richard Wilson's most ambitious essays in the Grand Style, a picture impressively entitled *Cicero and his Two Friends, Atticus and Quintus, at his Villa at Arpinum* (Fig. 1). To any viewer familiar with the artist's previous work, or indeed with the entire tradition of European painting, this must have seemed a decidedly unusual choice of subject. Although Wilson had been depicting stories from classical mythology at regular intervals over the past fifteen years, it had been almost two decades since he had last portrayed an episode from the history of ancient Rome.[1] Furthermore, no contemporary or earlier master appears ever to have painted Cicero in retirement at his villa at Arpinum, nor indeed to have found anything at all worth illustrating in Cicero's treatise *De legibus* (*On the laws*). Given the fact that this book consists of a prolonged philosophical discussion virtually devoid of either pictorial or narrative incident, one can easily understand why it attracted so little in the way of artistic interest. But why, then, after these centuries of neglect, should so traditionally minded a painter as Richard Wilson have embarked on this untrodden (and seemingly unpromising) thematic path? A simple answer might be that he responded to a patron's demand. Though perhaps not particularly likely,[2] this possibility cannot be dismissed out of hand. Yet even such a scenario would in no way diminish the novelty of the event. Whether initiated by the artist himself or stimulated by a patron, the emergence of an image of Cicero at Arpinum still remains to be accounted for, as does the considerable degree of success which Wilson's picture evidently achieved.[3]

Here I shall argue that the keys to understanding why a *Cicero and his Friends* appeared in the first place, and why it met with a favourable reception, lie in the precise historical moment when Wilson produced

his work and placed it on public display. In particular, I shall put forward
the idea that he conceived this composition in response to an ongoing
social controversy which came to a head in England during the late 1760s
and early 1770s – a controversy dominated by the single figure of John
Wilkes (1727–87). Moreover, I shall contend that Wilson's landscape
took up a definable position within the turbulent debates of its day; in
other words, that the *Cicero and his Friends*, despite or even because of its
classical form and antique content, played an active, albeit minor role on
the contemporary British political stage.

But first of all we should examine the image itself. The genesis of the
composition underlines its rather exceptional character within Wilson's
work as a whole. As far as we know, all of his other historical landscapes
are either purely imaginary inventions, or they derive in part from
topographical sketches which date from his Italian period (1750–56/7).
Neither is the case with the *Cicero*, however. Instead Wilson based his
scene on what must be a study drawn from nature in Britain, and
presumably towards the very end of the 1760s.[4] Only the left half of this
sheet, altered in numerous details, was adapted for use within the
finished oil; Wilson retained the distant overlapping areas of forest,
rounded hill, and mountain, as well as the cascading river which flows
out from under a bridge and around a spit of land to the left. In all
probability this sketch describes a site somewhere in northern Wales –
not an odd choice of model for antique Latium, considering that Cicero's
villa was situated within a similarly rugged and mountainous region.[5]
Since Arpinum itself lay beyond his reach, Wilson must have seized upon
his own native countryside as the most appropriate available substitute,
at least as the starting-point for his design. But obviously he did not feel
honour bound to respect the topography of the view he had sketched.
Instead he marshalled a number of its salient motifs into a pleasing
composition, with the help of at least one other drawing, a rather
approximate affair in coloured chalks now in the Ashmolean Museum.[6]
With this sheet he established the basic progression of fore-, middle-,
and background planes to be used for the painting itself. The way in
which Wilson developed his theme can offer us an object lesson in the
standard procedure of a classical landscape artist: essentially, he moved

---

**1** Richard Wilson, *Cicero and his Two Friends, Atticus and Quintus, at his Villa at Arpinum*. Oil on
canvas, exh. RA 1770. Private collection.

**2** Claude Lorrain, *Landscape with St George and the Dragon*. Oil on canvas, c. 1643, Wadsworth
Atheneum, Hartford, Connecticut.

from a particularised reality to a generalised, imaginative ideal that
conforms to a pattern first invented by Claude Lorrain and Gaspard
Dughet in seventeenth-century Rome. Wilson's specific compositional
source appears to have been Claude's *Landscape with St George and the Dragon*
(c. 1643; Fig. 2), which the final *Cicero* closely resembles in its overall
disposition of landscape motifs.[7] The significance of this appropriation
deserves further elaboration, which I shall attempt to provide below. But
for the moment we need only emphasise a fairly general and obvious
point: that the *Cicero and his Friends* is an imitation of the great classical
masters. According to Sir Joshua Reynolds, 'a painter of landskips in this
style, and with this conduct, sends the imagination back into antiquity'[8] –
which is precisely what Wilson wanted to do. At the same time, by
adhering to this approach he demonstrated his capacity as a moral artist
to reveal the existence of a perfect and immutable providential order
underlying the superficial confusion of the natural world.[9] The opening
lines of *De legibus* provide a rather neat analogy to the painter's process of
idealisation. Atticus begins the discussion by pointing to the Marian oak,
which Cicero had described in his earlier poem, *Marius*: 'I recognise this
as the very grove, and this oak, too, as the oak of Arpinum, the description of which I have often read in your poem on Marius. If that oak still
exists, this must certainly be it; and, indeed, it appears extremely old.'
Cicero's brother Quintus responds, 'Yes, my Atticus, it does exist, and
always will exist, for it is a nursling of genius. No such long-lived stock
can be planted by the care of an agriculturist as may be sown by the verse
of a poet.'[10] The gestures of the foreground figures in Wilson's *Cicero* may
allude to this specific interchange; although, as we shall see, he referred
his audience to a different passage from *De legibus*. In any case, the lines
just quoted may serve to remind us that there were hallowed precedents
indeed for a landscape artist who sought to use his imagination to make
nature's eternal truth manifest to his viewers. Aside from imitating
Claude Lorrain, Wilson had also emulated the ancient Roman writers –
and here Cicero in particular – by applying their rules for poetry to the
sister art of painting.

We are looking, then, at an ideal landscape, but one which also depicts
an event that took place at a particular time in history, and in a specific
place. Wilson made this very clear by including a page reference to *De
legibus* in the Royal Academy catalogue. The relevant passages read as
follows:

*Atticus*: Do you feel inclined, since we have had walking enough for the present,
and since you must now take up a fresh part of the subject for discussion, to

vary our situation; and if you do, let us pass over to the island which is
surrounded by the Fibrenus – for such, I believe, is the name of the other river –
and sit down, while we prosecute the remainder of our discourse?
Cicero: I like your proposal: for that is the very spot which I generally select when I
want a place for undisturbed meditation, or uninterrupted reading or writing.
Atticus: In truth, now I am come to this delicious retreat, I cannot see too much of
it. Would you believe, that the pleasure I find here makes me almost despise
magnificent villas, marble pavements, and sculptured palaces: Who would not
smile at the artificial canals which our great folk call their Niles and Euripi, after
he had seen these beautiful streams? Therefore, as you just now, in our
conversation on Justice and Law, referred all things to Nature, so you seek to
preserve her domination even in those things which are constructed to
recreate and amuse the mind. I therefore used to wonder before, as I expected
nothing better in this neighbourhood than hills and rocks (and, indeed, I had
been led to form these ideas by your own speeches and verses) – I used to
wonder, I say, that you were so exceedingly delighted with this place. But my
present wonder, on the contrary, is, how, when you retire from Rome, you
condescend to rusticate in any other spot.

Cicero responds by saying that Arpinum holds a special meaning for him
as his birthplace, and as the home of his ancestors. Then Atticus conti-
nues, in words that seem particularly applicable to Wilson's landscape:

But here we are arrived in your favourite island. How beautiful it appears! How
bravely it stems the waves of the Fibrenus, whose divided waters lave its verdant
sides, and soon rejoin their rapid currents! The river just embraces space enough
for a moderate walk, and having discharged this office, and secured us an arena for
disputation, it immediately precipitates itself into the Liris; and then, like those
who ally themselves to patrician families, it loses its more obscure name, and
gives the waters of the Liris a greater degree of coolness.[11]

From all this one can easily see that Arpinum embodies an ideal of
rural wholesomeness and tranquillity; it offers a moral retreat from the
turmoils of urban life on the one hand, and from the showy opulence of
great villas on the other. Here Cicero, Atticus, and Quintus enjoy the
opportunity for leisurely contemplation, which focuses less on their
immediate surroundings than on the far more complex world that they
have left behind.

Broadly speaking, then, we can recognise that the Cicero and his Friends
belongs to a long thematic tradition in European pastoral art, a tradition
most commonly associated with the Horatian beatus ille.[12] Wilson had
dealt with this topos before,[13] just as he had produced ambitious subject-
pictures based on classical literary sources; but since his return from
Rome he had never painted anything as 'historical' as the Cicero and his

Friends. By this I do not simply refer to his substitution of actual individuals from the past for the fictional characters of ancient poetry; more to
the point, I think, is that Wilson's protagonist was widely admired as a
man of public or civic virtue, and as one of the pillars of the Roman
republic – Cicero, in other words, was precisely the sort of exemplary
figure whom history-painters were meant to represent. As defined by
eighteenth-century English art theorists, the primary purpose of historical painting was to promote the public (and republican) virtues of
heroism and disinterested statesmanship by appealing to the rational
faculties of its (male) viewers.[14] Reason, not emotion, was to be
addressed by the most elevated form of art; and here we should note that
the *Cicero* entirely lacks that element of sentimental pathos which had
been a hallmark of Wilson's earlier poetic landscapes from the *Destruction
of the Children of Niobe* (c. 1759–60; Yale Center for British Art, New Haven)
onwards. By comparison with its predecessors, the *Cicero* is much more
rigorously a 'public' work of art – and not just in terms of its nominal
subject, but also in its character of a generalised Claudean prospect.[15]
Whereas throughout the sixties Wilson had always designed his imaginary landscapes in the manner of Gaspard Dughet (though none is based
closely on a particular Gaspard), the *Cicero and his Friends* loudly proclaims
its reliance on a celebrated picture by Claude.[16] What may strike us here
as an abdication of artistic independence must instead be read as a sign of
elevated ambition: for it was Claude, and not Gaspard, who most fully
met the criteria of excellence set down in academic art theory.[17] Those
criteria had always meant a great deal to Wilson, but perhaps never more
so than in the years immediately after 1768, when he had been appointed
a founding member of Britain's very own Royal Academy.[18] As a matter
of fact, the *Cicero and his Friends* is the first historical subject that he appears
ever to have shown at an RA exhibition.[19] What I would argue, then, is
that the formal and iconographic innovations apparent in Wilson's
painting – though not his specific choice of *De legibus* as a source, which I
shall explore below – speak for a deliberate attempt on his part to
produce a landscape truly worthy of a Royal Academician.

   Such a dignified painter had also to ensure that his art addressed an
appropriately exclusive public. In the early 1700s Lord Shaftesbury had
put forward an influential set of arguments which identified the true
'public' for serious painting with the political republic of 'independent'
citizens, i.e. those men who owned substantial property in land.[20] By
mid-century these criteria for citizenship had been diluted, as individuals
who possessed other forms of property pressed their own political

claims; and constructions of the art public altered accordingly, in the direction of a community of sentiment.[21] One could argue that Wilson had in fact addressed just such a community with his pathetic narratives of the 1760s. It seems clear, however, that the Cicero was primarily aimed at a much narrower and more traditional public of landed gentlemen.

This argument rests on two general criteria first of all: the fact that the wealthy landowners of eighteenth-century Britain took particular pride in their knowledge of classical culture, and more specifically, that they often liked to think of themselves as modern counterparts to the fabled patricians of ancient Rome. John Shebbeare stated the case as follows in 1756: 'No compliment, however well turned in its expression or elegant in its conception, can impart a more flattering idea to an Englishman, than that which compares him to an old Roman; the valour, prudence, love of liberty and country, with those other eminent qualities of our illustrious predecessors, are the attributes which he receives with most delight.'[22] As a Roman who could claim all these qualities and more, Cicero was admirably suited to play a part in this kind of sophisticated flattery. No wonder that Anton Raphael Mengs included the orator's bust in his portrait of the Grand Tourist Lord Brudenell,[23] nor that Richard Wilson found several patrons who wanted to acquire an image of Cicero as an implicit compliment to their own moral worth. In him they saw their own idealised reflection: the heroic statesman, the defender of liberty, the learned philosopher, etc. – all in all, a model patrician by any standard of measurement. And they could identify with Cicero all the more easily because he had been a landowner, just as they were, and just as he appears within the confines of Wilson's design.

Moreover, here we see Cicero engaged in virtuous retirement on his own rural property – an activity that was of paramount significance to the mythology of landowning in eighteenth-century Britain.[24] Contemporary writers and artists never tired of describing the private country estate as a type of moral paradise, where the landlord devoted his leisure-time to the acquisition of true wisdom. Like Cicero at Arpinum before him, in such a setting he could attune his thoughts to the rhythms of nature as well as to the wishes of God, before returning to take an active part in directing the nation's affairs. Perhaps it need not be said that this kind of virtue was one which only a landed gentleman could ever realistically hope to achieve. In much the same way, the moral content of Wilson's picture was equally exclusive of access, as the description he composed for the Royal Academy catalogue suggests in no uncertain terms. At issue here is the italicised reference following the Cicero's full title: *Vide Cic. de Leg. lib. 2, p. 74.*[25] While one would not wish to labour the point, this brief note does carry several pertinent connotations, beyond serving its obvious purpose as a means of identification. For one thing, it tells us that Wilson expected his chosen public to understand Latin, and to possess some degree of familiarity with Cicero's treatise (which, by the way, was not translated into English until the 1850s). And despite the fact that *De legibus* was far from being one of Cicero's more celebrated works, Wilson even presumed that his viewers could identify the particular Latin edition in which page 74 occurs in the second book (of three); this happens to be a text first published at Cambridge in 1727, and later reissued in 1745.[26] In a subtle way these assumptions complimented the artist's own cultural accomplishments, as well as those of that social group to whom the *Cicero* was addressed.

For a representative sample of the public which Wilson had in mind, we can call upon the men who bought the two major versions of the *Cicero and his Friends*. The first, exhibited picture was probably acquired by John Smith Esq. (1744–1807) of Sydling St Nicholas in Dorset; in a portrait of 1797 after Francis Lemuel Abbott he appears as the archetypal cultured gentleman *à la* Cicero at Arpinum, standing in front of a Palladian bridge on his own private estate.[27] Smith attained the rank of baronet in 1774, and the *Cicero* engraving of four years later was dedicated to him (presumably because he possessed the original work). Wilson's other patron was Sir Watkin Williams-Wynn, 4th Bt (1748–89),[28] whom Pompeo Batoni depicted in a particularly grandiose conversation-piece of 1768–71. Sir Watkin stands at the left, holding a drawing copied from Raphael's figure of *Justice* in the Stanza della Segnatura[29] – not an insignificant choice of attribute, in light of his roughly contemporary interest in the *Cicero and his Friends*. Smith and Williams-Wynn shared a considerable amount in common. Aside from being substantial landowners, both were also serious intellectuals. Sir Watkin was a major patron of the arts virtually from the moment he finished his schooling at Oxford;[30] he went on to hold numerous cultural offices, including memberships in the Royal Society and in the Society of Dilettanti. Smith, who attended Cambridge, also joined the ranks of the Royal Society; in addition, he belonged to the Society of Antiquaries, and in 1780 received an honorary Doctorate in Civil Law from Oxford University. So one might say that we have justice on the one side, and law on the other. This is no mere metaphorical conceit. For aside from being extremely erudite individuals, both of Wilson's patrons occupied positions of considerable social authority. In 1770, each was doubtless acting in the magisterial capacity traditionally demanded of a lord of the manor; two years later, Sir Watkin took his seat in the House of Commons and Smith began his term of office as High Sheriff of Dorset. Like most members of the British ruling class, these men did not simply own land, but played an active part in the administration of the laws. Thus they were ideally qualified to appreciate the novel twist that Wilson had given to the age-old subject of virtuous rural retirement. Instead of employing either Horace or Virgil, the standard classical sources for this type of theme, he had illustrated a book on jurisprudence, written by a man whom the English admired first and foremost as a model legislator. Perhaps the only surprising thing about this innovation is that no one appears to have thought of it before. But if we cannot account for that omission, I think we can suggest some very good reasons why Wilson's *Cicero* appeared and succeeded when it did. Here we can begin by making one simple observation: that in 1770, many English patricians were urgently, almost obsessively concerned with those very questions of law which Cicero had discussed with Atticus and Quintus at his villa at Arpinum.

Today we tend to think of the ancient Romans as figures of no real relevance to our own world, as dead names from a distant and fundamentally alien past. But for a literate Englishman of the later eighteenth century, this was anything but the case. Far from being confined to scholarly tomes on the subject, references to classical antiquity pervaded the entire field of discourse about current affairs. In the belief that a knowledge of history was essential for understanding both the present and the future, social commentators constantly cited relevant episodes from the rise and fall of Roman civilisation, drawing analogies with modern Britain for the purpose of strengthening their particular arguments. If we wish to assess just how alive Rome was for the English at that time, we need only glance at the period's daily or weekly newspapers. From a quick survey of the London press, one might almost be tempted to believe that the leading figures of antiquity had miraculously returned to life, in order to participate in the most pressing political and social debates of the day. Correspondents rarely signed their own names to letters to the editor, for fear of government prosecution or personal condemnation; instead they invariably employed Latin pseudonyms, which had the added advantage of giving their opinions an aura of time-hallowed cultural authority. Among the host of reborn Romans who held forth in print during 1769 and 1770 alone, we encounter such names as Messala, Marcellus, Vasa, Brutus, Gracchus, Agrippa, Sisenna, Cato Junior and, most notorious of all, Junius; the list goes on and on.

And as we shall see, there was a Cicero, not to mention a Tullius and an Atticus. Latin pseudonyms, it should be pointed out, were used by writers of all shades of political opinion, from the most radical to the most reactionary, just as analogies with Roman history were often exploited for quite contradictory purposes. But here we need only take one broad factor into account: that Wilson produced his *Cicero and his Friends* for viewers who had grown accustomed to reading the classical past in terms of the British present, and to seeing a historical figure like Cicero as someone whose words and deeds spoke to modern concerns. In 1770, those concerns focused above all on one man – John Wilkes.

Wilkes had first intruded into the public consciousness in 1763, when he had published an attack on the King's ministers in issue no. 45 of the *North Briton*.[31] This gained him the deep animosity of the government, which proceeded to embroil him in a series of highly visible legal battles. As an opponent of the extremely unpopular ministry directed by Lord Bute, Wilkes quickly attracted a host of passionate supporters, particularly among the middling and lesser tradesmen of London; its streets soon echoed to the cries of the first 'Wilkes and Liberty' mobs. In February of 1764 their hero fled to France to avoid being put on trial, and Parliament responded by declaring him an outlaw. Impelled by financial need, Wilkes returned home in the winter of 1768, in the hopes of securing a parliamentary seat and thus rendering himself immune to prosecution for debt. After an initial setback, he was returned to the Commons in March as a member for the county of Middlesex. A month later he submitted to arrest for outlawry, which was dismissed on a technicality, and was convicted on two other charges – that of seditious libel occasioned by *North Briton* no. 45, and one of obscenity, for having written and published a pornographic *Essay on woman*. Wilkes, to put it mildly, was something less than a paragon of moral rectitude in his private life. But this does not seem to have bothered the great majority of his admirers: Wilkes's confinement in the King's Bench Prison inspired a wave of mob violence during the summer and autumn of 1768, which stimulated Parliament to deprive him of his membership when the Commons reopened the following February. Then the sparks really began to fly. Before April had passed, the Middlesex voters had returned Wilkes to Parliament no fewer than three times, in defiance of a government resolution declaring him incapable of joining its ranks. Finally, on 15 April, the Commons unseated Wilkes in favour of the defeated candidate, Colonel Henry Luttrell. This move set off a frenzy of petitioning and agitation that continued well into 1770. Tempers were still high when

Wilkes was released from prison on 17 April of that year – about a week before the start of the Royal Academy exhibition – and his cause continued to occupy centre-stage on the English political scene for many months yet to come.

As has often been pointed out, the historical importance of the entire Wilkes affair lay far less in the man himself than in the issues raised by his case. He enjoyed remarkable success in propagandising his situation not as a personal problem, but as 'a clash between the forces guarding liberty and those working in favour of arbitrary power'.[32] Some of his supporters were country gentlemen who had traditionally been opposed to centralised government authority (and especially to the power of the Court); most Wilkites, however, came from that segment of the urban middle class which was frustrated by its lack of political clout. The most fundamental question raised by Parliament's repeated efforts to expel Wilkes, and by the final decision to replace him with Luttrell, was whether power should come from above or below. Who was in charge? – Parliament or the electors, the magistrates or the people? In his treatise on the laws, Cicero had taken a firm stand upon this very subject.

Cicero had lived at a time which virtually all English commentators regarded as the crucial turning-point in Roman history – the moment when they saw a free republic as having given way to a tyrannical empire, thus dooming a mighty civilisation to eventual collapse. Cicero had tried to stem the tide, most notably by leading the fight against Catiline's conspiracy; but no one individual, no matter how courageous, could have stopped the corrupted state of its citizenry from sealing the republic's fate. Foreshadowing that calamity was the rise of the tribune Clodius, a demagogue skilled at inflaming the passions of the mob. He incited Rome's plebeians to focus their fury on Cicero, who had to flee the city in fear for his life. Soon afterwards, according to an authoritative early biographer, the celebrated orator composed his book On the laws.[33] To quote from the introduction to an eighteenth-century French edition:

In a period when the ambition of the nobles and the spirit of independence and faction among the people were hastening on that terrible tragedy whose last act could only terminate in the loss of liberty, Cicero depicted before the eyes of his fellow-citizens the image of the Roman commonwealth in its best conceivable state, when laws, morals, discipline, subordination, patriotism, justice, disinterestedness, frugality, and other virtues were encouraged and patronised.[34]

Some eighteen hundred years later, Richard Wilson was to follow

Cicero's example by offering an idealised image of the past as a moral
lesson to a corrupted present.

Indeed, to many Englishmen of the late 1760s and early 1770s, their
own country's situation seemed little different from that which Cicero
had faced. Leadership had degenerated into faction; public morals were
in a bad way; a rabble-rousing demagogue was stirring up an insub-
ordinate people; all manner of dangers to liberty abounded. In a letter
published by the *Public Advertiser* in March 1770, the anti-Wilkite writer
'Tribunus' drew the following parallel:

Things, in short, are, on all hands, in a damned condition. . . . We have realised
that depraved state of affairs, ingenious writers feigned in better times. We possess
all the vices of the declining Romans, without any of those exalted virtues that
shone, at times, through the thickest cloud of their national depravity, and rapid
progress to a second barbarism.[35]

'Tribunus' painted a picture of a society in the throes of disintegration,
caused by the debility of the governors on the one hand, and the
rebellious tendencies of the governed on the other. Like the great
majority of spokesmen who argued against the cause of 'Wilkes and
Liberty', he called upon the men who ruled England to strengthen their
authority before it was too late. Anyone familiar with the writings of
Cicero must have realised that his message in *De legibus* was precisely the
same. As Cicero put it:

It is clear . . . that magistrates are absolutely necessary; since, without their
prudence and diligence, a state cannot exist; and since it is by their regulations
that the whole commonwealth is kept within the bounds of moderation. But it is
not enough to prescribe for them a rule of domination, unless we likewise
prescribe for the citizens a rule of obedience. . . . We would not, however, limit
ourselves to requiring from the citizens submission and obedience towards their
magistrates; we would also enjoin them by all means to honour and love their
rulers.[36]

According to Atticus, Cicero had amply demonstrated the soundness
of these principles during the period of his consulate; as a governor he
had realised 'the best state of the commonwealth', by ensuring that 'the
chief power in the hands of the aristocracy prevailed over that of the
populace'.[37] No statement could more succinctly encapsulate the main
bone of contention between the Wilkites and their opponents. By refus-
ing to heed the wishes of the Middlesex electors, both Parliament and
the King acted in defence of an aristocratic form of government which
was under siege by an uneasy alliance of disaffected landowners and a
radicalised stratum of the urban middle class.

The plebeian challenge to patrician rule took on a variety of forms, of which none was more prominent or threatening than mob violence. Eight major waves of Wilkite rioting shook the country between March 1768 and April 1769; a year later, another round of unruly celebrations greeted Wilkes upon his release from prison. These disturbances created a great deal of anxiety, even among individuals sympathetic to the Wilkite cause. For although they may have been opposed to the decisions taken by Parliament, such men saw greater dangers to both liberty and property in the unpredictable behaviour of an anarchic mob. Again, Cicero had been of much the same mind. For as he told Atticus and Quintus, 'nothing is more destructive in states, nothing so contrary to law and right, nothing less civil and humane, than to carry anything by violence and agitation in a sound and constitutional government'.[38]

I suspect that the arguments of De legibus were deliberately echoed by an English polemicist who actually signed his name 'Cicero' to a letter published by the Public Advertiser in October 1769. This latter-day Tully saw

but one Means of Salvation for us in our present calamitous Circumstances. If the persons to whom our most amiable Sovereign has intrusted the Reins of Government, dare boldly face these bursting Storms of Sedition, and continue unshaken by the vague Threats of a misled and enraged Multitude, we still may escape; but it is beyond a Doubt, that if the least Compliance is shewn to the unreasonable Requests with which they have dared to disturb the Throne, and insult the whole Legislature, we must inevitably sink into Perdition; and that beautiful Structure, which our glorious Ancestors have built and cemented with their Blood, shall fall (O piteous change!) into an undistinguished Heap of Ruins.[39]

The situation might yet be saved, in other words, if the King's ministers stood firm against the fury of the mob, and if they refused to heed the petitions in support of the Middlesex electors. But neither these assertions, nor those penned by the original Cicero himself, would have passed without challenge in the English political climate of 1769–70. Many of those who defended Wilkes argued that rioting was the only recourse left to a people whose freedoms had been unjustly usurped by a tyrannical and arbitrary government. For a fairly typical articulation of this point of view, we can turn to a letter signed 'Albanus', which appeared in the Public Ledger in September 1770:

To what are we to impute these disorders? and to what cause assign the decay of a state, so powerful and so flourishing in past times? The reason is plain, the servant is now become the master. The magistrate was subservient to the people; punishments and rewards were the properties of the people . . . But what are that people now? What their suffrages, their elections, their rights, or their privileges? All, all lost. – The magistrate has ... usurped your right, and exercises an arbitrary authority over his ancient and natural Lord.[40]

The notion that nature puts the people *above* their magistrates runs precisely counter to the spirit of the parliamentary resolution to expel Wilkes in favour of Luttrell; in the most fundamental terms, this move was justified on the grounds that the legislators' superiority to their electors was based upon natural law. And natural law is, of course, what we see Cicero and his friends discussing in the rugged setting of Wilson's Arpinum. Their inspiration comes directly from nature herself, as their postures in the landscape are clearly meant to suggest. Not surprisingly, this trio of ancient patricians reached the same conclusions which motivated their much later English counterparts. The basic point of Cicero's argument is that the laws of the commonwealth, especially in so far as they assign authority to the magistrates and obedience to the citizens, form part of the eternal pattern of nature as established by an omniscient God. To quote from *De legibus* for the last time:

This, then, ... has been the decision of the wisest philosophers, – that law was neither a thing contrived by the genius of man, nor established by any decree of the people, but a certain eternal principle, which governs the entire universe, wisely commanding what is right and prohibiting what is wrong. Therefore they called that aboriginal and supreme law the mind of God, enjoining or forbidding each separate thing in accordance with reason.[41]

Once the laws are equated with nature, reason, and God, then they cannot be challenged on either moral or rational grounds. This kind of argument crops up over and over again in many English treatises on jurisprudence; as one might expect, it was restated with particular frequency by writers who saw a serious threat to the nation's proper social structure in the persons of Wilkes and his plebeian supporters. As phrased by one such commentator in 1771:

Let everyone therefore remain where nature has placed him. Let us respect the sublime intelligence that reigns in the most grand and magnificent picture that ever was. What a ridiculous dissonancy must we not see, if being able to displace the order of the ground-work and details, of the lights and the shades, those personages who fly back and seem to disappear in it, should exhibit themselves on more advanced plan[e]s, and we should transmit to their place such as are appropriate for receiving the greatest illustrations of light?[42]

Curiously enough, this writer used the language of landscape painting to illustrate his point that men should respect the established social hierarchy, if they wished to order their lives in agreement with natural and divine law. And surely it would seem most improper if Cicero and his friends were to switch places with the unseen shepherd who must be guarding his flock in the background of Wilson's view.

We have seen, therefore, that Cicero's book *On the laws* had something quite specific to say about England's most pressing social issues during the period around 1770. But does it then necessarily follow that a painting based on this text would have functioned in more or less the same way? Even if we are willing to accept the notion that Wilson's public had a fairly clear idea of what *De legibus* was all about, and that cultured Englishmen were in the habit of connecting ancient Roman themes to modern historical events, we may seem to invade more problematic territory when it comes to assigning a political role to a fine example of Grand Style landscape art. In order to try and bridge this gap, certain more specifically artistic factors should be taken into account.

First of all, it would be a grave mistake to assume that the pictures on display at the Royal Academy were somehow insulated from the world outside. In fact, the Academy itself had been very much of a political issue ever since it had come into being in 1768. By abandoning their membership in the Society of Artists of Great Britain, the first Academicians had provoked a great deal of dissension within the artistic community as a whole. This furore expressed itself in a series of pamphlets, and of letters to the London press which took on the dimensions of a major public debate during 1769 and 1770 especially. The Academy's opponents appear mainly to have been disgruntled artists, who felt betrayed by some of their more eminent colleagues.[43] But while the critics may have been motivated by personal reasons, it has never been pointed out that many of their arguments were overtly political. In particular, they singled out the Academy as yet another example of that pernicious tendency towards arbitrary power which was trying to stamp out the cleansing flame of 'Wilkes and Liberty'. This is made perfectly clear in a letter addressed to the King by the pseudonymous polemicist 'Fresnoy', which was published by the Wilkite *Middlesex Journal* in May 1770; 'You disdain, then, sir, to mingle your royal favour with the vulgar, honest, ardent wishes of the people, in support of the society of artists of Great Britain; and therefore instituted the royal academy, so that the plumes of prerogative might wave in triumph over the cap of liberty.'[44] 'Fresnoy' further castigated the academicians themselves as 'old' men who had turned courtier, in return for being made 'knights' and 'esquires'.[45] Their works, he asserted, were not truly English but 'Parisian', suited to the tastes of a despotic regime.[46] 'The mean, slavish, and selfish arts practised by the

Foreign academy in Pall-Mall'[47] – this was how one of 'Fresnoy's' allies, writing under the name of 'Paul Varnish', described the RA exhibition of 1770. Thus, in the eyes of the radicalised middle class, the Academy belonged to the enemy camp, as an instrument of those who believed that all power should be exercised from the top.

Many of the Academicians themselves were perfectly happy to confirm the impression that their institution represented a bastion of privilege. Some years later, the painter William Collins was to make the proud claim that the rank of Royal Academician 'was equal to a patent of nobility'.[48] Perhaps a more noteworthy symptom of the RA's sense of their elevated status is the effort they made to attract viewers only from the respectable ranks of society. As started in the catalogue for the first exhibition, entrance fees were charged in order to prevent 'The Room being filled by Improper Persons, to the entire exclusion of those for whom the Exhibition is apparently intended'.[49]

Those 'Improper Persons' did have an art of their own – engraved illustrations in magazines, for example, or the cheap and often defiantly crude satirical prints which sold for pennies in the streets. And when the early Academy exhibitions were in progress, the outsiders held their own counter-exhibitions, at least in fictitious form. Usually described as the work of sign-painters, in reference to Hogarth's famous alternative display of 1762, these shows were reviewed – or rather brought into being – in the pages of such periodicals as the *Middlesex Journal*. Their 'contents', as one might expect, stood in stark contrast to what could actually be seen at the RA. The imaginary pictures were usually political in theme, and were either anonymous or attributed to popular heroes or villains. One such 'show', concurrent with the Academy exhibition of 1770, included a portrait described in the following manner: 'Mr. *Wilkes in a Roman habit* – a bold, majestic figure; in his right hand the Bill of Rights, and in the other, the sword of Justice.'[50] Here we can envision a Roman orator, akin in type to those Catos, Juniuses and Brutuses who speak from the pages of the Wilkite press. That this construct was phrased in ostensibly pictorial terms suggests a form of radical alternative to a painting like Wilson's *Cicero and his Friends*.

In addition, a number of real images from 1770 questioned certain basic premises of his design, by fashioning some of the same thematic materials into entirely different political statements. When that year's Royal Academy exhibition was in progress, for instance, the pro-Wilkes *London Magazine* published an engraved portrait of Edmund Burke, boldly captioned *The British Cicero*, which shows the Irish-born orator brandishing the Magna Carta and flanked by a full-length statue of his Roman counterpart.[51] The criterion of oratory does not fully explain just how such a connection came to be made. Although not overly enamoured of Wilkes himself, and distinctly suspicious of the motives of many of the 'Liberty Boys', Burke played a major public role in galvanising nationwide support for the cause of the frustrated Middlesex electors.[52] He did so in the belief that Parliament's refusal to heed their desires was symptomatic of a far broader and more serious problem: the growing power of the Court, which Burke saw as threatening to replace a form of government responsible to the electors with one controlled by royal favouritism. Burke's purposes, of course, were not entirely unselfish. One of his major purposes was to justify the role of an Opposition party, and specifically that of his own faction, the Rockingham Whigs. Yet no matter what his reasons may have been, Burke's actions made him something of a Wilkite hero. He was often praised as a defender of liberty – and herein lay the rationale for associating his name with that of Cicero.[53] For among all of the latter's celebrated deeds, none commanded greater respect in the eyes of eighteenth-century Englishman than his heroic struggle against the forces of tyranny, as embodied in the conspiracy led by Catiline.[54] It was in this, what one might aptly term his dominant guise, that Cicero was enlisted into the Wilkite ranks, and assigned to Edmund Burke's symbolic retinue. But more than one type of Cicero took part in the political fray. The pseudonymous 'Cicero' who wrote to the Public Advertiser in late 1769 (see above) was fundamentally opposed to all that Burke and the Wilkites were striving to achieve; unlike theirs, his chosen model was not the fighter of tyrants, but rather the apologist for patrician authority who had composed De legibus. As an illustration of that specific text, Wilson's painting joined forces with one side of a veritable battle of the Ciceros which had already entered into the mainstream of the Wilkes debate.

His Royal Academy exhibit, however, had more than just rival images of Cicero to contend with. By 1770, in response to the ongoing dispute over the actions taken by Parliament, certain contemporary artists had begun to produce works which radically challenged the basic moral presumptions of aristocratic government in general. One particularly incisive example came from the pen of John Collet, in the form of a small landscape print that appeared a few months before the Cicero made its public debut (Fig. 3). Collet (c. 1725–80) is a little-known but nonetheless fascinating figure, perhaps the only English painter of his generation who was able to straddle the dividing-line between polite and popular art.

During the 1760s and 1770s he exhibited a mixture of pastoral landscapes and satirical subjects at the Free Society of Artists; significantly, he never made the jump to the RA. Where the academicians generally aspired to be seen as gentlemen, Collet obviously had no such pretensions. Instead he often took it upon himself to lampoon some of the gentry's most deeply cherished myths. In this instance he has described a rather repulsive country squire who is trying to seduce an eminently wholesome farm girl; their posture derive from the first plate of Hogarth's *A Harlot's Progress*, a visual echo which accentuates the overtones of moral corruption.[55] These are further emphasised by the prominently positioned goats, a conventional symbol of lust in eighteenth-century English political prints.[56] The animals' presence, and that of the smirking peasant beyond, may contribute to an initial impression that Collet's message is fairly innocuous – little more than a mild satire of patrician power, translated into the easily recognisable terms of sexual exploitation. But this satire takes on a dimension of malignancy once we follow the landlord's gesture to the gibbet which dominates the middle distance, precisely where our vision comes to rest. The hanged man's presence tells us something of utmost importance: that the landed gentry controlled the law, and could exploit that control as a means of constraining the liberty

**3** Samuel Smith after John Collet, *Landscape with a Squire and a Farmgirl*. Engraving, 1770.

of their poorer subjects. The message is one which frequently appeared in the contemporary radical press; to cite only one such assertion, taken from the *Middlesex Journal* of 1769, 'Liberty is a phantom, and so is truth. The only rule of – Right, – Justice, – and Law, is Power.'[57]

This cynical statement strikes at the very heart of that idea of patrician rule which the *Cicero and his Friends* so fervently supports. Whereas Wilson presents the landlord-cum-legislator as personifying virtue in authority, Collet endows the identical figure with the attributes of oppressive and arbitrary vice. There is no need to conclude that either statement is true – only that neither takes a neutral stand. Essentially, we are looking at a pair of conflicting pictorial responses to the same historical situation. And that conflict, it should be pointed out, also takes place on the level of form.

Both compositions rely on lateral framing elements to direct our vision into the centre – but what meets us there is entirely different in each case. In Wilson's landscape we literally ascend towards the heavens; as indeed must seem only appropriate, since Cicero and his friends are discussing how the contemplation of nature must inevitably lead men to an awareness of the wisdom of God. But when we try to move through Collet's prospect, we immediately encounter some formidable obstacles, notably the bulk of the squire who blocks the horizon, and the gibbet silhouetted against the sky. Even the overhanging branches push us downwards, keeping us very much on the earthly plane with little or no room for escape. Here the landlord and the signs of his authority function not only as formal intrusions, but as intruders, forces that evidently disrupt the natural order of things. We could never say that about Cicero, Atticus, and Quintus. In formal terms, they simply complete the arrow-shape of the waters moving in from the left-hand side; even the gesture of the rightmost figure seems to follow the bidding of the broken log behind. The villa also pays homage to its surroundings by echoing the lines of the bridge beneath and the overlapping contours of the receding hills. Though this building represents a visible stamp of human possession, it is neither obtrusive nor dominant; instead, like the three men in front, it remains subject to the natural pattern. What Wilson's picture is suggesting, I believe – and this would be fully consistent with his textual source – is that patrician ownership and authority are part and parcel with the order of nature. Collet asks us to arrive at precisely the opposite conclusion.

Furthermore, one doesn't need to be much of a connoisseur to realise that Collet's print owes as much to the heritage of seventeenth-century

Dutch naturalism as Wilson's painting does to the grandiose heights of the classical tradition. The *Cicero*, as we have seen, describes a generalised ideal based only vaguely on a particular place; Collet's scene, on the other hand, speaks in emphatically contemporary and individualised terms.[58] This formal contrast is perfectly in keeping with the content of each image: while Wilson deals with abstract concepts of morality, natural law, providential pattern, etc., Collet ignores abstractions in favour of making a very specific point. Moreover, he has phrased his message in a pictorial language that virtually any of his viewers would have been able to understand – the implication being that no one part of his audience is in any way superior to the rest. But Wilson has made just such an assumption, and not simply by referring to a Latin source or by invoking the example of Claude Lorrain. In the *Cicero and his Friends* he has fused an elevated style with an equally artistocratic philosophical approach in order to suggest the special status of his chosen public, as individuals who are morally, socially, and intellectually superior to that part of mankind which is tied to more vulgar, material concerns. As James T. Boulton has observed, this was precisely the strategy employed by the leading spokesmen for the government cause in the press and pamphlet war of the late 1760s and early 1770s.[59] While they tended to favour generalised arguments about universal truths, often buttressed by Latin quotations, most of their opponents discussed highly topical issues in the defiantly simple language of the common man. On the battleground of political discourse, questions of style and questions of substance were debated with equal intensity[60] – and the visual arts were divided along closely comparable lines. If a painter set out to identify himself with one polarity or the other, he had to play by the rules of a game which restricted his choice of both form and content. Clearly, John Collet was well aware that he was taking sides. Why should Richard Wilson have been any different?

I don't wish to imply that politics were uppermost in Wilson's mind when he sat down to paint the *Cicero and his Friends*. I imagine that he was more immediately concerned with the forthcoming Royal Academy exhibition, and with producing a new sort of landscape appropriate to that dignified institutional setting. Thus Wilson may simply have regarded his picture as a *tour de force* of classical erudition, and perhaps at the same time as more truly and thoroughly a history-painting than any of his earlier works. Or possibly he was only aware of one aspect of his *Cicero's* meaning, that having to do with the conventional theme of rustic retirement. But even if a patron had supplied him with the subject, could

Wilson have been totally ignorant of the fact that his novel iconography lent itself so readily to the purposes of propaganda?After all, he had already come under personal attack by one Wilkite polemicist: in one of his tirades against the Royal Academy, 'Fresnoy' had cruelly caricatured Wilson as a drunkard, and had placed him within the ranks of the toadies to despotism.[61] Furthermore, throughout 1770 Wilson was engaged on a series of major commissions for Sir Watkin Williams-Wynn, whose opposition to the cause of the Middlesex electors was sufficiently prominent to merit special condemnation in the radical press.[62] To assume that neither the artist nor his patron would have thought to connect an illustration of De legibus with the Wilkite agitations seems to fly in the face of probability. And we should keep in mind that Wilson addressed his composition to a group of highly educated individuals who knew their Cicero, and who were anything but short of political awareness. It is hard to imagine that such a public could simply have missed the picture's topical connotations. Although Cicero may have had only two companions at his villa at Arpinum, in eighteenth-century Britain he could boast a tumultuous throng of admirers; and at no other time did they listen more closely to his words, nor compete more bitterly for his friendship, than during the heyday of John Wilkes.

## Notes

1 In January 1752, shortly after his arrival in Rome, Wilson was commissioned by Ralph Howard to paint a *Summons of Cincinnatus* and a *Departure of Regulus* (both now in a private collection, London); see W. G. Constable, *Richard Wilson* (Cambridge, Mass., 1953), pls. 15a, 15b. These two works and the *Cicero* make up the known total of paintings by Wilson of Roman historical subjects.

2 As Michael Kitson has kindly suggested to me in conversation, the idea of amplifying the meaning of a classical landscape by incorporating a textual reference of this type would be more in keeping with a painter's than with a patron's way of thinking.

3 The *Cicero*'s success can be judged by the fact that the original version (probably Fig. 1) spawned several repetitions, of which at least three autograph examples are now extant (one in the National Gallery of South Australia, another in a Canadian private collection, and a third which passed through Sotheby's on 6 July 1983, lot 270). None of Wilson's other late historical landscapes appears to have been as prolific a 'breeder'. Furthermore, the version illustrated here was published as a print in 1778 – and the expense of engraving was rarely undertaken unless a composition had attracted attention sufficient to promise a broad market appeal. The questions of identifying the public for this print, and of analysing the reasons for their interest, lie outside the chronological scope of this paper. Undoubtedly, however, by 1778 the *Cicero* had lost most if not all of the specifically topical connotations which I shall be discussing here.

4 For a discussion of the two known studies for the *Cicero*, see D. H. Solkin, 'Some new light on the drawings of Richard Wilson', *Master Drawings*, XXI, no. 4 (1978), pp. 409–10. The nature study is reproduced as pl. 15 in the first version of this essay (*Art History*, vol. 6, no. 4 (December 1983), pp. 406–22, to be referred to hereafter as Solkin, *Art History*).

5  In a letter to Atticus, Cicero had once described that part of Latium in which Arpinum was situated by quoting Homer's lines on the land of Ithaca (*Odyssey*, IX, 27): 'Rough land, but breeds good men.' See D. R. Shackleton Bailey, ed., *Cicero's letters to Atticus*, 5 vols. (Cambridge 1965), I, p. 231. Perhaps the northern Welsh flavour of Wilson's landscape was one factor which stimulated the great Denbighshire landowner, Sir Watkin Williams-Wynn, to purchase a version of the *Cicero and his Friends*.

6  Solkin, *Art History*, pl. 16; also reproduced in Constable, *Wilson*, pl. 27c.

7  Wilson may have based his composition on the actual picture by Claude, or on Barrière's etching of 1688, after a finished drawing now in the Rospigliosi collection. The painting was still in Rome (in the Palazzo Barberini) when Wilson was studying there, though he probably had a better opportunity to examine it after its arrival in England by the mid-1760s. Curiously, the *St George* is itself based on an earlier model: the Domenichino of the same subject now in the National Gallery, London. See M. Röthlisberger, *Claude Lorrain: the paintings*, 2 vols. (New Haven, Conn., 1961), I. pp. 191, 217–18.

8  Sir J. Reynolds, *Discourses on art*, XIII, 1786, ed. R. Wark (New Haven, Conn. and London, 1975), p. 237.

9  On the moral basis for classical landscape art as articulated in eighteenth-century England, see D. H. Solkin, *Richard Wilson – the landscape of reaction* (London, 1982), esp. pp. 58–76.

10  Cicero, *De legibus*, in *The treatise of M. T. Cicero*, trans. C. D. Yonge (London c. 1853), p. 398. All subsequent references to *De legibus* are taken from this edition.

11  *Ibid.*, pp. 427–9.

12  On the innumerable variations on this theme produced by English writers during the seventeenth and eighteenth centuries, see M.-S. Røstvig, *The happy man: studies in the metamorphoses of a classical ideal*, 2 vols. (Oslo, 1954 and 1971).

13  Wilson's *Solitude* of 1762 is a pictorial emblem of the Horatian retirement ideal, and like the *Cicero* may have had certain specific political connotations; see Solkin, *Wilson*, pp. 70–4, 102.

14  This all too brief summary of the functions of history-painting is based on John Barrell, *The political theory of painting from Reynolds to Hazlitt – the body of the public* (New Haven, Conn. and London, 1986), pp. 1–23 and passim.

15  On the politics of the Claudean prospect, see John Barrell's essay in this volume, pp. 19–40. In eighteenth-century Britain, this most public form of landscape was more often constructed in literature than it was in painting, where Wilson's *Cicero* represents an exceptionally thorough and ambitious realisation of the type.

16  Sir William Beechey once recalled Wilson as saying that he admired Claude for 'air' and Gaspard for 'composition' (quoted in W. T. Whitley, *Artists and their friends in England 1700–1799*, 2 vols. (Cambridge, 1928), I, p. 380). This remark obviously does not apply to the *Cicero*, nor to Wilson's Italian-period landscapes of c. 1754–55, which are just as thoroughly Claudean in handling as they are in design; on these pictures, see Solkin, *Wilson*, pp. 38–49, 187–91. Here it may also be worth pointing out that the renewal of Wilson's interest in Claude during the early 1770s is marked not only by the *Cicero and his Friends*, but also by his other historical landscapes from the same years: notably the engraved version of *Apollo and the Seasons* (first published in 1772, and reproduced in Constable, Wilson, pl. 26a), and the *Athens in a Flourishing State* of c. 1772 (engraving in reverse of original, repro. Constable, pl. 29b), which is essentially an imaginative pastiche of several works by Claude, including the famous '*Altieri' Landscape with the Father of Psyche Sacrificing at the Milesian Temple of Apollo* (1663; The National Trust, Anglesey Abbey; see Röthlisberger, *Claude Lorrain*, II, fig. 259).

17  While Reynolds mentions Claude on numerous occasions in his *Discourses* (e.g. Wark, ed., pp. 69–70), he never once refers to Gaspard – perhaps because the latter produced a large number of specific views, whereas the great preponderance of Claude's works consisted of ideal landscape compositions.

18 Of course Wilson was not the only founding member of the Academy to produce works of an exceptionally ambitious character during the period just after 1768; the best known example of this tendency is Reynolds.

19 In 1769, at the first Royal Academy exhibition, Wilson exhibited three pictures which are simply described in the catalogue (nos. 122–4) as 'landskips'. As far as I know he never used such basic terminology to describe pictures with a significant narrative component, so these are likely to have been either Italian views or pastoral compositions.

20 For a discussion of Shaftesbury's construction of the 'public' and its impact on subsequent art theory, see Barrell, *Political theory*, introduction.

21 See, for example, my 'Portraiture in motion: Edward Penny's *Marquis of Granby* and the creation of a public for English art', *Huntington Library Quarterly*, vol. 49, no. 1 (winter 1986), pp. 1–23.

22 'Battista Angeloni' (J. Shebbeare), *Letters to the English nation*, 2nd edn, 2 vols. (London, 1756), I, p. 1.

23 Coll. The Duke of Buccleuch and Queensberry, KT, Boughton House, Northants. See F. .Russell, 'The British portraits of Anton Raphael Mengs', *National Trust Studies* (1979), pp. 11–12, fig. 3.

24 On the importance of the notion of virtuous rural retirement to the landed gentry of eighteenth-century England, see Røstvig, *Happy man*.

25 *The exhibition of the Royal Academy. MDCCLXX. The second* (London, 1770), p. 19. No other entry in the catalogue included a textual reference in any language but English.

26 The catalogue reference is to Cicero, *De legibus* (Cambridge, 1727, reprinted 1745). I have been unable to determine whether this was the most commonly used edition of the period, though certainly it was far from being the only available one.

27 Solkin, *Art History*, pl. 18.

28 On 5 June 1770 Sir Watkin gave Wilson a partial payment in advance for a 'Capital Landskip with Cicero at his Villa' (the Adelaide version, see n. 3 above; repro. Constable, *Wilson*, pl. 27b). This work, together with several others, appears to have been completed by 3 July of the following year, when the painter received the balance due. The relevant receipts are now in the National Library of Wales, Aberystwyth, and have been fully reproduced in W. G. Constable, 'Richard Wilson: some pentimenti', *Burlington Magazine*, XCVI (1954), p. 140. For a discussion of the chronological relationship between the two main versions of the *Cicero*, as established by the Williams-Wynn documents and the extant preliminary drawings, see Solkin, 'Drawings', p. 413, n. 26.

29 On the iconography of this portrait, see The Iveagh Bequest, Kenwood, *Pompeo Batoni (1708–87) and his British patrons* (London, 1982), no. 28, pp. 58–61. The Batoni is also reproduced as pl. 19 in Solkin, *Art History*.

30 The basic source on Sir Watkin's art patronage remains B. Ford, 'Sir Watkin Williams-Wynn, a Welsh Maecenas', *Apollo*, 99 (June 1974), pp. 435–9.

31 My analysis of the Wilkes affair is largely based on G. Rudé, *Wilkes and liberty* (Oxford, 1962, paperback edn 1965), and on J. Brewer, *Party ideology and popular politics at the accession of George III* (Cambridge 1976).

32 Brewer, p. 168.

33 C. Middleton, *The History of the Life of Marcus Tullius Cicero*, 8th edn, 3 vols. (London, 1768), II, p. 161.

34 F. Morabin, preface to Cicero, *De legibus* (Paris, 1719), quoted in C. D. Yonge's edn, p. 390.

35 'Tribunus', 'To the printer of the *Public Advertiser*', Public Advertiser no. 11019 (8 March 1770).

36 Cicero, *De legibus*, p. 462.

37 Ibid., p. 478.

38 Ibid., p. 480.

39 'Cicero', To the Printer of the *Public Advertiser*', *Public Advertiser*, no. 10909 (20 October 1769).

40 'Albanus', 'An Address', *Public Ledger*, no. 3350 (22 September 1770).

41  Cicero, De legibus, p. 431.

42  Anon., 'Discourses on the principal causes that obstruct our success in the present age for attaining greater perfection in arts, sciences, and literature', Universal Magazine, vol. 49 (July 1771), p. 4.

43  For the best (albeit still inadequate) discussion of the disputes following the establishment of the Royal Academy, see W. T. Whitley, Artists and their friends in England 1700–1799, 2 vols. (Cambridge, 1928), I, chs. 14, 15; II, pp. 272–9.

44  'Fresnoy', 'To the K + + +', Middlesex Journal, no. 171 (3–5 May 1770). Whitley (Artists and their friends, ii, pp. 272–5) makes a strong but inconclusive case for identifying 'Fresnoy' with the Reverend James Wills, the Chaplain of the Incorporated Artists. In 1769–70 Wills was curate of Whitchurch in Middlesex, where he would have had the opportunity to observe Wilkes's disputed elections at first hand.

45  'Fresnoy', 'For the Middlesex Journal', Middlesex Journal, no. 59 (15–17 August 1769); and 'To Sir Joshua R + + + + + + +, K + + + + +, P + + + + + + + + of the Royal Academy', Middlesex Journal, no. 85 (14–17·October 1769).

46  'Fresnoy', 'To the K + + +', Middlesex Journal, no. 171 (3–5 May 1770).

47  'Paul Varnish', 'To Mr. Fresnoy', Middlesex Journal, no. 169 (28 April–1 May 1770).

48  E. Fletcher, ed., Conversations of James Northcote R. A. with James Ward (London, 1901), p. 164.

49  The exhibition of the Royal Academy, MDCCLXIX. The first (London, 1769), p. 2.

50  'Decimus', 'To the Publisher of the Middlesex Journal', Middlesex Journal, no. 180 (24–26 May 1770).

51  London Magazine, XXXIX (April 1770), opp. p. 174, repro. Solkin, Art History, pl. 20. I am grateful to Dian Kriz for bringing this print to my attention. Since I wrote the first version of this article, I have come across two full-length painted portraits of Wilkite heroes in the guise of Roman orators, both, perhaps significantly, by American-born artists: Charles Willson Peale's William Pitt as a Roman Consul (1768; Westmoreland County Museum, Montross, Virginia) and Benjamin West's Alderman John Sawbridge in the Character of a Roman Tribune (by 1772; destroyed). The Peale is reproduced in Lillian B. Miller, ed., The selected papers of Charles Willson Peale and his family. I – Charles Willson Peale: artist in revolutionary America, 1735–1791 (New Haven, Conn. and London, 1983), p. 75; Thomas Watson's mezzotint of the West (which was shown at the Royal Academy in 1773) is illustrated in Helmut von Erffa and Allen Staley, The paintings of Benjamin West (New Haven, Conn. and London, 1986), p. 551.

52  See Rudé, Wilkes and liberty, passim.

53  The London Magazine was not alone in connecting Burke with Cicero – the same link was made, for example, in an engraved popular broadsheet of 1770 entitled Political electricity, or, An historical & prophetical print in the year 1770 (see F. G. Stephens and D. George, Catalogue of prints and drawings in the British Museum – division I. Political and personal satires, 11 vols. (London, 1870–1933), IV, 1883, pp. 649–60, no. 4422). This print is made up of a series of thirty-one vignettes which either describe contemporary events (including one Wilkite riot) or allude to political issues from a radical point of view. At top is a scale of justice, which holds six members of the Ministry on one side and six opposition speakers on the other; thanks to the help of George Grenville (who vacillated in his support of Wilkes), and to the presence of two bags of Treasury money, the Administration's representatives outweight their opponents. The most prominent figure in the Opposition group is Edmund Burke, shown in the act of speaking; but, as the extensive caption informs us, the 'Scale of Virtue is outweighed by that of Vice. & thy speech, O Cicero availeth thee nothing'. It was probably with Burke specifically in mind that Samuel Johnson scornfully referred to 'the Cicero of the day, [who] says much, and suppresses more, and credit is equally given to what he tells, and what he conceals'. This statement comes from Johnson's anti-Wilkite pamphlet, The false alarm, which was issued in four impressions between 17 January and 12 March 1770; see S. Johnson, Political writings, ed. D. J. Greene (New Haven, Conn. and London, 1977), p. 337. Perhaps we should also note here that quotations from Cicero

were often flung out by polemicists on either side of the Wilkes debate; e.g. 'Atticus', in the St. James's Chronicle, no. 1396 (6 February 1770) (on the side of the Middlesex electors), and 'Mentor', in the Independent Chronicle, no. 48 (17 January 1770) (in support of Parliament). I suspect that one reason why Cicero's name was never linked to that of Wilkes himself had to do with the fact that the latter was a notoriously poor orator.

54 For a brief encapsulation of the most commonly held view of Cicero in eighteenth-century England, see pp. xii–xiii of Middleton's Life.

55 I would like to thank Michael Rosenthal for pointing out this Hogarth reference to me. The gibbet in the background of Collet's scene derives from a Hogarth source as well, in this case his Tail-piece, or The Bathos from 1764. To judge by his collars, Collet's squire also appears to be a clergyman, as Timothy Clifford has kindly suggested.

56 H. M. Atherton, Political prints in the age of Hogarth (Oxford, 1974), p. 219. Here the help of Dian Kriz once again deserves grateful acknowledgment.

57 'Suscitabulum', 'To the Publisher of the Middlesex Journal', Middlesex Journal no. 7 (15–18 April 1769).

58 Here it may be worth recalling the political implications of the distinction between the generalised prospect and the particularised view, as analysed by John Barrell in his essay in this volume.

59 J. T. Boulton, The language of politics in the age of Wilkes and Burke (London and Toronto, 1963), pp. 24, 34–44, and passim.

60 Ibid., esp. pp. 21, 35–7.

61 'Fresnoy' likened Wilson to a 'Malmsey butt' in his letter 'To sir Joshua Reynolds', Middlesex Journal, no. 135 (8–10 February 1770).

62 For attacks on Sir Watkin's political conduct in the Wilkes affair, see Middlesex Journal, no. 13 (29 April–2 May 1769), and no. 169 (28 April–1 May 1770). Wilson was distantly related to Williams-Wynn, and had begun to work on two immense Welsh views for him by February of 1770; drawings for these pictures were presumably executed at some point during the previous summer or autumn. For information on this commission, see Constable, 'Pentimenti', p. 140, and n. 28 above.

# 5

# The implications of industry:
# Turner and Leeds
## Stephen Daniels

Turner's *Leeds* (Fig. 4) is one of the few pictures of an industrial city in early nineteenth-century English water-colour. In this essay I want to show what a complex and knowledgeable picture it is: empirically precise, analytically intelligent and resonant with literary and political associations.

The viewpoint is Beeston Hill, about one and a half miles south of the River Aire. Many of the buildings in view are located south of the river and the political boundary of Leeds in the out-township of Holbeck. Holbeck was functionally part of the city; in 1806 a local clothier described it as 'joining to Leeds like the suburb of a town.'[1]

There are three preparatory sketches for the picture. These were probably done on the spot in September 1816, after Turner's sketching tour of the Dales undertaken to collect material for illustrations to the *Richmondshire* volume of Thomas Dunham Whitaker's History of Yorkshire.[2] Turner's *Leeds* was almost certainly intended to be engraved for Whitaker's volume on Leeds, entitled *Loidis and Elmete*, and why it was not published there is an issue to which I will return.

The sketch which is the basis for the whole area depicted beyond the foreground is a sharply drawn, meticulously detailed and annotated panorama extending over three pages of sketchbook (T.B. CXXXIV, ff. 79v, 80r, 38r). The sketches of the foreground are much more free and made from a different viewpoint further down the road (T.B. CXXXIV, ff. 37v, 38v, 45r). These two viewpoints are conflated in the finished picture.

Compared with the panoramic sketch the water-colour is cropped and compressed; the road is severely foreshortened, the slope of the hill steepened, connecting foreground and middle distance more directly and suddenly. The water-colour is more selective in its detail than the panoramic sketch. The effects of smoke and mist obscure many buildings and what emerge prominently are the large textile mills and churches, picked out by the colouring of their respective materials, red brick and pale stone. The emphasis on these features is reinforced by the realignment of the road to lead directly to the mill in the centre and by the placement of two figures in the left foreground to frame the mill to the left.

In the foreground sketches there is just shorthand indication of some of the human activity in the finished picture. This does not mean that Turner was casual about the figures, that the figures are incidental to the meaning of the picture. On the contrary, Turner was in his water-colours extremely careful about details of the dress, disposition, and activity of figures, their position in the landscape and role in its working. And *Leeds* is no exception.

On the left of the picture two tentermen are hanging newly woven and washed cloth to dry. It is the kind of morning – sunny and breezy – that local clothiers welcomed.[3] The large pile of cloth still to be hung confirms that the men are working at the end of a line of tenter frames crowning the crest of Beeston Hill. These may be indicated in one of the foreground sketches (T.B. CXXXIV, f. 45r) by a line of slanting strokes. A keen and knowledgable observer of industrial tasks, Turner portrayed industrial drying in two other pictures – the drying of cloth in his 1811 oil of Whalley Bridge and Abbey (B.J. 117) and the drying of paper in a watercolour of Egglestone Abbey and Mill (w.565) dating from 1816.

To the tentermen's right, and further downhill, two figures are picking mushrooms. They occupy a similar position, and strike similar poses, to the couple picking mushrooms in Turner's view of Gledhow Hall. (This water-colour is exactly contemporary with *Leeds* and shows a landscape on the northern side of the city in a similar early morning atmosphere. The fact that it was published in *Loidis and Elmete* suggests *Leeds* was intended to be, too.)

At the focal point of the foreground are two masons who can be partially identified in one of the sketches (T.B. CXXXIV, f. 37v). They stand at the apex of a wedge-shaped composition with its base at the bottom edge of the picture, one side described by the edge of the wall, the other by the edge of the shadow of the wall, a spade and a pile of mortar. Standing each side of the wall, the masons are about to lift a slab into place. The elbow of one and the turned head of the other direct attention to the figures coming uphill.

The leading figure is a clothworker shouldering a roll of cloth. Logically he has come from the row of workshops just down the hill, (their weaving chambers clearly visible on the upper storey) and he is perhaps

about to turn into the field on the left to have the cloth tentered.

Turner would have been aware of the different stages of cloth manufacture and their organisation in the landscape. He knew Leeds and its locality well. Since 1808 he had stayed there every year with his patron Walter Fawkes, the local clothiers' radical political representative.[4] In addition, informative descriptions and illustrations of each branch of cloth manufacture and other occupations associated with it were provided in *The costume of Yorkshire* by George Walker, published in Leeds and London in 1813 and 1814. Circumstantial evidence suggests Turner knew Walker personally[5] and it is likely that Turner based his depiction of four figures in Leeds directly upon illustrations in Walker's book. The milkcarriers seem closely modelled on Walker's *Milk Boy*. The couple between the clothworker and the mason standing to the right of the wall resemble Walker's *Factory Children*. The milk-carriers are returning from an early morning delivery to Leeds, a quickening activity at this period that Walker connects directly with urban industrial growth. If the two figures trudging uphill are factory hands they could be returning from a night shift in one of the large mills in the valley – the one in the centre was gaslit in 1815.[6]

Although the main concentration of industrial building is in the valley there is nothing bucolic about the foreground. The stone pavement at the edge of the road and the rebuilding of the wall indicate that we look down an important economic artery. By the early nineteenth century fields in the southern outownships of Leeds had been turned over to the grazing of milkcows, an intensification of land use that was, in its way, as 'urban' as the building of mills and houses. Indeed, so valuable was land for grazing milkcows or for tentering cloth that these activities inhibited residential development.[7] What Turner depicts is not a contrast between 'country' and 'city' but an integrated, wholly industrialised landscape. He illustrates various processes, some mechanised, some not, and their interconnection, from the spinning of yarn in the valley to the weaving and tentering of cloth on the slopes of the hill. In explicating the workings of the landscape Turner pays particular attention to the weather conditions and the time of day. As much as the drift of dispersing mist and rising smoke,[8] the activities of tenterers, mushroom pickers, milk-carriers and factory hands characterise the atmosphere of the early morning. It is a scene of concerted energy – meteorological,

4 J. M. W. Turner, *Leeds*, 1816, watercolour heightened with bodycolour over pencil. Yale Center for British Art, Paul Mellon Collection.

technological and human – harnessed to industrial expansion. The brightening sunlight, freshening breeze and rising smoke empower the scene and endow it with optimism.

Having specified the empirical and analytical aspects of Leeds I now want to examine its political and literary associations. In doing so I will first return to the question of why it was not published in Whitaker's Loidis and Elmete. The picture was probably intended to be the frontispiece of the book and so complement Place's prospect of Leeds, the frontispiece to Ralph Thoresby's history of the city, Ducatus leodiensis (1714), which Whitaker reissued to pair with his own. The contrast between Whitaker's appraisal of modern Leeds in his text and Turner's in his picture may have been sufficient for Whitaker to reject Turner's Leeds as an illustration. An emphatically conservative cleric, Whitaker deplored the effect of industrialisation on the landscape of the Leeds locality and the morals of its inhabitants. Holbeck had been overrun in 'the general calamity'. Recalling Holbeck as a village happily separated from the city by 'an interval of many pleasant fields planted about with tall poplars', Whitaker observed, 'verdure and vegetation are now fled'. He yearned for the more polite regime of the cloth industry a generation before when it was controlled by the 'gentlemen merchants' of Leeds, a group who were withdrawing their capital from the industry. The only modern landscapes Whitaker admired were those of the villas that, 'dread of smoke and desire of comfort', had promoted retired merchants to develop on the northern, more prestigious, side of Leeds. This was precisely the kind of landscape that Gledhow exemplified, a landscaped estate with a fine house owned by the Dixons, formerly a leading merchant family in Leeds. Turner's view of Gledhow which Whitaker did publish shows to advantage the 'beautiful plantations' Whitaker singled out in his text. Quoting a phrase from Cowper's conservative poem The task, Whitaker characterised grimy Leeds and its ring of parks as 'a swarth indian with his belt of beads'.[9]

The society that Whitaker admired, namely the Tory and Anglican oligarchy of gentlement merchants, was losing ground at the time. When Turner depicted Leeds, economic and political power in the city were shifting discernibly to Whigs and Dissenters.[10] Their economic figurehead was John Marshall. It is Marshall's mill and that of his former partners the Beyons that are the dual focal points of Turner's view of the city. Leeds was the leading flax-spinning centre in England. When a Prussian factory inspector visited the city in 1814 he reported that the Continental blockade had stimulated the production of yarn and that six large new mills had recently opened. Many workers had been taken on and employers and employees were prospering.[11] Marshall's mill had become a showpiece for progressive visitors to Leeds and the Benyons' mill was also renowned for its advanced and safety-conscious construction. The thread the flax mills produced was turned locally into rope and canvas for which there was a quickening demand in the war years, notably by the navy.[12] Marshall had waving sheds attached to his mill but he also put out yarn to domestic weavers in Holbeck.[13]

The prospect of Leeds prospering after five years of depression would have aroused Turner's patriotism – in August 1816 he was regaling the company at Fawkes's house with a song, 'Here's a health to honest John Bull' which he had copied down on the inside cover of his sketchbook (T.B. CXLVIII). The manufacturers of Leeds, notably John Marshall, had overcome the Continental blockade. At a time when British tourists were admiring scenes of allied triumph over Napolean abroad, Turner was admiring one at home.

Turner's wartime patriotism was directed as much to British artistic achievement as to its industrial and scientific know-how[14] and in this respect also Leeds had proved itself worthy of Turner's enthusiasm. The formation in 1808 of the Northern Society for the Encouragement of the Fine Arts made Leeds the main provincial centre for the exhibition and marketing of modern painting. George Walker was instrumental in establishing the Society, Fawkes assisted in running it, and it was probably Fawkes who encouraged Turner to exhibit at the Society in 1811. Turner would surely have concurred with William Carey's praise of Leeds as the first city 'to form a Provincial society, upon the patriotic principle of patronizing the British School. The Artists of England owe much to Leeds, and Leeds to the Artists of England.' Exhibitions lapsed after 1811, apparently because of the adverse commercial climate, and so in 1816 Turner had even further reason to relish the prospect of Leeds prospering.[15] Turner would have seen a general cultural expansion where Whitaker saw only decline.

George Walker's The costume of Yorkshire expressed a cultural outlook that accorded with Turner's own. Turner would have been in sympathy with Walker's introduction which hoped that 'the British heart will be warmed by the reflection that most of the humble individuals here depicted . . . contribute essentially by their honest labours to the glory and prosperity of the country'. He would also surely have been moved by Walker's affirmation that textile factories 'are essentially requisite for the widely extended commerce of Britain and furnish employment, food and raiment to thousands of poor industrious individuals'. In Walker's illustrations and descriptions items of advanced technology (including a pioneering steam locomotive near Leeds) do not degrade workers, rather they enhance the dignity of labour in promoting industriousness throughout the country. His account of the woollen industry links skilled and unskilled, handworkers and machine operators, small masters and large employers in concerted effort. There were tensions between various sectors of the industry which Walker acknowledges but his account overall is a harmonious one. It agreed with the consensus of testimony from the Leeds locality to the 1806 Commons Select Committee on Woollen Manufacture which maintained that technology did not and would not disrupt the domestic system. By increasing the local supply of yarn mechanised mills dovetailed into the domestic system and arguably energised it.[16] It was still reasonable for political economists to argue that rather than replacing skilled work, machinery and the division of labour would enhance it. The source of Britain's economic advance was still 'the wonderful skill and ingenuity of her artisans' working in concert with advanced technology.[17] This, as opposed to the alarmist view of Whitaker, seems to me to be the political economy of Turner's Leeds.

In addition to The costume of Yorkshire it seems the political economic imagery of Leeds is specifically influenced by an earlier picture and a poem: Samuel Buck's prospect of Leeds published in 1722 and 1745 (Fig. 5) and John Dyer's poem The fleece, first published in 1757.

Buck depicts Leeds from Chevalier [Cavalier] Hill to the east of the city where clothmaking was in his time developing. The clockwise circulation of cloth in Turner's Leeds replicates the directional movement in Buck's prospect of the city. Like Buck, Turner positions weaving-shops to the right and a figure shouldering a roll of cloth moving towards the two figures unrolling cloth on the tenter frames on the left. The direction and elevation of Buck's viewpoint enables him to complete his narrative of the cloth industry by highlighting in the city the cloth hall and merchants' mansions and the main export artery of River Aire with its sailing barges. A second edition of the prospect, published in 1745, is glossed by a written account of the cloth trade of Leeds.

Buck's prospect belongs to an idiom of eighteenth-century topography which highlights features signifying the commercial progress of a locality and by extension the benign implications for the nation as a whole. The most famous example in prose is Daniel Defoe's description of the Yorkshire woollen industry. Completing his survey of the stages of clothmaking in Calderdale, Defoe observes from a height 'almost on every tenter a piece of cloth, or kesie or shalloon, for those are the three articles of that country's labour, from which the sun glancing, and, as I may say, shining (the white reflecting its rays) to us, I thought it was the most agreeable sight I ever saw'.[18] As Britain's most valuable industry, and one which linked agriculture, manufacture and trade, the woollen industry provided a paradigm for the nation's well-being. This appraisal of the woollen industry is expressed most forcibly as a political economic prospect in The fleece.

In the tradition of Virgil's Georgics, The fleece is an instructive poem.[19] It prescribes the most advanced procedures for the production and distribution of cloth. It does so as it traces the progressive transformation of 'Britannia's fleece' into cloth 'uphung/On rugged tenters, to the fervid sun ... it expands / Still bright'ning in each rigid discipline, / And gathered worth'.[20] It is a process that takes the poem from the hills of Herefordshire to the Yorkshire Dales, to the port of London, connecting all social ranks and a variety of specialised workers from artisans to factory hands. Having pictured Britain as a nation united through industry Dyer goes on to chart its influence overseas. Packed into sailing barges 'with white sails glist'ning', then taken by 'tall fleets into the wid'ning main . . . every sail unfurl'd', the cloth carries the benevolence of 'Britain's happy trade, now spreading wide / Wide as th' Atlantic or Pacific seas, / Or as air's vital fluid o'er the globe'.[21] Two things threaten Britain's moral geography: the rivalry of France and, more seriously, the allure of luxury which undermined the empires of antiquity.

A zealous reader of English poetry, Turner possessed a copy of The fleece in Volume 9 of his Complete edition of the poets of Great Britain (1794) edited by Robert Anderson.[22] As it contained also the works of James Thomson and Mark Akenside (whose formative influence on Turner is well documented), this volume of Turner's must have been well read. The fleece is glossed by Anderson's emphasis on the patriotism of the poem and his enlisting of Akenside's admiration of Dyer. There are echoes of The fleece in Turner's own verse of about 1811–12. In Book II of The fleece Dyer interpolates the legend of Jason and the Argonauts, noting the fashioning of the hero's wondrous ship, 'in th' extended keel a lofty mast / Up-rais'd and sails full swelling'.[23] Turner too applies the Jason legend to Britain, transfering to the construction of ships the narrative scheme that Dyer employs for the making of cloth, following the course of British oak from plantations to the building and launching of warships to engage the French fleet, 'ensigns broad displayed / Britannia's glory

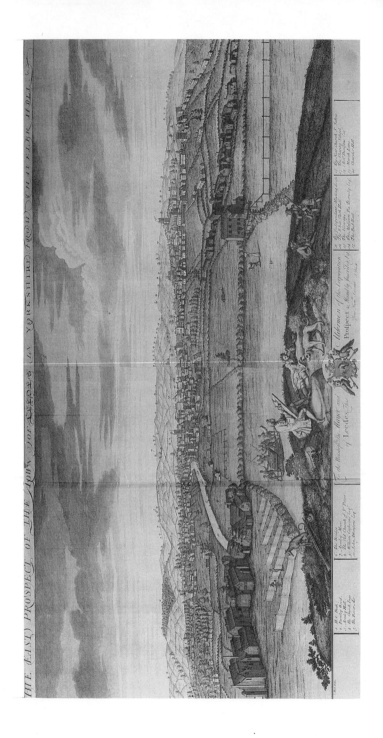

THE (EAST) PROSPECT OF THE TOWN OF LEEDS IN YORKSHIRE FROM (CHARTER HILL)

To the Worshipfull the Mayor and Aldermen of this Corporation of Leeds this Prospect is Humbly Inscribd

waved arrayed' (T.B. CVIII, f. 23v). In Book III of The fleece Dyer describes the processing of flax and hemp in a mill in Calderdale by both children and adults, 'all employ'd / All blithe'.[24] In verses on Birdport in Dorset, a centre for the manufacture of naval sailcloth and rope, Turner explicates the flax industry again with the idiom of The fleece, beginning with the 'breaking' (crushing) of flax in a scutch mill.[25]

> Here roars the busy mill called breaks
> Through various processes o'ertakes
> The flax in dressing, each with one accord
> draw out the thread, and meed the just reward
> Its population great, and all employed,
> And children even draw the twisting cord
> Behold from small beginnings, like the stream,
> That from the high raised downs to marshes breem [?]
>
> First feeds the meadows where grows the line,
> That drives the mill that all its powers define,
> Pressing . . .
> On the peopled town who all combine
> To throw the many strands in lengthened twine;
> Then onward to the sea its freight it pours,
> And by its prowess holds to distant shores,
> The straining vessel to its cordage yields:
> And Britain floats the produce of her fields.
> Why should the Volga or the Rubicon
> Be covetted for hemp? why such supply'd
> The sinew of our strength and naval pride . . .
>
> Plant but [?] the ground with seed instead of gold
> Urge all our barren tract with agricultural skill,
> And Britain, Britain, British canvas fill;
> Alone and unsupported prove her strength
> By her own means to meed the direful length
> Of Continental hatred called blockade . . (T.B. CXXXIII, ff. 102v, 105v, 110v)

If Turner's appraisal of Bridport echoes The fleece, Dyer's poem resonates more powerfully in his appraisal of Leeds. Turner had already transcribed the flax industry into the idiom of The fleece before he depicted the city that was in 1816 the industrial centre for flax as well as wool. Leeds occupies a key position in the argument of The fleece. Dyer builds up

5 Samuel Buck, engraved I. Harris, The East Prospect of the town of Leedes, 1720, line engraving, two sheets conjoined. Society of Antiquaries, London.

an image of the city that raises its status beyond any other in Britain, to the point where Leeds stands as the exemplar of British expansion and influence. Some of the features in Turner's view of Leeds confirm Dyer's imagery of the city from a similar, perhaps the same, vantage point, coming over the brow of the hills from the south:

> And ruddy roofs, and chimney-tops appear,
> Of busy Leeds, up-wafting to the clouds
> The incense of thanksgiving: all is joy;
> and trade and business guide the living scene . . .

The inhabitants of Leeds come out to work 'As when a sunny day invites abroad. The sedulous ants . . . o'er high, o'er low, they lift, they draw, they haste':

> . . . th' echoing hills repeat
> The stroke of axe and hammer; scaffolds rise,
> And growing edifices; heaps of stone
> Beneath the chisel, beauteous shapes assume
> Of frize and column. Some with even line,
> New streets are marking in the neighb'ring fields,
> And scared domes of worship. Industry,
> Which dignifies the artist, lifts the swain.

The imagery of building – 'beauteous shapes assume of frize and column' – is already classicised before Dyer connects the development of Leeds first with a city in antiquity, then with that of other British industrial cities:

> . . . such was the scene
> of hurrying Carthage, when the Trojan chief
> First view'd her growing turrets. So appear
> Th'increasing walls of busy Manchester,
> Sheffield, and Birmingham, whose redd'ning fields
> Rise and enlarge their suburbs.[26]

Dyer's extended prospect not only glosses the smoking chimneys in Turner's Leeds as emblems of urban aspiration – a trope Turner had already employed in verse on 'the extended town' (T.B. CII, f. 4v) – but also endows the masons with a symbolic importance commensurate with their pictorial prominence. In magnifying the expansionism of Leeds by analogy with Carthage Dyer discloses a prospect of decline as well as prosperity. In Book II of The Fleece he had observed 'the dust of Carthage' in a survey of ancient cities ruined by luxury, monuments 'to those / who toil and wealth exchange for sloth and pride'.[27] This would have confirmed (perhaps it was the origin of) the cautionary analogy

Turner himself made between the fortunes of ancient Carthage and modern Britain[28] and it infuses his view of Leeds with the gravity of the scenes he painted a year before and a year after of the building and of the ruin of Carthage.

Masons are also prominent in a later watercolour of the Leeds periphery, *Kirkstall Lock on the River Aire* (T.B. CCVIII-L), which can be seen to complement Turner's prospect of the city. As in the view from Beeston Hill the masons flank a main artery into Leeds, the city being named on the barge. Sailing barges on the River Aire were an essential ingredient of the iconography of Leeds in topographical depictions of Leeds. Buck shows them and Dyer exhorts, 'Roll the full cars down the winding Aire / Load the slow sailing barges'.[29] In *Airedale*, a poem contemporary with *Kirkstall Lock*, John Nicholson celebrates 'the populous and flourishing town of LEEDS' (eclipsing Kirkstall Abbey which once overshadowed it) in terms of the barges on the river Aire, 'sails unfurling in commercial pride'.[30] Contrary to the title of Turner's picture he has not actually depicted the River Aire (which flows in the background by Kirkstall Abbey) but the Leeds–Liverpool Canal;[31] that he knew as much because he had written the word 'canal' on the sketch (T.B. CCX, f. 61). The displacement of the name makes sense if we recognise that it was the River Aire that had the topographical associations, not the Leeds–Liverpool canal.

Unlike Turner, practitioners of the Picturesque could scarcely cope with industrialisation, notably those who fashioned a conservative politics with the Picturesque. For Humphry Repton and Uvedale Price textile mills were disturbing features in the landscape, storehouses of volatile social and economic energies which threatened landed interests and tastes.[32] For the itinerant Tory John Byng textile mills were redeemed in wartime by their patriotic associations. In a striking analogy he likened them to those established emblems of British power: warships. The rows of windows on a mill reminded him of the ranks of gun ports on a First Rate Man of War.[33] Materially this analogy is not so fanciful. Naval dockyards were the largest industrial sites in the country and large warships harnessed as much human and natural energy as many a textile mill. The analogy may have been in Turner's mind too, not to redeem an industrial landscape but to enhance it. Warships were a favourite subject of Turner's and in his verse, sketches and paintings he expressed their power and patriotic iconography (*Victory Returning from Trafalgar* (B.J. 59, New Haven) he sold to Fawkes in 1806). Considering also Turner's view that industry was ultimately realised in seaborne trade and that ships were the main vehicle of Turner's views on industrialism, it is plausible that Turner's view of the industrial landscape of Leeds was infused with naval associations. The flax mills in Turner's view of Leeds had overcome the Continental blockade. What the tentermen are raising to billow in the wind might be sailcloth made from mill-spun yarn, and even if not in fact Turner would have been aware of Dyer's use of tentered cloth and spreading sails as dual ensigns of British dominion. To recall Turner's couplet:

> Urge all our barren tracts with agricultural skill
> And Britain, Britain, British canvas fill . . .

In terms of Turner's watercolour *oeuvre* Leeds can be seen to have as much connection with coastal scenes like Saltash and Devonport as urban scenes like Dudley and Coventry.[34] Or, to enlarge the point, Leeds can be seen to occupy a central place in a series of over 350 water-colours that Turner produced between 1810 and 1827 which Turner himself saw as a coherent network of landscapes.[35]

If Leeds is an eccentric picture in terms of early nineteenth-century water-colour as a whole, it is not in terms of Turner's *oeuvre*. In many, if not most, of his topographical works Turner seems to have grasped the workings of a place and its implications in a style which interpenetrates general themes and particular observations.[36] In his view of Leeds Turner concentrates the complex implications of local industry – economic, geographical, social, moral and political implications – in a naturalistic impression of a late autumn morning. The range of research required to recover these implications testifies to the extensiveness of Turner's topographical knowledge.

## Abbreviations

T.B.  Turner Bequest.
B.J.  Numbering of oil-paintings in Martin Butlin and Evelyn Joll, *The paintings of J. M. W. Turner*, 2nd edn (London and New York, 1984).

## Notes

This essay was first published with fuller illustration in *Turner Studies*, vol. 6, no. 1 (1986), pp. 10–17.

1  Report and minutes of evidence on the state of the woollen manufacture, *Parliamentary Papers* (1806), III, p. 75 (testimony of Robert Cookson).
2  David Hill, *In Turner's footsteps* (London, 1984), p. 104.
3  A kind of day always noted by a local scribbling and fulling miller Joseph Rogerson in his diary of 1808–14, published in *Thoresby Society Publications*, vol. 32 (1929), pp. 59–106.
4  Hill, p. 18.

5 Walker knew Fawkes well. A neighbouring landowner, he shared Fawkes's love of hunting on the moors and painted panels in Fawkes's Farnley Hall with some hundred sporting scenes. Turner would surely have met him there. Gordon Nares, Farnley Hall, Yorkshire I, Country Life (20 May 1954), p. 1620. I owe this reference to David Hill. See also n. 15 below for Walker's connection with Fawkes and probably Turner through the Northern Society for the Encouragement of the Fine Arts.

6 E. J. Connell, 'Industrial development in south Leeds 1790–1914' (unpublished Phd. thesis, University of Leeds, 1975), p. 87.

7 Maurice Beresford, 'The face of Leeds 1780–1914', in Derek Fraser, ed., A history of modern Leeds (Manchester, 1980), pp. 72–112; reference on p. 82.

8 The naturalistic atmosphere of Leeds resembles another panorama which may have influenced it, Girtin's Eidometropolis as described by the Monthly Magazine:

> he [Girtin] has generally paid particular attention to representing the objects of the hue with which they appear in nature, and by that means, greatly heightened the illusion. For example, the view towards the East appears through a sort of misty medium, arising from the fires of the forges, manufacturers, &c. which gradually lessens as we survey the western extremity.

Monthly Magazine, vol. XIV, pp. 254–5. I owe this reference to Scott Wilcox.

9 Thomas Dunham Whitaker, Loidis and Elmete (London, 1816), pp. 78–80, 87, 97–8, 100, 115, 131, 380, 390; quotations on pp. 97 and 87.

10 R. G. Wilson, Gentlemen merchants: the merchant community in Leeds 1700–1830 (Manchester, 1971), pp. 111–32; Derek Fraser, 'Politics and society in the nineteenth century', in Fraser, ed., pp. 270–300; reference on p. 273.

11 J. G. May, 'Report on a journey to England', in W. O. Henderson, ed., Industrial Britain under the Regency: the diaries of Escher, Bodmer, May and de Gallois (London, 1968), pp. 139–41.

12 W. G. Rimmer, Marshalls of Leeds, flax spinners 1788–1886 (Cambridge, 1960), pp. 53–124; Connell, pp. 86–115.

13 P. J. Hamerton's Life of Turner (London, 1895), albeit not a reliable source, reports that Marshall purchased fourteen of the water-colours Turner made for Whitaker on his 1816 tour; and if so, Leeds may well have been among them.

14 Jack Lindsay, J. M. W. Turner: his life and work (London, 1966), p. 137.

15 Trevor Fawcett, The rise of English provincial art: artists, patrons and institutions outside London (Oxford, 1974), pp. 89, 168–70; quotation on p. 168.

16 Stephen Daniels, 'Moral order and the industrial environment in the woollen textile districts of West Yorkshire 1780–1880' (unpublished Phd. thesis, University of London, 1980), p. 55.

17 Maxine Berg, 'Political economy and the principles of manufacture 1700–1800, in Maxine Berg, Pat Hudson and Michael Sonenscher, eds., Manufacture in town and country before the factory (Cambridge, 1983), pp. 33–58; quotation from Dugald Stewart on p. 58.

18 Daniel Defoe, A tour through the whole island of Great Britain (1724–26), ed. Pat Rogers (London, 1971), p. 492.

19 My reading of The fleece owes much to John Barrell's in English literature in history 1730–1780: an equal wide survey (London, 1983), pp. 90–109.

20 All quotations are taken from the revised edition of the poem in Poems by John Dyer (London, 1761). These lines are from p. 131.

21 Ibid., p. 188.

22 Mentioned in the list of Turner's library on p. 255 of B. Falk, Turner the painter (London, 1938).

23 Dyer, p. 100.

24 Ibid., p. 135.

25 This process, along with other details of flax-growing and processing in the Bridport area and the importance of the industry are described in William Stevenson, General view of the agriculture of Dorset (London, 1812), pp. 294–303, 446–7. Stevenson collected his material in 1811 and so his appraisal is exactly contemporary with Turner's as well as agreeing with it

in most particulars. Turner may have known of the sequence of twelve illustrations by
William Hincks of the Irish Linen Industry, published in London in 1782 and 1791, which
follows the progress of flax-processing from the sowing of flax seed to the baling of linen
for export and includes (pl. 5) a perspective view of a scutch mill showing the machinery
for breaking the flax.

26  Dyer, pp. 137–9.
27  Ibid., pp. 118–19.
28  Lindsay, p. 117.
29  Dyer, p. 137.
30  John Nicholson, *Airedale in Ancient Times* (London, 1825), pp. vi, 31. I owe this reference to
    John Barrell.
31  Eric Shanes, *Turner's rivers, harbours and coasts* (London, 1981), p. 32.
32  Humphry Repton, *Observations of the Theory and Practice of Landscape Gardening* (London, 1803),
    pp. 201–2; *Fragments on the Theory and Practice of Landscape Gardening* (London, 1816), p. 207;
    Uvedale Price, *Essays on the Picturesque* (London, 1810 edn), p. 198. Repton's personal
    aversion to textile mills and their social associations did not prevent him accepting a
    commission from the Leeds woollen manufacturer Benjamin Gott to design Gott's park
    at Armley to the west of Leeds to frame his client's mills. For the tensions of this
    commission see Stephen Daniels, 'Landscaping for a manufacturer: Humphry Repton's
    commission for Benjamin Gott at Armley in 1809–10', *Journal of Historical Geography*, vol. 7
    (1981), pp. 379–96.
33  *The Torrington Diaries*, ed. C. Bryn Andrews (London, 1935–36), vol. III, pp. 81–2; vol. II, pp.
    194–5.
34  See Eric Shanes, *Turner's Picturesque views in England and Wales* (London, 1979), nos. 1, 27, 66
    and 58 respectively.
35  Eric Shanes, *Turner's rivers*, p. 15.
36  Ibid., pp. 13–16 and *passim*; Andrew Wilton, 'Introduction' to Shanes, *Turner's picturesque
    views*, pp. 5–9; Shanes, *Turner's Picturesque Views*, passim.

# 6

# Aesthetic and commodity: an examination of the function of the verbal in Turner's artistic practice
## Marcia Pointon

Representations are not rooted in a world that gives them meaning; they open of themselves on to a space that is their own, whose internal network gives rise to meaning. And language exists in the gap that representation creates for itself.
—M. Foucault, *The Order of Things* (1966) (London, 1974), p. 78

This essay is concerned with language: its relation with, and effect on imagery,[1] My purpose is to demonstrate the centrality of the verbal in Turner's practice and in our accession to that practice. Fundamental to my argument is the notion that the commercial and the aesthetic (the world of buying and selling art and the world of visual pleasure) cannot be separated out by varying procedures such as style analysis, iconography, reception and patronage studies, but are imbricated in the verbal. I want to show that the apparent contradiction between the assumed specialness of the work of art and the work as product of a set of economic circumstances is a contradiction that Turner himself was obliged daily to negotiate as well as one through which he is constructed as artist and producer in history. I will be suggesting that his grasp and development of language was the precise and only means at his disposal for forging a way of working within these contradictions.

Three propositions underpin this essay. The first is the notion that we construct the past from our own perspective in the present, as a (potentially limitless) series of narratives. As art historians we may believe our concerns to be primarily with material culture but access to a visually constructed history is always regulated by the verbal. It is always mediated by acts of writing that are themselves subject to the same historical determinants.

The second proposition is that any act of writing is the sum of conscious intent and the working of the unconscious. It is never a simple act but necessitates a deal of some kind between the writer and the reader even if the latter is never specified.

The third is that literacy in general and the book in particular occupy a specially powerful place in nineteenth-century culture. Olivia Smith has pointed out that 'between 1790 and 1819, the hegemony of language was severely challenged. Because ideas about language justified class division and even contributed to its formation by accentuating differences in language practice, they were sensitive to any political movement which threatened to disturb class boundaries.'[2] The overall cultural dominance of word over image needs, therefore, to be examined to discover how the word interpellates the image, how image creation and the making of an artist's reputation respond to the imperatives of the word.

What ways do we have of evaluating these differences of language in cases where Turner is the speaking subject (i.e. in his letters) and in cases in which he is the spoken subject (i.e. in writing about him)? I shall be seeking a framework within which to register these differences that is historically located and which does not depend on impressionistic readings ('He sounds cross, doesn't he') or expressionistic readings ('That letter tells me how sensitive Turner was.' 'That statement shows how unsympathetic that biographer was.') I do not regard these verbal constructions as revelatory of a hidden truth about Turner the man but as a domain of communication which functions according to certain rules, which formulates and gives prominence to particular problems and effectively excludes others, which develops characteristic vocabularies and orders of priorities.

Turner's letters are my starting point. John Gage, their editor, declared, 'there are many reasons for gathering and publishing [Turner's] letters'. In fact he articulates only one: 'that such a collection will help to dispel the impression still left by his earliest biographers, that Turner was an unsocial being, that he wrote infrequently and reluctantly, & that he showed a habitual distrust of, and incapacity with words'. Reviewing the Letters, Luke Herrmann expressed the view that 'Compared to the correspondence of Constable, that of Turner . . . will pay only a minor role in the study of British art history.'[3]

The issue of language is present in historiography (as Gage and others have recognised); we do not choose to put it there. It is there from the start as a series of ways of defining Turner, ways of constructing the man and his work: Turner speaker, writer and maker. Linguistic theory may highlight the issue but it doesn't create it. The historical framework for an inquiry into language and Turner is that defined by questions of literacy, class, rhetoric, convention, biography and communication in all its forms. To put it very simply Turner, the man in history, is caught between (and must function within) the terms of a written language of craft, technology and the market on the one hand and, on the other hand, a rhetoric of the aesthetic, a language of learning and cultivation which, like the language of business, has its own rules and conventions.

Language has always been a vital means by which the artist established his or her status; the distinction between *ingegno* or practical skill oriented talent and the kind of academic and theoretical knowledge postulated by Reynolds in the *Discourses* needed to be constantly reaffirmed. It was this second, ekphrastic language, learned language which marked out the artist from the artisan. There are other languages too that are relevant here: the rhetoric of *belles lettres*, the language of poetry, the language of technology.

The language of poetry and that of technology can be seen as the terms within which the titles of Turner's Royal Academy contributions function. They alternate between the informative/technological and the poetic/imaginative. A look at examples from one year will serve to make the point: in 1832 Turner exhibited at the Royal Academy six paintings, three of which have factually informative titles and three of which offer poetic verbalisations. The first three are: *The Prince of Orange, William III, embarked from Holland and landed at Torbay, November 4 1688, after a stormy passage. The yacht in which his majesty sailed was, after many changes and services, finally wrecked on Hamburgh sands while employed in the Hull trade* (no. 153); *Van Tromp's Shallop at the entrance of the Scheldt* (no. 206); and *Helvoetsluys – the city of Utrecht, 64, going to sea* (no. 284). The three poetically worded titles are: *Childe Harold's pilgrimage – Italy.* 'And now, fair Italy / Thou art the garden of the world, etc.' – Byron (no. 70); 'Then Nebuchadnezzar came near the mouth of the burning fiery furnace, and said, Shadrach, Meshac, and Abednego, come forth and come hither, etc.' – Daniel iii, 26 (no. 355); and *Staffa, Fingal's Cave.* 'Nor of a theme less solemn tells, etc.' *Lord of the Isles.* (no. 453). There is no doubt that for a contemporary audience the linguistic differences between the informative and the poetic signalled different categories of response.

Turner's age is the age of the biography and of the lecture; two genres that define status and power within a community of learning and achievement, one eye constantly on posterity, as it were. Turner, in terms of class and professional identity, is *contemporaneously* defined by his words just as he is by his painting; the fact that they were few only serves to indicate how powerfully they signified and still do signify. So once we acknowledge our subject, Turner, suspended in what Geertz calls 'webs of significance' which he, in common with the collective cultural practice of his age, has helped to spin,[4] what tools can we devise to examine and interpret this phenomenon?

It is here that linguistic theory can help us. Let us look at a passage from one of Turner's letters:

The picture was Exhibited at the British Institution about 8 years ago – 30 years between the two makes Lord Egerton Pict the first about 1806 – Lord Gower bought it and thereby launched my Boat at once with the Vandervelde – I should wish much the Duke of Sutherland to see it – but in regard to the price that is the greatest difficulty. With me the price was not sent with it to the Institution – so I escape condemnation on that head – and any who likes may offer what they please.[5]

Traditional art historical practice, quite correctly, would extrapolate from this letter a variety of factual information about Turner and his work:

1 Turner has a good memory for his own work.
2 He is able to produce a chronological account of his own career in which certain key works can be seen as markers.
3 He is sensitive about money and his reputation as a businessman but he is also prepared to be defiant.

But if we look at this passage as discourse we might make some further observations that will be historically illuminating. By discourse I mean those sequences of linked and cohesive speech acts the understanding of which requires more than simply knowing what any particular linguistic act refers to. Discourse alerts us to ideology in language and to questions of who controls language (and, therefore, forms of knowledge); it defines its object and there are, therefore, no criteria of truth external to it.

1. The structure and syntax in Turner's letter is fragmentary and abrupt; it thus offers a discourse of discontinuity that undermines or at least challenges the notion of chronological continuity that the listing of works establishes. So one might say that the text is continuity – the continuous existence of Turner's paintings as well as the continual production of paintings by Turner – and the sub-text is discontinuity.

2. The one figure of speech, 'the launching of the Boat', is embedded in a sequence of factual statements, summary and even legalistic in their brevity.

3. The discourse of commerce (which this whole passage may be taken to exemplify) has no place for the 'I'; the market is the imperative

and Turner does not, therefore, appear as 'I' until half-way down the passage. However, once this discourse of commerce is recognised the 'ship launched' can be seen as part of the commercial discourse, a metaphor for financial investment as well as career progress. In the terms of ship-building and ship-launching Turner must be designer, builder, financier and master mariner.

4. The dominant discourse, that of commerce, once recognised, can then be seen to be suddenly undermined by the introduction of another, conflicting, discourse, that of the confessional subject with its neatly framed disavowal of its own involvement: 'So I escape condemnation on that head.'

5. The discourse of commerce is finally reasserted as the object being bartered over (the painting) is thrust by its producer on to an open market: 'And any who likes may offer what they please.'

Now an analysis such as the one I have just undertaken can tell us much about the constraints within which Turner as an artist must operate. I am not suggesting that we can know what Turner was thinking or how he was responding as an individual (we can never actually know such things as this though we might wish to try to deduce them). What we can know, by recognising discourse in this way, is something of that complex cultural web in the formation of which language works as a systematic practice. Artists, like everyone else, live and work at any particular time in a relationship with ideology; the fact that beliefs, aspirations and regulations are unwritten or undeclared does not make them any the less powerful.

I now want to go somewhat further and suggest that language is inextricably linked to image production. I want to look at the discontinuities and spaces (linguistically defined) within which art is shaped. I am not implying that these are the only considerations deserving of attention in relation to Turner's images, but they are the ones that interest me for this project. I am going to take as my example three of a series of letters written by Turner in connection with the production of his *View of the High Street, Oxford* (commissioned in 1809 and finished in 1810). The circumstances of the commission as known are as follows: the 'View of the High Street' was commissioned by the Oxford dealer and frame-maker James Wyatt in November 1809 as the basis for an engraving. Late in December Turner went to Oxford to make a drawing. The picture was finished in March 1810, sent to Oxford before 6 April but returned for the opening of Turner's gallery on 7 May. Some alterations were made to the figures and the spire of St Mary's was raised at Wyatt's request. It was subsequently engraved by John Pye and S. Middiman, with figures by C. Heath, and published by Wyatt on 14 March 1812. A smaller print by W. E. Albutt was published in Paris in 1828.[6]

*Letter 1, Turner to Wyatt, 4 February 1810*

Sir / You may prepare a frame 2 feet 3 inches high by 3 feet 3 long, but I think that it must be cut less, having at present too much sky, so do not put the frame together until you hear again from me. By way of consolation let me tell you the picture is *very forward*, but I could wish you to send me back the annexed sketch with information how the several windows are glazed, and those *blank* in front of the All Souls entrance, particularly those in the *large Gable part*, if they project in a bow, like the two by the gateway, as I find two marked in my second sketch more than in my first, and therefore suppose some alteration has taken place since the first was made. /Pray tell me likewise if a gentleman of the name of Trimmer has written to you to be a subscriber for the print.[7]

In what ways is the visual being negotiated here via the verbal? What is immediately striking with these texts is precisely how shifting, how unstable and changeable is this declared subject of Turner's painting, that is, *Oxford*. To begin with, the fenestration of the very buildings he is recording appears to change: 'I could wish you to send me back the annexed sketch with information how the several windows are glazed, and those *blank* in the front of the All Souls entrance . . .'

*Letter 2, Turner to Wyatt, 28 February, 1810*

Sir/ I did not receive yours yesterday early enough to answer by Post, but with respect to the picture, I have continued it on the same size, viz 2F 3 1/4 i by 3F 3i utmost measure. Yet the sky I do think had better be an inch at least under the top Rabbit [rebate], therefore I should advise you to make the Rabbit deep, so that it can be hid. Therefore the sight measures may be as follows – 3 Feet 2 1/2 by 2 Feet 2 1/2. / The Picture you may inform Mr. Middiman can be seen if he will favour me by calling, and with a line when it will suit him, that I may be sure to be at home. I am afraid it will not be finished as early as you mention'd, but I shall not long exceed that time March 7, for it certainly would be desirable to you to have it while *Oxford* is full./ The figures introduced are as follows . . . two Clericals, one in black with a master of arts gown, the other with lawn sleeves for the Bishop (being in want of a little white and purple scarf) preceded by and follow'd by a Beadle – Hence arise some questions – first? Is it right or wrong to introduce the Bishop crossing the street in conversation with his robes, whether he should wear a cap? What kind of staff the Beadles use, and if they wear caps – in short, these are the principal figures, and if you will favour me with answers to the foregoing questions and likewise describe to me the particularities of each dress I should be much obliged to you, for I could wish to be right.[8]

Oxford may be full of people or empty; houses are demolished and a gateway removed: 'The figures taking down the old Houses are not only admissable but I think explains their loss and the removal of the gateway.'[9] The discourse is one of flux, change and transformation, a language which (at one and the same time) both describes an actual changefulness (houses being demolished, etc.) *and* provides an analogue to that slow cumulative process of brushstroke, amendment, correction, affirmation, by which the surface of the painting slowly comes into being. The image comes to represent the permanent element in a world that shifts and changes before one's very eyes; the task of the painter is manifestly to maintain the illusion of permanence and agelessness in forms which his eye has already registered and verbally recorded as changeful and decaying. The verbal provides the key to the transition between those two contradictory states.

'You may prepare a frame 2 feet 3 inches high by 3 feet 3 long, but I think it must be cut less, having at present too much sky, so do not put the frame together until you hear from me,' Turner tells Wyatt in the first letter of the series. The frame must be prepared but not put together, made but left unmade. The picture is *very forward*, Turner tells Wyatt in the next sentence, but immediately asks Wyatt to send *back* the sketch with the information about the windows. In other words, the picture is forward but instantly things are to move backwards, that is, in the wrong direction, if we take the trajectory from artist to patron, from painting to production as engraving, from Turner to Wyatt. In the next letter continuity is affirmed ('I have continued it on the same size') and then instantly undermined with the change of mind about the sky ('Yet the sky I do think had better be an Inch at least under the top Rabbit'). The figures are in procession: 'two Clericals, one in black with a master of arts gown, the other with lawn sleeves for the Bishop . . . preceded by and follow'd by a Beadle . . .' . They are in temporal sequence just as the painting is but the latter is (unlike the beadles) a little late ('it will not be finished as early as you mentioned').[10]

*Letter 3, Turner to Wyatt, 14 March 1810*
Sir/ I have not heard or seen Mr. Middiman, and not being so fortunate as to meet with him at home yesterday evng., I now write to ask – how to proceed, *the Picture being finished*, and in a day or two can be varnished for the last time. The packing case is likewise ready. Therefore be so good as to say what conveyance you wish me to use to send it by, and whether you positively wish Mr. M. to see it first? In which case you had better write to him again, or perhaps my delivering the Picture to him, you may consider the same (sending you a receipt for it)./ As to

the figures introduced, I have made use of those you sent, and therefore hope you will find them right. Yet I took the hint, for the sake of color, to introduce some Ladies. The figures taking down the old Houses are not only admissable but I think explains their loss and the removal of the gateway. In short, I hope that the Picture will *please* and that you will find your endeavours seconded and prove ultimately very advantageous.[11]

In the third letter the question is how to *proceed*; here the discourse of 'completion' takes over from that of transformation. The painting caught up in time is *finished* but its narrative is not complete just as the frame is to be made but left incomplete: varnish, packing case, etc., await it. Looking back to the first letter where Mr Trimmer, a potential subscriber, is mentioned we find this discourse of the *completed work* (launched like one of Turner's ships) already present. The painting itself becomes a narrative, a story to engage an audience, and that is Turner's point of exit: 'I hope the picture will *please*', he says, 'and that the market will justify the investment.'

Clearly on one level all this toing and froing was inevitable if two people at a distance were to collaborate over a work in which some topographical accuracy was required and there was no chance of a telephone conversation. But the act of writing is always more than the mere imparting of information. What is, I think, intriguing is how the art of naming and defining plays such an important part in this process: windows are to be glazed or blank, gables projecting or in a bow, lawn sleeves, caps, master of arts gowns and so on. Turner could not have produced the painting without the words to define the categories of objects he is painting. The almost desperate enumeration in this writing should alert us to the problem of the relationship of words to the production of visual imagery.

In support of my hypothesis about the function of the verbal in the configuration of the visual in this particular instance I want to draw attention to a second discourse that is present within these letters. This is the discourse of Authority which encompasses the invocation of a whole series of authorities. Turner, the young artist here without authority in the public sense, issues what amounts to an instruction: 'You may prepare a frame.' Wyatt's (and Middiman's) authority underlies the anxiety to complete. The authority of artist is in interplay with the authority of patron. But the real authority is Oxford, town and institution, the embodiment of learning and knowledge which is linguistically constructed and verbally experienced. Oxford, to put it bluntly, is full of words and it is with a cascade of words about bishops, beadles, clerics and their *proper* attributes that Turner seeks approval of this ultimate authority 'for', as he says, 'I could wish to be *right*'.[12] Within the public domain of learning, a domain which we have already remarked upon in relation to Turner's careful imparting of information in the titling of paintings, knowledge is constituted by the ability to name correctly and in proper order. Only that ability lends authority.

I want to conclude by addressing the same kinds of questions to writing not by Turner but about Turner. And as the thematic underpinning of this essay has been the intersection of art as aesthetic with art as commodity, I propose to turn to the *Liber studiorum*. The first text I want to examine is a curious hybrid affair about which much could be said in terms of historiography. It consists of a clutch of notes about Turner written by the engraver and author, John Pye (who probably never intended to publish them) which have been collated, edited and augmented by a third person with a claim to artistic knowledge and special access to Turner's works, John Lewis Roget, proto-historian of the English water-colourists and their institutions.[13]

Whilst our starting point, Gage's edition of Turner's collected correspondence, presents itself as a series of fragments which turns out to have the authority of a whole, the *Liber studiorum* presents itself as a named whole which, on inspection, turns out to comprise only fragments. The *Liber studiorum*, a collection of plates and texts which aspires to be a book (though it never quite became one) is thus framed first by Pye and then, in an outer casing as it were, by Roget. One is reminded of the framing devices of the *Liber's* own frontispiece in which *Tyre at Sunset with the Rape of Europa* is framed against Gothic blind arcading above a pile of fragments of human civilisation. An account of Turner is constructed in Pye and Roget via a series of fragmentary and conflicting statements. The empirical explanation for this fragmented discourse must lie in the note-taking, memoranda and accretions of the various authors and editors. But I would suggest that the narrative is contradictory and ruptured also because it addresses the conflicting concepts of the aesthetic and the commercial, those terms that in Turner's writing acts are already seen to be reconcilable only by a wrenching and determined use of language.

Pye's account of the origin of the *Liber studiorum* tries to bridge this gap. He gives two reasons for Turner having commenced his series of engraved works: deficiency of employment as a result of a slack market and desire on the part of Turner to show that he could depict everything in the visible world:

Instead, therefore, of painting more pictures 'to increase the dead stock in hand',
he in 1807 entered upon the *Liber Studiorum*. He commenced that work 'in consequence of having deficiency of employment' and 'to demonstrate that in a work
of elementary composition and chiaroscuro' he 'could demonstrate everything
that is visible beneath the sun.'[14]

The pragmatic and speculative (dead stock, deficiency of employment) here confronts the symbolic search for a demonstration of omni-
science (everything that is under the sun). Art can do everything and
there is nothing that it cannot encompass.

The same contradiction reappears a few pages later when we are told
that 'the neglect of the public caused [Turner] to abandon the work when
fourteen parts . . . had been published.'[15] Market forces had intervened.
Yet the artist allegedly insisted on the wholeness of the fragmented work
and the oft-quoted 'What is the use of them but together', Turner's
plaintive refrain upon finding his plates scattered in print shops and
collectors' portfolios, is the voice of the artist mediated and repeated,
framed in the observations of others. The discourse of wholeness is most
clearly enshrined in the declared taxonomy of the *Liber's* preface: 'It is
intended in this publication to attempt a classification of the various
styles of landscape, viz, the historic, the mountainous, pastoral, marine,
and architectural.' This classifying system challenges the overall Genre
system within which all academic art functioned to a greater or lesser
degree. The system thus by implication subsumes *all* artistic practice.[16]
What else could be left to do once that was completed, one may ask?

There is a perpetual promise of wholeness, of completeness, in the
formation of the *Liber studiorum* which is, let us remember, a collection of
pages which never quite attains the status of 'Liber', a book, Turner
having had to content himself with issuing a fragmentary collection of
prints and a frontispiece. This promise of wholeness derives both from
the sense that it is formed of parts and from the sense that it purports to
display the whole of nature. The promise, an unfulfilled promise, is
repeated in the Pye-Roget search for a whole account, a whole 'portrait'
of Turner.

The crucial moment in the biographical account of the artist (whether
declared or implicit) is the moment of the origin of the work of art.
Whilst neglect and the market are invoked to account for the failure of
Turner to complete the series, that very failure simultaneously generates
the account of artistic originality:

'During that time [i.e., the eleven years from 1807–1818 when the Liber was in course of publication] it was that Turner threw off all deference to the works of Claude, Gainsborough, Wilson and others, to repose solely on his own learning and genius . . .'[17]

The Liber thus becomes a place of innovation and the point at which the artist frees himself from his ancestral lineage, becomes original. Free of Wilson, Gainsborough, et al. it is now imperative for the narrative to proceed to establish the Liber itself as the foundation of a new lineage, a new artistic genealogy. Thus the language is that of legacy, ownership and association. 'Permit me to say that it [the Liber] was first thought of at the house of his friend, Mr. Wells.' Mr Wells is defined as the person '. . . at whose house the Liber was projected'. Turner's first twentieth-century biographer appropriates this discourse (a testimony to its power) re-presenting the Liber as 'not intended to reproduce anything that was already in existence'.[18] Accordingly he heroicises Wells for providing the location: 'The conception of the undertaking was so bold and unprecedented . . . only a disinterested friend, like Wells, sublimely confident in Turner's genius . . . only a friend like Wells whom Turner loved and esteemed. . . .'[19] Wilton, however, writing in the era of the recently opened Clore Gallery (1987), dismisses Wells's role.[20] The authenticity of the Pye account of the Liber's origins is envinced by reference to Turner having left a legacy to Mr Wells's three daughters. Nothing establishes the idea of continuity and wholeness like genealogy and family trees. So the Liber is grafted firmly to a lineage and sealed with a cash bequest.

Pye and Roget may thus be seen as collaborators in the production of a discourse which proposes the Liber as a principle rather than as a commercial or artistic undertaking. 'Originality' and 'wholeness' are the key concepts that underpin their joint account. Both concepts are, however, major currency in the art market; there the authenticity of the work, its value as an 'original', and the wholeness or material completeness of an object affect its monetary value.

The question can be further explored by turning to what is, if not precisely a collaborative publication, certainly an account of Turner that fully declares its affiliation to an authority external to the text. This is Walter Thornbury's The life of J. M. W. Turner, R.A. first published in 1862 and the first full-length biography of the artist. It is significant for a discussion centred on the Liber studiorum that this was the year the copyright bill was passed, one culmination of over a century of debate about 'originality'. Thornbury's book opens with a letter from Ruskin of four years earlier, written in response to an enquiry from Thornbury, intended to ascertain whether or not Ruskin himself intended to write on Turner. Ruskin, giving Thornbury the go-ahead, instructs him to fix the main characteristics of Turner in his mind as the key to the secret of all the artist *said* and *did* (my italics):

Uprightness
Generosity
Tenderness of Heart (extreme)
Sensuality
Obstinacy (extreme)
Irritability
Infidelity

Here, then, we have Turner constructed by Ruskin, a master of the discursive translation of image into words, as seven contradictory categories. Thornbury writes with the authority of Ruskin whose own reputation was founded upon his writing about Turner, about what Turner *said* and *did*, equally weighted thus. In a sense, therefore, the whole of Thornbury's account becomes an attempt to resolve the contradiction between 'uprightness' and 'infidelity', between 'generosity' and 'irritability'.

The *Liber* plates, by 1862, eleven years after Turner's death, had become one of the registers for the artist's reputation in the market. The *Liber* could, in Thornbury's account, be seen as an ideal model for a commercial age, that is an investment which would accrue in monetary value:

The 'Liber' was not successful in the business sense of the term. But the price that a fine and perfect copy will fetch at the present time would seem almost fabulous. Engraved by Charles Turner, and others, at a cost varying from five to seven guineas only per plate, proof impressions of single plates have recently sold for upwards of 10 l and proofs touched on by the artist himself for more than double.[21]

The *Liber* was engraved on copper plates which wore very quickly; the metal being soft, the surface rapidly deteriorated. Thus the 'proofs' or the first set of impressions would be much clearer than later ones. It is, however, not the empirical, technical, history of Turner's engravings that concerns me but the discourse of the commercial and the aesthetic upon which these contemporary accounts are predicated.

Great difficulty is experienced in both the Pye–Roget and the Thornbury account around the issue of Turner's own relationship to the *Liber* prints. Not only is the artist seen as having thwarted the imperatives of completion and wholeness, he is also perceived as subverting the concept of the 'original' within the already difficult framework of the original engraved reproduction. As far as it is possible to ascertain, the situation was that eleven of the plates were engraved by Turner himself, others were put out to engravers but even in these cases Turner is also alleged to have worked on them himself; all the outlines were done by Turner and Finberg stresses the artist's control over the whole process.[22] Most notoriously, Turner repaired the plates when they became worn, thus creating confusion in the terms of the market between 'proofs' and the less valuable 'prints'. The only distinction made by Turner was between proofs and prints but, as Finberg says, exactly what he meant by these terms is difficult to discover.[23] Certainly not all his proofs were first states and collectors started classifying the engravings in their own way. In short Turner disrupted the system and rendered the language inadequate as a result.

Turner also removed from the margins the marks that distinguished one class of impression from another.[24] The very disjuncture between 'uprightness' and 'infidelity' is thus most fully manifest in accounts of the production of the Liber. Moreover, the allegedly subversive practices that undermine the principle of wholeness and originality (that is, the imperative of the aesthetic) are attributed by Thornbury to 'tradesman-like' practice.[25] The discourse is one in which genius is under attack from commercial pressure: 'Turner superintended the printing and publication in a most minute and yet in a most capricious manner . . .'[26] Yet Turner, being the man he was, we are told, 'sometimes the result would be, but very seldom, a patchwork of incongruous intentions. Sometimes the design was so perfect and grand, it could not be changed or injured . . .'[27] The 'art' of Turner is here construed as being deployed to deceive: 'Generally speaking, the alterations were made with consummate art merely to hide the wear and tear of the copper; the faintness, the blur, or the pallor of the plate's old age. It would have bordered slightly on sharp practice, had it not been for Turner's inventive genius.[28]

These actions allegedly made it extremely difficult to form a complete set of first impressions of the Liber. In fact, as we now know, Turner kept for himself all first impressions as a form of private investment. They were released on to the market only after his death. The demands of collecting, the need to assemble a coherent whole from many parts, are thus seen by his early biographers to be countered by Turner's practice. Turner himself is presented as undermining those very concepts of wholeness and originality upon which the market depended. Whilst Turner is by one definition 'tradesmanlike', the manner of producing and printing the Liber was 'unbusiness like, fitful and peculiar'. Thornbury, referring to an account that is repeated in the Pye–Roget text[29] about the woman employed by Turner to sew the prints together in numbers and whom the artist allegedly refused to pay except in kind, says: 'We can scarcely wonder that, as is generally reported, some female servant of Turner employed to stitch the numbers, stole many of the plates and sold them privately.'[30] It is as though the contradictions can only be explained by the introduction, into the narrative, of a dishonest female servant.

It is historically significant that this debate should take place around questions of engraving. Oxford High Street was produced for an engraver; it was designed with mass reproduction and dissemination in mind. The Liber studiorum paradoxically was tied to the notion of originality; it was, after all, conceptually related (at least by the analogous title) to the so-called Liber veritatis of Claude, a drawn record of his own work made popular through the engravings of Earlom, published by Boydell in the 1770s.[31] Claude's series was intended as a means of verifying his own work as original and distinct from forgeries or imitations. Yet Turner's Liber was also, by its very medium, reproductive. Engravings, and especially engraved series, formed the backbone of the vast commercial empire of buying and selling art in nineteenth-century Britain, a market that catered for an unprecedentedly wide audience. Thus whilst Earlom is described by Finberg as 'an enterprising publisher who skilfully exploited Claude's reputation',[32] Turner is construed as one who seizes the exploitative medium and turns it to his advantage, uniting the commercial and the aesthetic in an unprecedented act of visionary boldness.

Susan Lambert points out that 'formal definitions of the print were not promulgated until the 1960s and then ostensibly to help tax inspectors and customs and trading standards officials to distinguish original work from reproductions so that the former could receive privileged treatment and to protect the public from reproductive work which masqueraded as "original".[33] The complex history of printmaking and the shifting definitions of originality which are part of that history are outside the scope of this essay. Nonetheless it is instructive to note that the aftermath of the nineteenth-century debate that has been the subject of this essay is a form of classification in the fiscal domain rather than in what is more recognisably a cultural arena. Turner's tradesmanlike action in repairing and regenerating his plates is construed as one that confounds the market's own system of classification. It also confounded

Finberg, who argued that questions of morality that interest a modern print-dealing public were 'less clearly defined at the time'.[34] Turner's marginal marks he cannot comprehend: 'I must confess I find it impossible to unravel all the details of the business.'[35] Thus a response to the market on the part of the artist – for this, according to the accounts of Pye, Roget and Thornbury, is one of the points of origin of the Liber prints – results in the destruction of that very system that allowed for the commoditisation of the work, a system analogous to, and as significant as, the genre system that safeguarded the aesthetic hierarchy in the Academy. In its place, Turner introduced a private system of marking plates to distinguish different states, a system which challenged the language of recognition and classification through which the market operated. The market was thus exploited – Turner's engravings could only be recognised by the science of connoisseurship then evolving.

Assumptions about the artwork as commodity in a market underpin Turner's discourse. Here, moreover, language is a working practice accommodating the visual construction within a system – the market economy – defined by and dependent upon the verbal. In contemporary writing about Turner, the interdependency of the commercial and the aesthetic is disavowed and a polarisation produced through a discourse of 'originality' and 'wholeness' which the biography, as genre, itself reinforces. This discourse of 'originality' and 'wholeness' contains within it an opposing and contradictory discourse of fragmentation within which the artist is construed as breaking up the system of signification, blurring the necessary distinctions and threatening the equilibrium. Turner's commoditisation of his own work was contingent with, and exploitative of, language and system. The politics of current art–historical practice, whether in academic discourse or within the institution of the museum further works to expel from the definition of art the principle of commodity with which it is imbricated.

## Notes

1 Parts of this essay have appeared in Art History (December 1987); the arguments are based on a paper given at the conference of the Social History Society of the UK in York in January 1988.
2 O. Smith, The politics of language, 1791–1819 (Oxford, 1984), p. 3.
3 L. Herrmann, review, Turner Studies, 1/2 (1981).
4 C. Geertz, The interpretation of cultures: selected essays (New York, 1973), p. 5, drawing on Max Weber.
5 Collected correspondence of J. M. W. Turner with an early diary and a memoir by George Jones, ed. John Gage (Oxford, 1980) (hereafter Gage), no. 264 (1 February 1844).
6 Turner, 1775–1851 (Tate Gallery, 1974), no. 160.

7  Turner to Wyatt, 4 February 1810, Gage, no. 29.

8  Turner to Wyatt, 28 February 1810, Gage, no. 30.

9  Turner to Wyatt, 14 March 1810, Gage, no. 31.

10  Turner to Wyatt, 28 February 1810, Gage, no. 30.

11  Turner to Wyatt, 14 March 1810, Gage, no. 31.

12  Turner to Wyatt, 28 February 1810, Gage, no. 30.

13  J. Pye, *Notes and memoranda respecting the liber studiorum of J. M. W. Turner, R.A., written and collected by the late John Pye, landscape engraver. Edited, with additional observations, and an illustrative etching by John Lewis Roget* (1879).

14  Ibid., pp. 19–21.

15  Ibid., p. 22.

16  Rather than merely 'all the forms of landscape painting which he had hitherto practised', as stated by A. J. Finberg, *The history of Turner's liber studiorum with a new catalogue raisonné* (London, 1924), p. xxxvii.

17  Pye, p. 22.

18  Finberg (1924), p. xxi.

19  A. J. Finberg, *The Life of J. M. W. Turner, R.A.* (Oxford, 1939, 1961), p. 128.

20  A. Wilton, *Turner in his time* (London, 1987), p. 74.

21  W. Thornbury, *The life of J. M. W. Turner, R.A.* (London, 1862), p. 286.

22  Finberg (1924), p. xxii.

23  Ibid., p. lxiii.

24  Pye, pp. 68–9.

25  P. 275: 'These crafty tradesmanlike alterations which, when studied, are the strongest proofs I know of his genius and of his thriftiness, were made under his own eye, if not by his own hand.'

26  Thornbury, p. 274.

27  Ibid.

28  Ibid., p. 275.

29  P. 61.

30  Thornbury, p. 274.

31  Finberg's insistence that the idea of any relationship with the Earlom production is 'positively misleading' is a protectionist position on the part of the biographer. A. J. Finberg (1924, p. xxi).

32  Finberg (1961), p. 129.

33  S. Lambert, *The image multiplied*, (London 1987), p. 32.

34  Finberg (1924), p. lxv.

35  Ibid.

# 7

# Reading Constable
## Ann Bermingham

I would like to address the question of meaning, or rather the production of meaning, in Constable's landscapes, for it seems significant that so much of what we have come to believe about Constable's art derives from his own accounts of it to family and friends as preserved in his correspondence, and remarkable that these statements should be accepted so unproblematically.[1] I am not made uneasy by the use of the raw 'data' the letters supply, the evidence of dates, projects, trips, exhibitions and the like (although the sheer quantity of this kind of information I would suggest is in and of itself, meaningful), but rather what disturbs me is the use of certain passages from the letters as textual glosses for the paintings, as if they constituted the last critical word for what it is we see before us on the canvas. This primitive matching of word and image represents an abdication from critical analysis and interpretation, one which until recently has uncontestedly closed off Constable's art from other methodological approaches.[2]

It is not my intention to do away with the correspondence as a means of discussing the art, nor do I wish to urge that it simply hold equal place among the other strategies of interpretation. Such negation and pluralism share with the older traditional use of the correspondence a peculiar blindness with regard to the crucial role it plays in the creation of a critical discourse that is highly ideological and that infuses Constable's whole approach to landscape painting. Rather, I would like to demonstrate how the letters collaborate with the art in order to maintain a particular set of meanings as a way of forestalling others. These meanings, I believe, form the basis of what we have come to accept as Constable's 'naturalism,' a naturalism which erases all its cultural signs. The letters assist and finally can be said to direct this project of naturalisation by imposing on the art a rhetoric of personality, or, more exactly and profoundly, a rhetoric of authenticity. It is the ideological matrix created by the art and the letters, and merely re-presented in the traditional readings of his landscapes, that I wish to explore.

I would like to discuss what Constable called his 'natural painture', that is, the naturalistic effects produced in his landscapes by certain stylistic, and finally, ideological choices, in order to analyse the formal means or figure that not only provides the foundation for the construction of this naturalism but also repeats and reaffirms in the landscapes' style the same rhetoric of personality that we find in the letters. Such a figure exists in the sketch-like finish which functions as evidence of both a naturalistic observation and a subjective response. Its dual signification works to collapse the distinction between Constable and the landscape that he paints. In its most radical form, it makes it impossible for us to decide which is being represented. Constable's fusion or confusion of himself with his object is of a piece with other cultural practices of the time which sought to conflate themselves with the natural structure of the world.

As part of this pattern of naturalisation there develops a mythology of the oil sketch. Its most succinct formulation comes in Diderot's *Salon* of 1765 when he writes: 'Sketches possess a warmth that pictures do not. They represent a state of ardour and pure verve on the artist's part, with no admixture of the affected elaboration introduced by thought: through the sketch the painter's very soul is poured forth on the canvas.'[3] By the nineteenth century, this view of the sketch as a mirror of the artist's soul made the seasoned exhibitor at the Salon or Academy reluctant to exhibit them. As Albert Boime has explained, the artist 'hesitated to disclose what he felt were the intimate recordings of feelings and personality. He was in a sense as self-conscious about his preliminary studies as he would be self-conscious about his own body. . .'.[4]

This naturalisation of the sketch as a reflection of feelings and personality coexisted with another notion of the sketch as a transparent rendering of natural phenomena. These two different interpretations were, in the Academic tradition, given two different forms, the *esquisse* and the *étude*. Both forms were part of the generative process of the final work of art. The *esquisse* could represent an artist's first thoughts about a subject or his final orchestration of major formal elements before embarking on the actual painting. Unlike the *étude*, it was not painted directly from the motif. Instead it was the imaginary working out of the composition, colour, and light. Often the formal solutions arrived at were derived from the work of other artists, and in this way, the artist of the *esquisse* put himself in relation to the history of art. In the *étude*, on the other hand, the artist competed with nature, attempting to capture, through a direct and rapid rendering *alla prima*, the transitory effects of light and atmosphere pervading the scene. Like the *esquisse*, it too was rough and unfinished, not, however, as the inevitable result of the process of preliminary formal conceptualisation, but the better to represent the immediate and actual sensations of light and atmosphere which could then be idealised in the finished painting. Unlike the *esquisse*, the *étude* was not devoted to sharpening the artist's powers of invention and composition but rather his powers of observation and documentation. Opposed as these two modes of sketching were, both were naturalised as the transparent renderings of either the artist's mind (the *esquisse*) or of his object (the *étude*).[5]

In addition to the difference between the documentary *étude* and the more conceptual *esquisse*, a distinction should also be drawn between the studio *étude* and the more radically naturalistic landscape *étude*. Unlike the landscape *étude*, the studio *étude* was made indoors; hence it was a factual rendering of a highly controlled situation, in which the model or still-life objects could be posed or arranged with the lighting, background, and props adjusted accordingly. While this kind of painted study demanded a factual and descriptive rendering of the motif, the very circumstances under which the rendering took place made the studio *étude* already approximate to the idealised and artificial aspects of the finished painting. In *plein-air* landscape sketching, by contrast, there is very little control over the motif or the circumstances under which it is painted. Light and atmosphere, which are fundamental to the colour, composition and mood of the landscape, were precisely its least controllable elements and as such presented the landscape sketcher with his greatest challenge. As the eighteenth century drew to a close, with *plein-air* landscape sketching widely practised by professional and amateur alike, the technical writing on landscape painted burgeoned and was increasingly given over to the problem of rendering light.[6]

In his famous treatise on landscape painting, *Eléments de la perspective pratique* (1800), Pierre Henri de Valenciennes insisted on the importance of the sky in setting the tonal scale for the landscape. The sketcher should begin his *étude* with the sky, which Valenciennes claimed would give a 'background tone', and 'from this advance to the middle distance and by degrees to the foreground, which will always be in harmony with the sky, from which the local tone is taken'. '*Progressing in this way,*' he tells the artist, '*you will not be able to fill in any detail: for all études from Nature should be done within two hours at the outside, and if your effect is a sunrise or a sunset, you should not take more than an hour.*'[7]

As his remarks suggest, landscape painting came increasingly to demand for itself technical procedures which not only differed from traditional Academic practice, but which were gradually perceived by artists as being incompatible with it. Unlike other genres of painting, landscape was divided technically from within. While in the case of history painting or portraiture the studio *étude* could be more easily accommodated to the idealised form of the finished work, in the case of landscape, the naturalism of the *plein-air étude*, arrived at through different conditions and procedures from those governing the studio *étude*, could not be adjusted to the final work without a serious compromise of visual truth and original purpose. The internal tension in landscape painting between the initial, 'objective' *étude* and the final, 'idealised' painting distinguished it from other genres in terms of the procedural and theoretical problems it posed for the artist. While these problems would eventually manifest themselves in all genres of painting as realism came to be increasingly prized in art, they first arise in landscape and it is there that the Academic tradition is seriously undermined.

Symptomatic of the eventual split between landscape practice and Academic practice is the amount of emphasis given in the biographies of landscape painters to the artist's struggle to become versed in 'the art of seeing nature', as Reynolds would call it. In these biographies landscape practice becomes heroic and the accounts of artists painting out of doors take on mythic qualities. As early as Sandrart's *Teutsche Academie* (1675) we hear how Claude 'tried by every means to penetrate nature, lying in the fields before the break of day and until night in order to learn to represent very exactly the red-morning sky, sunrise and the evening hours . . . This hard and burdensome way of learning he pursued for many years, walking daily into the fields and the long way back.'[8] A more colourful account of the landscape artist's dedication to the study of nature comes from an anecdote about Claude-Joseph Vernet, the teacher of Valenciennes, who according to his 1788 obituary had himself lashed to the mast of a ship crossing the Mediterranean, the better to witness and record the effects of a storm at sea.[9] There are similar stories in the nineteenth century; one thinks particularly of the tales of Turner and the genesis of his *Snow Storm – Steam Boat off a Harbour's Mouth* (RA, 1842) and *Rain, Steam, and Speed – The Great Western Railway* (RA, 1844).[10] Such stories describe, in addition to an almost fanatical devotion to the truthful *reportage* of natural phenomena, a relationship between the artist and his object that is quite unlike the traditional one. It is difficult to imagine the portrait painter or history painter undergoing similar kinds of quasi-heroic/quasi-masochistic ordeals, unless perhaps one is talking of Géricault. For the ordinary exhibitor at the Academy, whose repertoire ran from face to face or from nymphs to satyrs, such experiences of physical discomfort and danger in the name of art were unheard of. The physicality of the landscape painter's encounter with his object stressed in the accounts of Claude and Vernet underscores the fact that his relationship to landscape was one not of intellectual distance but of material proximity.

Because it originated in actual physical experience of the object, landscape painting not only demanded technical procedures different from Academic practice, but also a critical language separate from traditional Academic discourse. With its empirical bias, landscape theory departs from the Academic preoccupation with idealism and the ranking of genres. The concepts of Beauty, Sublimity and Picturesqueness, categories used in the eighteenth century to discuss landscape, are based on the physical characteristics (smoothness, vastness, irregularity) of the actual object, and share with science a concern with the classification of observable features.

The theoretical objectification of nature, as that thing outside the self which is contained within our field of vision and limited by it, is compatible with the assumptions supporting the practice of *plein-air* landscape sketching. In the literature of both empirical science and landscape painting, we find the body described as a receiver of stimuli, as an organ that both protects one from and exposes one to the shocks of external reality. The inevitable joining of sensation and observation in the practice of *plein-air* sketching laid stress on the importance of the artist's physical and mental disposition when in the act of perceiving nature. Significantly, the posture of defence is not recommended. Instead the sketcher's physical and mental attitude before what we might call the assault of nature, as the stories of Claude and Vernet suggest, was meant to be a passive one. Useful only in their receptive states, the sketcher's body and mind were the substances upon which nature impressed itself.

In recommending the sketcher's subjugation to nature, Valenciennes drew an important distinction between the open (or 'simple') mind necessary for the true apprehension of nature and the closed (or 'clever') mind which only blinded one to nature. He wrote: 'The first artists, to whom everything was new, observed Nature with a simple mind and caught glimpses of truth. But before long they grew tired of exact observation and sought to be clever as well, and, from that moment truth gave way to error.'[11] It does not require a great leap to move from Valenciennes's portrait of the primitive artist to Constable's description of the true landscape painter in his 1835 lecture to a Hampstead audience where he said, 'The landscape painter must walk in the fields with a humble mind.

No arrogant man was ever permitted to see nature in all her beauty.'[12] Valenciennes's simple mind and Constable's humble mind were minds for which the act of perceiving landscape was not predetermined or mediated by theoretical expectations. This open-minded objectivity insured that what was represented would be a transparent transcription of nature. However, while Valenciennes was describing the proper approach to preparing a landscape *étude*, Constable made transparent realism a standard for a finished landscape painting. Moreover, for Constable this transparency was an index of the artist's moral character, a sign not just of open-minded objectivity, but of personality and authenticity as well. Here and elsewhere in Constable's writings on landscape we find naturalistic landscape painting described as both the objective mirror of the world and the mirror of the artist's soul.

A number of important issues that will concern us are raised by the ambiguous dualism of Constable's naturalistic landscapes. To try to explain this dualism as simply a dialectical tension between Constable's 'romantic' and 'naturalistic' tendencies is to overlook the fact that both the romantic and naturalistic interpretations of Constable turn on the assumption that his writings and his art are the results of a direct, unmediated response to nature either as something deeply felt or as accurately observed. In this sense, the romantic and naturalistic readings reveal themselves to be essentially the same. Nowhere are the art–historical consequences of the transparent realism they assume more evident than in the problems raised in the thirty-year unresolved and unresolvable controversy over the Hampstead cloud studies.[13] While the 'romantics' tend to reject outright the possibility that Constable's cloud studies were influenced by scientific treatises and/or earlier artistic schemata, preferring instead to see his art as existentially motivated, the 'naturalists,' who readily admit such outside 'influences,' conclude in a romantic vein by insisting on Constable's 'genius' in surpassing these sources, changing them, depending on their nature, into something either more artistic or more naturalistic. Thus even when mediation is admitted it is immediately naturalised, turned into a reflection of Constable's mind or sensibility. This is because within the system of transparent realism the evidence of mediation is seen as a threat to the quality and originality of the art, yet wholly to deny mediation risks emptying the art of meaning and tradition and turning it into a mechanical reflection of nature, not unlike that found on the ground glass of a camera obscura. Hence for the romantic/naturalistic reading of Constable, based as it is on a theory of transparent realism, the problem of mediation remains

central and unresolved, and mediation functions as both an embarrass-
ment and a necessity.

The problem of mediation is crucial to our discussion of Constable's
correspondence not only because the letters mediate the art, but also
because they, along with the art, are mediated by the same theory of
transparent realism that characterises the romantic/naturalistic reading
and that is merely reiterated by it. The part of the correspondence that
has played the greatest role in the study of Constable's naturalism is the
portion comprising the letters he wrote to his friend John Fisher in the
1820s during the time when he was seeking full admission to the
Academy by exhibiting six-foot-wide canvases of rural country scenes
from his native Suffolk. By examining these letters I wish to show how
Constable both mediated his naturalism and naturalised this mediation.
By this I mean that his naturalism both responded to a specific public
discourse about landscape painting and its performative role in art and
culture, and effaced this response by making it appear to be the result of a
private experience of nature. This particular strategy of denial helps to
account for the change that Constable's naturalistic style underwent at
this time and that was signalled by the increasingly sketch-like finish of
his landscapes. I hope to explain the significance of this change by first
setting out some of the more obvious mediating influences we find in
Constable's discussions of his landscapes with Fisher, showing how they
work themselves into the formal language of the paintings and how
Constable's response to these influences describes his perception of
himself vis-à-vis the Academy and the critics. I then wish to take up the
larger theoretical question of mediation as it relates to the supplemental
role the correspondence plays in the interpretation of Constable's art.

The correspondence to Fisher is more allied to the technical writing
on landscape and to the biographies of landscape painters than to the
Academic discourse of, say, Reynolds. Like the biographies and the
technical writing which not only detail procedure but also fabricate auras
of artistic personality, heroic difficultas or, in some cases, religious
mysticism in order to compensate for landscape's ostensible lack of
'serious' subject matter, Constable's discussions of landscape can be read
as responses to the Academic hierarchy of genres which prized history
painting while relegating landscape to an inferior status. Along these
lines it is important to recall that in his lecture on 'The Origin of Landscape' given before the Royal Institution in 1836, Constable began by
announcing that 'The history of painting may be divided into two main
branches, history and landscape; history including portrait and familiar

life, as landscape does flower and fruit painting.'[14] He then bodly
claimed, in a remarkably subversive passage, that

Landscape is the child of history, at first inseparable from the parent. Gradually it
advanced until, from being the humble attendant on history, it became able to
stand side by side with it on the same eminence, and you could hardly tell which
was the most distinguished or the most indispensable. In time it went alone, and
afterwards, in the decline of history, it may be seen like a dutiful child supporting
its aged parent (as in the works of Pietro de Cortona), and lending its aid to uphold
the feebleness of decay.[15]

Constable attributed landscape's superiority to the fact that it was more
naturalistic and was not encumbered by the literary references or narrative constructions basic to history painting. The decline of Italian art in
the seventeenth century, he claimed, for instance, was owing to artists
imitating art instead of nature. 'The deterioration of art,' he maintained,
'has everywhere proceeded from similar causes, the imitation of pre-
ceding styles, with little reference to nature.'[16] In contrast to this 'mannerism', the great art of the seventeenth century was created by painters
whose profound study of common nature resulted in works of great
truth and sentiment. We hear of the 'poetry' and 'sublimity'[17] of Poussin's landscapes, of Claude's 'calm sunshine of the heart',[18] of Rubens's
'joyous and animated character',[19] of Rembrandt's 'sentiment'[20] and
Ruysdael's 'understanding'.[21] The qualities Constable discovered in their
landscapes are emotional, intellectual and spiritual as well as purely
formal. Moreover, the advantage their landscapes enjoyed over history
painting was that these qualities could be communicated directly to the
beholder without the mediating presence of literary narrative. Discussing Poussin's The Deluge he said, 'The good sense of Poussin, which was
equal to his genius, taught him that by simplicity of treatment, the most
awful subjects may be made far more effecting than by overloading them
with imagery',[22] and he cited the paintings as 'greater proof of the
effective power of landscape alone, the figures being few and entirely
subordinate'.[23] The negative criterion that Constable used to evaluate
seventeenth-century art is mediation. The less mediated the art was,
either by past styles or by literary narrative devices, the better. Landscape,
originating as it did in the direct experience of nature and the naturalistic
plein-air étude, was therefore not only distinct from history painting but, for
Constable, superior to it. In this sense, his lectures on the history of
landscape painting were a form of revisionism. Constable rejected the
traditional Academic favouring of idealistic modes of representation
over realistic ones, basic not only to the hierarchy of genres but also to

studio practice, in order to reserve the superiority of the one term over the other.

I have dwelt on his lectures of the 1830s in order to highlight certain themes that first preoccupied him in his letters to Fisher a decade earlier. The letters contain initial formulations of many of the ideas more powerfully and publicly expressed in his lectures. From the letters, it is clear that Constable wished his landscapes to distinguish themselves from other genres of painting, and from other landscapes, by their naturalness, and, in addition, that he wished to infuse this naturalism with connotations as profound as those found in history painting but which could never be expressed in any other genre *except* landscape. In the 1820s, when he was seeking admission into the ranks of the Academicians by exhibiting his six-foot Stour valley landscapes, it was apparent to him that his naturalism was seen simply as a reflection of nature and not as an expression of individual consciousness and experience. The goal he set for himself at this time was to make his landscapes the sign of both nature and human nature, of both optical sensation and emotional response. He did this by counterfeiting the formal appearance of the oil sketch in the final work. The sketch-like finish Constable fabricated for his landscapes is something of a fiction in that it combines characteristics of both the *étude* and the *esquisse*. It suggests not only the *plein-air* effects and the detailed rendering of natural objects but also the more hasty, synthetic generalisations that for Diderot mirrored the artist's soul. It is in the context of both signifieds, human nature and nature, that this sketch-like finish transforms the indivi-dualised descriptions of natural objects into a general scientific descrip-tion of natural forces, and the individual experience of natural pheno-mena into a universal statement of feeling.

Not only were the *étude* and *esquisse* important models for the finish of Constable's six-footers but they also played a crucial role in their gene-sis.[24] For although he continually emphasised to Fisher the importance of studying nature for landscape painting, his own 'grandes machines' were made in his London studio, not from nature, but from earlier oil sketches done in Suffolk and from cloud studies done at Hampstead. Thus what the letters detail was not so much Constable's actual painting procedure in constructing the works he hoped would gain him full membership in the Academy, but rather the critical point of view through which he wished these landscapes to be seen and understood. Just as the sketch-like finish of the six-footers does not embody an immediate encounter with an actual landscape scene but merely signifies

one, so too do the letters discourse less of actual experience than of
ideological meaning. In one of them he writes, 'I hope you will not think
I am turned critic instead of painter',[25] yet it is precisely this turning critic
that is so significant and that must be explored if we are to understand the
relationship between his writing and his painting.

In order to understand Constable's turning critic it is helpful to begin
by examining the kind of critical reception his six-footers received at the
Academy. Constable's dissatisfaction with this reception is first
expressed in 1821, the year he exhibited *The Hay Wain*. The painting was
ignored by the majority of London newspapers. One finds no mention
of it in the reviews of the *Chronicle*, *The Times*, the *Morning Chronicle*, the *Sun*,
the *Morning Post*, the *Globe*, or the *Morning Herald*. It did, however, receive
two flattering reviews. The *Observer* said of it:

There is a fine freshness of colouring, and a great tact in the disposition of the
figures and the relief of the different objects, so as to make the entire harmonise,
as apparent throughout. The still-life is excellent, and the great masses of foliage
have a peculiar but not unnatural richness. If we were to make any objection we
should say that the foreground was perhaps a little too light, but this might have
been necessary for the relief of the masses at the back of the landscape. There is
much skill shown in this performance, of which Ruysdael has evidently been the
model. It is however, original enough to escape the servility with which imitations are generally branded. Mr. Constable is certainly not one of the *servum
pecus*.[26]

A more substantial review appeared in the *Examiner*.

No. 331, *Landscape – Noon*, is a picture of Mr. Constable's which we think
approaches nearer to the actual look of rural nature than any modern landscape
whatever. An able judge of art, who saw and admired it with us, thought it a little
mannered, from a certain sparkle there is over it. We do not think so, but, granting
the objection to be just, it is a mere slight flaw in a diamond; for what an open air
and fresh and leafy look it has, with its cottage and foreground so brightly and yet
so modestly contrasting their reddish hue with the green and blue and yellowish
tints of the trees, fields and sky – a sky which for noble volume of cloud and clear
light we have never at any time seen exceeded except by Nature. How tastefully is
the bit of red introduced upon the collar of the team of horses, in the sky and tree
reflecting water, and how does the eye delight to peep, with the luxurious feeling
of a Faun or a Sylvan, under and through the clustering foliage into the meadows
and hills beyond. How completely in keeping is the work throughout in its
unaffected pencilling, colour and character. We challenge the Dutch Masters to
show us anything better than this.[27]

The *Examiner* critic's lavish praise represents the climax of several years of
his observing and commenting on Constable's works.[28] As early as 1812

the critic made a point of noticing Constable's landscapes and from that time to this he never failed to remark favourably on his exhibition pieces. His reviews are remarkably consistent, stressing two aspects of Constable's work, his naturalism and his finish (or, as the case might be, lack of it). In the 1815 review he sets the theme and tone that would guide the rest, writing, 'It is a pity that Mr. Constable's pencil is still so coarsely sketchy. There is much sparkling sunlight and general character of truth in No. 268 *A Village in Suffolk* and No. 215 *Boatbuilding*.'[29] The following year, reviewing Constable's now lost *A Wood: Autumn*, he approves of his improved eye for portraiture of nature but laments that 'his execution is still very crude'.[30] Remarking on the lost *Harvest Field with Reapers and Gleaners*, Constable's exhibition piece for 1817, he concludes that 'his finishing and drawing are better than formerly, though still far below the standard of his colouring and general effect. They are beautiful, inasmuch as they are a close portraiture of our English scenery.'[31] In 1819, he selected *The White Horse*, the first of the six-footers, for praise in the Academy exhibition. After extolling Turner's *England: Richmond Hill, on the Prince Regent's Birthday*, he goes on to compare Constable with him and says:

Of a very different style, though equally successful of its kind, is Mr. Constable's, who, though he also is still far from pencilling with Nature's precision, gives her more contracted features, such as a wood or a windmill on a river, with more of her aspect. He does not give a sentiment, a soul, to the exterior of Nature as Mr. Turner does; he does not at all exalt the spectator's mind, which Mr. Turner eminently does, but he gives her outward look, her complexion and physical countenance. He has none of the poetry of Nature like Mr. Turner, but he has more of her portraiture. His *Scene on the River Stour* (251) is indeed more approaching to the outward lineament and look of trees, water, boats, etc., than any of our landscape painters.[32]

The important distinction the critic draws between the poetry and portraiture of landscape derives from Reynold's *Fourteenth Discourse* on Gainsborough. There Reynolds defended Gainsborough's naturalistic style of landscape by saying that it was perfectly suited to the humble rural subjects he chose to represent. Observing that Gainsborough's style was his own and did not derive from a study of the old masters, Reynolds says:

It cannot be denied, that excellence in the department of the art which he professed may exist without them [the old masters]; that in such subjects, and in the manner that belongs to them, the want of them is supplied, and more than supplied, by natural sagacity, and a minute observation of particular nature. If

Gainsborough did not look at nature with a poet's eye, it must be acknowledged that he saw her with the eye of a painter; and gave a faithful, if not a poetical, representation of what he had before him.[33]

As the resemblance between these two passages suggests, the *Examiner* critic was judging Constable's landscapes by the accepted Academic standards of the day. His admiration and understanding were limited by the standards set out by Reynolds and were the tools he used to 'process' Constable's landscapes within an accepted Academic lexicon. Reynolds's tone was evident again the following year when the *Examiner* critic reviewed *Stratford Mill*, declaring: 'We shall arouse the jealousy of some professors, and some devotees of the Old Masters in saying that the *Landscape* by Mr. Constable has a more exact look of nature than any pictures we have ever seen by an Englishman, and has been equalled by very few of the most boasted foreigners of former days, except in finishing.'[34] Had he been able to suppress his disappointment with Constable's finish we might take his remark for Reynold's avowal that 'I am well aware how much I lay myself open to the censure and ridicule of the academical professors of other nations, in preferring the humble attempts of Gainsborough to the works of those regular graduates in the great historical style.'[35]

The Academic standard the *Examiner* critic applied to Constable's landscapes was a mixed blessing, for while it secured a place for his work it also worked to keep it there. By containing Constable's work within the tradition of English naturalism developed by Reynolds in his *Fourteenth Discourse*, the critic tended to close off other possibilities for Constable's landscapes. Thus his portraiture excluded nature's poetry and his rural scenes precluded sublime effects. The most serious exclusion, however, was the one broached in the comparison of Turner and Constable, whereby Constable's portraiture of nature, his naturalistic recording of the optical effects of light and colour in nature, could never exalt the mind of the spectator. In short, this naturalism ensured that his landscapes could never rise above the status of mere portraits. As for Reynolds, landscape for the *Examiner* critic did not really exist: it could be subsumed under the categories of either portraiture or history painting. But whereas Turner's historical landscapes could at least compete at the Academy on the same ground as history painting, Constable's portraits of nature could not. The critic's emphasis on Constable's technical achievements in naturalism, his lights, colours and tones, represents a serious limitation of critical response as much as an actual exercise of it.

By 1812, the date of *The Hay Wain*, Constable was in the strange position of finding that the more his art was praised the more it was diminished. Art historians have often been puzzled, given the generally favourable critical response to his landscapes in the press at this time, that Constable should have felt so continually and bitterly disheartened. Yet I think it must have been particularly disconcerting to him to realise that the naturalistic style that he had so painstakingly developed and that was so warmly praised was finally the very thing that prevented the critics from seeing beyond the rendering of natural appearances into the deeper meaning of the work. The sudden flurry of letters in autumn 1821, outlining to Fisher the meaning of his art and the goals he set for himself in landscape, was an attempt for formulate a response to the critical problem his naturalistic style presented. At this time Constable sought to clarify the meanings of his landscapes and to develop a style that would make them not only explicit but also universal in their implications.

He had spent the early part of the summer of 1821 travelling and sketching with Fisher in Berkshire and Oxfordshire. Thus the letters of August, September and October can in some respects be seen as continuations of their preambulatory discussions of art and landscape. In Constable's second surviving letter after their return we find him expressing impatience with his art or rather with the perception of it. After describing the oil sketches he had made since his return, he went on to say:

I wish it could be said of me as Fuselli [sic] says of Rembrandt, 'he followed nature in her calmest abodes and could pluck a flower on every hedge – yet he was born to cast a steadfast eye on the bolder phenomena of nature.' We have had noble clouds & effects of light & dark & colour – as is always the case in such seasons as the present.[36]

The abrupt disjunction between the wistful remarks about Rembrandt's painting of nature's bolder phenomena and the matter-of-fact notation of the September sky is one of those fractures in Constable's epistolary style that does not signal a change of subject so much as its continuation on another plane. In this case, his remarks about Rembrandt and his own 'skying' are related, to become finally joined under that elusive term he so often used in later life, the 'Chiar-oscuro of Nature'. Rembrandt's steadfast eye is thus not unlike his own, which is also sensitive to the bolder phenomena of nature, particularly as they are manifested in the 'noble clouds' and in the effects of light and dark they produce.

In his next letter, the famous letter of 23 October, he returns to the subject of skies. Responding to Fisher's defence of his sky in *Stratford Mill*, he wrote:

That landscape painter who does not make his skies a very material part of his composition – neglects to avail himself of one of his greatest aids. Sir Joshua Reynolds speaking of the 'Landscape' of Titian & Salvator & Claude – says *'Even the skies seem to sympathise with the Subject'*. I have often been advised to consider my Sky – as a *'White Sheet drawn behind the Objects'*. Certainly if the Sky is *obtrusive* – (as mine are) it is bad, but if they are *evaded* (as mine are not) it is worse, they must and always shall with me make an effectual part of the composition. It will be difficult to name a class of Landscape, in which the sky is not the *'key note'*, the *standard of 'Scale'* and the chief *'Organ of sentiment'*. You may conceive then that a *'white sheet'* would do for me, impressed as I am with these notions, and they cannot be Erroneous. The sky is the 'source of light' in nature – and governs everything.[37]

The passage from Reynolds to which Constable refers is from the *Thirteenth Discourse* were Sir Joshua describes the superiority of the landscapes of Claude, Titian and Rosa to the more minutely finished and detailed portraits of nature by lesser artists. He wrote:

If we suppose a view of nature represented with all the truth of the *camera obscura*, and the same scene represented by a great Artist, how little and mean will the one appear in comparison of the other, where no superiority is supposed from the choice of the subject. The scene shall be the same, the difference only will be in the manner in which it is presented to the eye. With what additional superiority then will the same Artist appear when he has the power of selecting his materials, as well as elevating his style? . . . Like the history-painter, a painter of landskips in this style and with this conduct, sends the imagination back into antiquity; and, like the Poet, he makes the elements sympathise with his subject: whether the clouds roll in volumes like those of Titian or Salvator Rosa, – or, like those of Claude, are gilded with the setting sun . . .[38]

The distinctions Reynolds drew between the portraiture and poetry of landscape, between minute naturalism and more synthetic descriptions, between tight and loose finishing, and between the description of appearances and the expression of sentiment, were the criteria used by the *Examiner* critic to discuss Constable's art, and with which Constable himself was now preoccupied. Significantly, he cited his skies to Fisher not as the means of making his landscapes more naturalistic, but as the means of rendering them more expressive in the terms set out by Reynolds. He attempted to make a natural feature of the landscape signify something more than itself. The sky becomes both a signified and a signifier, both the thing represented and the thing which represents, both the natural 'element' and the 'chief organ of sentiment'.

He then went on, after mentioning the rough criticism of Ward and Haydon in the *John Bull*, to return to the subject of his own landscapes, and to the question of their origin. He wrote:

the sound of water escaping from Mill dams . . . old Willows, Old Rotten Banks, slimy posts & brickwork. I love such things. . . . As long as I do paint I shall never cease to paint such Places. They have always been my delight. . . . I should paint my own places best. . . . Painting is but another word for feeling. I associate my 'careless boyhood' to all that lies on the banks of the Stour. They made me a painter (& I am grateful) that is I often thought of pictures of them before I touched a pencil. . . .[39]

Just as his discussion of skies is usually interpreted to be a simple profession of naturalistic interest in atmospheric phenomena, this passage too is often read in the context of his naturalism as a pure expression of feelings and associations which are mediated by nothing more than his deep personal attachment to the landscape of his youth. Nevertheless, like his discussion of clouds this explanation of the origin of his art has an older literary source. Constable's words to Fisher strongly echo Philip Thicknesse's 1788 biographical account of the young Gainsborough. Thicknesse wrote: 'there was not a picturesque clump of trees . . . hedgerow, stone or post for some miles round about the place of his nativity, that he had not so perfectly in his mind's eye, that had he known he could use a pencil, he could have perfectly delineated'.[40] Central to both Thicknesse's and Constable's statements is an idea of the young artist's profound attachment to his native landscape, the strength of which enabled him to previsualise its scenes as paintings long before he had grasped the actual techniques for rendering them. The myth is, of course, inspired by picturesque theory which in prescribing an approach to landscape sketching substituted sensibility for knowledge and presented simple formulas as alternatives to Academic training. Given Constable's discomfort with Academic standards for landscape it is not surprising that he should be sympathetic to the picturesque as personified by Thicknesse's Gainsborough. The picturesque fascination with the minutiae of landscape is echoed by Constable's fondness for 'slimy posts & brickwork', and was mediated early on by the example of Gainsborough. Writing to a friend from Ipswich in 1799, he claimed, 'I fancy I see Gainsborough in every hedge and hollow tree.'[41] That Constable should here unblushingly admit to seeing landscape through what he believed to be Gainsborough's eyes and should twenty years later, in his letter to Fisher, suppress this important source of his vision suggests a process of mediation more complex than his response to Reynolds's

*Discourses.* Clearly it was a statement made for posterity as much as for
Fisher. With it Constable placed himself in a tradition of rustic landscape
misunderstood by Reynolds and the Academy, but by failing to acknowledge explicitly that he was doing this, he made that tradition appear to
begin with himself; in short, he reinvents it. Just as Thicknesse's accounts
of Gainsborough's previsualising of landscape elide questions of artistic
influence and Academic training, so too does Constable's paraphrase of
Thicknesse make such questions seem irrelevant to the fact of his own
autobiographical experience and artistic personality.

Constable thus distances himself from a tradition still held to be
inferior by contemporary critics, while, at the same time, reinventing it in
response to this criticism and to his own desire for meaning in his art. His
later remarks about Gainsborough in his lectures would seem to be a
continuation of this revision of history. For Constable, unlike Reynolds,
Gainsborough's landscapes were full of poetry and sentiment. 'On looking at them,' he told a lecture audience in 1836, 'we find tears in our eyes,
and know not what brings them.'[42] By insisting on the poetry of Gainsborough's works, he was insisting on that of his own. What Constable began
in his letters to Fisher as a formulation of his aesthetic of landscape
became in his lectures a rewriting of the history of landscape, a counter-
history to that offered in Reynold's *Discourses.*

In rewriting this history, Constable stressed that an experience of the
materiality of things, their sounds, smells, textures, and surfaces, created
associations which in turn could be communicated through painting in a
way that was universally legible. In this respect, Constable's landscapes
represent an important encoding of one myth of bourgeois realism
which held that meaning and truth could be read on the surface of things,
could be expressed through appearance alone. This idea, which as T. J.
Clark has shown culminated in Impressionism, did not allow for the
possibility that meaning might have no visible effects. It also muted the
fact that a reproduction of reality was only a reproduction and *not* reality,
and that as a reproduction, it could create meanings quite different from
those originally perceived or intended by the artist.[43] While Constable
certainly subscribed to the myth of bourgeois realism he also, as the
evidence of his correspondence and style suggests, comprehended
(consciously or unconsciously) its limitations. For this reason, he
supplements one kind of transparency – landscape painting as a mirror
of nature – with another – landscape painting as a reflection of sensibility.
While the first notion made landscape painting superflous to real nature,
the second gave it a reason for being by making it a vehicle for

expression.

Given the particular cultural expectations regarding the externalisation of meaning and emotion in art, it is hardly surprising that Constable's paintings of the 1820s should point beyond the luminous and quietistic transcriptions of natural incidents in landscape scenery that characterised his work of 1810–20, to evolve into theatrical re-enactments of a personal response to nature, or, in short, into simulacra of artistic presence. Constable's formal solution to the problem of signification which his naturalism presented was to adjust his style, substituting for the individual descriptions of natural phenomena and effects a more general controlling and unifying principle, which could be read both as nature or naturalistic effect and as personal expression. Inevitably, the sky, as both the 'source of all light' in the landscape and its 'chief organ of sentiment', became the key element Constable used to reformulate his naturalism. Thus, in the close of the 23 October letter in which he discusses his skies, he announced that he had retouched The Hay Wain. 'My last year's work,' he wrote, 'has got much together. This weather had blown and washed all the powder off. . . .'[44] When The Hay Wain was exhibited at the British Institution in January 1822, the Examiner critic noticed the change and remarked: 'We doubt whether Mr. Constable has improved No. 197, Landscape-Noon, by putting out certain lights, refraction of the sun's rays from the polished parts of vegetation, etc., but it still remains an extraordinary example of verisimilitude and rivalry to pastoral nature.'[45] Judging from these remarks and from the work as it appears today, Constable must have toned down the individual highlights (the 'powder') which tended to individuate his objects too much and to unify them instead through a broad pattern of chiaroscuro, with the result that the work was, as he said, 'much got together'. If I correctly understand this shorthand explanation of his method to Fisher, he accomplished this by observing the light of the wet and windswept September sky, using the dramatic patterns of light and shadow cast by the moving clouds to suggest a naturalistically plausible chiaroscuro for the The Hay Wain scene.

In a complementary move, Constable began at this time to adjust the 'coarse' and 'sketchy' brushwork which had so disturbed the Examiner critic to this new, more generalised orchestration of lights and darks. The result is the diverse and complex technique of paint application found in the six-footers. As in the étude, with its focus on specific objects and their individualised textures and appearances, we find in Constable's six-footers (particularly in the foreground) strokes which are intended to mimic the actual surfaces of natural objects (leaves, grasses, rocks, tree trunks, etc.). Finally, however, these passages of individualised description are subsumed in the finish used throughout the painting. This finish describes the distribution of highlights, as they are scattered throughout the landscape, and its roughness thus unites the more individual system of notation found in the foreground into a uniform surface. In this systematic treatment of surface and patterning of light, Constable's works have the qualities of an *esquisse*.

In this context, Constable's discussion of finish in his Royal Institution lectures takes on greater clarity. In remarking on Reynolds's criticism of the 'minute description of leaves and plants in the foreground' of Titian's *St Peter Martyr*, he concluded:

Sir Joshua was swayed by his own practice, of generalising to such a degree that we often find in his foregrounds rich masses of colours, of light and shade, which, when examined, mean nothing. In Titian there is equal breadth, equal subordination of the parts to the whole, but the spectator finds, on approaching the picture, that every touch is the representative of a reality; and as this carries on the illusion, it cannot surely detract from the merit of the work.[46]

Whereas on closer inspection Reynolds's finish reveals simply itself, Titian's disappears to reveal its object. Constable's defence of Titian at the expense of Sir Joshua is a defence not only of his own elaborated *étude* – like foregrounds, but also of a principle of naturalistic style which, embodied in a technique that rendered it simultaneously visible and invisible, proclaimed the presence of both the artist and the object.

This new kind of handling was quite different from the earlier one to which the *Examiner* critic objected. That finish, while more transparent and less rough, was also less systematic. Because of its inconsistency, one could complain that it was not a *finish* at all, and this may have been the objection to it. While Constable's finish of the 1820s was less criticised than his unsystematic handling of 1810–20 or the exaggerated impasto of his finish of the 1830s, it was, nevertheless, not understood. Its very roughness and generalised aspect seemed inappropriate to the portraiture of nature for they destroyed the naturalistic illusion of transparency between the viewer and the object. It was precisely this transparency that critics had come to expect of rural landscape as exemplified by the Dutch masters of the seventeenth century; hence the *esquisse*-like aspects of Constable's finish seemed inappropriate to the subject matter of his work which traditionally demanded a consistent *étude*-like handling throughout. Because it did not fit into traditional

Academic preconceptions of what was appropriate to the genre of rustic landscape, Constable's finish of the 1820s remained culturally illegible at the same time that it was being culturally responsive.

What the period eye failed to see was the synoptic principle of the sketch-like finish which united the immediate apprehension of natural effects of light and weather (the *plein-air étude*) with the personal response of the artist (the *esquisse*). Constable, of course, discusses his finish with Fisher in both ways, as a sign of nature and of human nature. In a letter from 1824 he described the critical reception of his painting of *A Boat Passing a Lock* in terms that makes this clear:

My picture is liked at the Academy. Indeed it forms a decided feature and its light cannot be put out, because it is the light of nature – the Mother of all that is valuable in poetry, painting or anything else – where an appeal to the soul is required. The language of the heart is the only one that is universal – and Stern says that he disregards all rules – but makes his way to the heart as he can. My execution annoys most of them and all the scholastic ones – perhaps the sacrifices I make for lightness and brightness is too much, but these things are the essence of landscape.[47]

As both the 'light of nature' and an 'appeal to the soul', his sketch-like finish became the means whereby 'painting becomes but another word for feeling', and these feelings became the universal 'language of the heart'.

What this natural, transparent, and universal language of the heart sought to bypass, by naturalising its signifiers as 'common sense', 'feelings', 'humanism', etc., was the culturally determined language of society. By encoding the language of the heart into his paintings, Constable attempted to make them intuitively understood (by virtue of our shared humanity) and intellectually unanalysable. If we take Constable's paintings on their own terms, we are continually thrown back on to a discourse which they inscribe which his correspondence reinforces and which we merely repeat. Thus to continue to speak this language of the heart in discussing Constable's work is to remain trapped within the limitations of Constable's own naturalism, that is within the formal and verbal strategies he devised to control the production and reception of meaning in his art.

Moreover, it insures that we accede to the ideological implications of this naturalistic language and the naturalistic style it generates. Both turn on the belief that private experiences and associations are publicly relevant because they are universally shared, and that this sharing forms the basis of a public discourse.[48] We might begin by asking who shared this language, to what class and sex did they belong, and, to go further, whether they were not perhaps from the same class and sex whose pursuit of private economic interest had created and sustained the social order that now validated this 'language of the heart' as 'universal'? While I cannot pretend to offer this as a conclusion to what I have done here, I would like to suggest its relevance for our reading of Constable. For, if we merely represent the ideological assumptions of Constable's naturalism as criticism and art history, then not only have we dignified a questionable tactic of cultural and political control as 'scholarship', but also by denying his art its specific ideological assumptions, we deny it its place in history, its significance as both a product and index of culture, and its power to shape not only the history of art but our own critical consciousness.

As we have seen, Constable, in his paintings and his writings, continually implies two opposing yet mutually supportive claims for his naturalism: the constative 'it is' and the performative 'I feel it to be thus.' The difference between the two is both absolute and indistinct, the slippage between them occurring, for instance, in his discussion of skies, in the *étude*- and *esquisse*-like finish of his landscapes, and even in the ontological impossibility of a phrase like 'the chair'oscuro of nature'. Within such a system, which proposes both a transparent relationship between nature and art and between art and emotion, questions of cultural mediation are awkward. The influence of Gainsborough and Reynolds, for instance, becomes problematic for Constable, to be acknowledged only as a confirmation of his own ideas while simultaneously suppressed and made secondary to his own direct experience of nature. Similarly, the role of landscape painting as mediating the experience of nature must both be allowed and disallowed. Thus in his last Hampstead lecture on landscape, Constable offered this parable:

I will imagine two dishes, the one of gold, the other of wood. The golden dish is filled with diamonds, rubies, and emeralds – and chains, rings and brooches of gold, while the other contains shell-fish, stones, and earths. These dishes are offered to the world, who chooses the first; but it is afterwards discovered that the dish itself is but copper gilt, the diamonds are paste, the rubies and emeralds painted glass, and the chains, rings, counterfeit. In the meantime, the naturalist has taken the wooden dish, for he knows that the shellfish are pearl oysters, and he sees that among the stones are gems and mixed with the earth are the ores of the precious metals.[49]

The naturalist chooses the wooden bowl over the gilded one because he sees past the rough aspects of its contents to the pearls, gems and precious metals. If one applies the parable to landscape painting, one could say that the naturalistic painter both looks at and through nature, his knowledgeable vision mediates between nature's common surface and hidden treasures. This mediating knowledge is not a culturally determined taste – for the 'world' chooses the gilt dish – but derives from a more profound (innate, original, natural, moral, spiritual, etc.) perception of 'truth,' and is in this sense anti-cultural.

The problematic role landscape painting played in supplementing and mediating real nature was focused for Constable on the issue of style. To his mind certain styles were truer to nature than others by virtue of the fact that they imitated its appearance and conveyed the effects of these appearances on the artist to the viewer. Ideally, for Constable, the *étude*-like quality of his finish should reflect nature's surfaces while its *esquisse*-like aspect should correspond to nature by itself being an embodiment of emotion, sensation, and associations.[50] The tension Constable felt between the constative and performative aspects of his style is expressed in his correspondence with Fisher. In a letter of 1830, he confessed his fear that his finish had deteriorated into a 'manner'. He wrote:

I have filled my head with certain notions of *freshness* – *sparkle* brightness till it has influenced my practice in no small degree, & is in fact taking the place of truth so invidious is manner, in all things – it is a species of self worship – which should always be combated – & we have nature (another word for moral feeling) always in our reach to do it with – if we will have the resolution to look at her.[51]

Just as culture for Constable had always obscured the transparent rendering of nature, so now he felt had the self silvered the window of the painting so that it mirrored only the artist. Thus meaning in his late works is no longer constituted by the disparity between the real landscape and its representation (i.e. between nature and culture), but by the difference between the constative and performative aspects of his own style. While he continually struggled to contain the *esquisse*-like aspect of his finish, by frequent disavowals of 'manner' and resolutions to look more closely at nature, his late paintings reveal his difficulty in controlling it. As a supplement to his naturalism, the *esquisse*-like finish finally threatened to replace that which it was only intended to augment.

By merely repeating Constable's own naturalistic interpretation of his art, the traditional reading of the correspondence reveals itself to be radically paradoxical. On one hand it relegates the letters to a position of secondary importance to the paintings, while on the other it relies on them to 'complete' the images. Besides positing the correspondence as both superfluous and necessary it describes the paintings as both complete and incomplete. This paradox which deeply subtends Constable scholarship is also deeply repressed by it. Moreover, the same paradox lies at the heart of Constable's landscape painting, for just as the correspondence supplements the images, the lectures supplement the correspondence, so too do the images supplement nature – the real landscape. His naturalistic painting is predicated on the fact that the originary plenitude it prizes – nature – is, by the act of representing it, revealed to be incomplete. Thus while traditional Constable scholarship both appeals to and suppresses the supplementary role of the writings in 'completing' his art, Constable in his writings both acknowledged and suppressed the role his landscapes played in 'completing' nature. In reading Constable therefore we must preoccupy ourselves, as much as he did, with the problematics of this relationship between the writings and the paintings and between the paintings and nature, for it is here that his art and his modernity begin.

## Notes

First published in *Art History*, vol. 10, no. 1 (March 1987), pp. 38–58.

1  *John Constable's correspondence*, ed. R. B. Beckett and (for vol. 7) Leslie Parris, Conal Shiels and Ian Fleming-Williams, 7 vols. (Ipswich, Suffolk, 1962–75).

2  Since C. R. Leslie's biography (1843) and until recently, Constable scholarship has attended to the details of his personal life as revealed in the letters in order to identify his landscapes and interpret his naturalism. More recently, John Barrell (*The dark side of the landscape: the rural poor in English painting 1730–1840* (Cambridge, 1980)), Ronald Paulson (*The literary landscape: Turner and Constable* (New Haven, Conn. and London, 1982)), and Michael Rosenthal (*Constable: the painter and his landscape* (New Haven, Conn. and London, 1983)) have discovered in the correspondence expressions of social and political ideology (Barrell and Rosenthal) and Constable's psychology (Paulson and Rosenthal). While they do not address the interpretive role the correspondence has played in Constable criticism they, nevertheless, approach the letters critically.

3  Denis Diderot, *Salons*, ed. Jean Seznec and Jean Adhemar, 4 vols. (Oxford, 1960–75), vol. 2, pp. 135–54. Quoted in translation by Albert Boime, *The Academy and French painting in the nineteenth century* (London and New York, 1971), p. 84. Diderot uses the word 'esquisse' for all sketches. For an explanation of the technical terms for sketching see note 5 below.

4  Boime, p. 84.

5  In traditional Academic practice oil sketches were intended to assist the artist in learning how to render in colour and in preparing a finished painting. Unlike the finished painting they were loosely painted and it was their rough finish that in the eighteenth century came to be read as a sign of the artist's 'soul' or personality.

There were three categories of sketches. The first, the *étude* or study, was the careful or exact rendering of the motif. Usually, but not always, the *étude* was limited to a single model, object or detail, or in the case of landscape, a single effect such as a sunset or a rainbow. There were two kinds of *études*: the studio *étude* made indoors and the *plein-air* *étude* (usually a landscape) made outside. *Études* could be used as *aides-mémoire* by an artist in constructing the final painting where they were not exactly copied but, rather, adjusted to the more idealised style of the finished work.

The *esquisse* was a sketch made in preparation for a finished painting. It was not usually painted directly from the motif. Instead, it was an imaginary working out of the composition, colour, and light. Paintings by other artists as well as real scenes could be used as inspiration for the *esquisse*. For the most part, however, in the *esquisse*, the artist put himself in competition with history rather than nature. The *esquisse* could represent an artist's first thoughts about a subject or his final orchestration of major formal elements before embarking on the actual painting. In French, the word *esquisse* is often used by artists and critics (as in the case of Diderot) to refer to all kinds of sketching – to sketching in general.

The *ébauche* was a sketch made directly on the canvas used for the final work and was a form of underpainting that guided the artist in laying in the composition and building up his tones. The *ébauche* could be in colour or *grisaille*. It was usually obliterated by the final work.

This rather simplified description of the categories of Academic sketching should be supplemented by reading Albert Boime's more fully developed and annotated study (pp. 79–89, 149–65).

6 See, in particular, Edward Dayes, 'Instructions for drawing and colouring landscapes', in E. W. Brayley, ed., *The work of Edward Dayes* (London, 1805); Henry Richter, *Day-light: a recent discovery in the art of painting* (London, 1817); and William Varley, *Observations on colouring and sketching from nature*, 2nd edn. (London, 1820).

7 Pierre Henri de Valenciennes, *Eléments de la perspective pratique* (Paris, 1800), pp. 338–9, quoted in translation by Albert Boime, p. 138. For a discussion of Valenciennes's own sketches see Paula Rea Radisch, 'Eighteenth-century plein-air painting and the sketches of Pierre Henri de Valenciennes', *Art Bulletin*, 64 (March 1982), pp. 98–104.

8 Quoted by Philip Conisbee, 'Pre-romantic plein-air painting', *Art History*, vol. 2, no. 4 (December 1979), p. 416.

9 Conisbee, p. 424. See George Levitine, 'Vernet tied to a mast in a storm: the evolution of an episode of art historical folklore', *Art Bulletin*, 49 (March 1967), pp. 92–100.

10 Both stories were told to Ruskin. Walter Thornbury records the story about *Snow Storm* in his *Life of J. M. W. Turner, R.A.* (London, 1877), pp. 457–8; the *Rain, Steam, and Speed* story is given in A. M. W. Stirling's *The Richmond Papers* (London, 1926), pp. 55–6.

11 Quoted in translation by Boime, p. 137.

12 John Constable, *John Constable's discourses*, ed. R. B. Beckett (Ipswich, Suffolk, 1970), p. 72.

13 The controversy erupted over Kurt Badt's belief that Constable's cloud studies were influenced by Luke Howard's scientific classification of clouds (*John Constable's clouds* (London, 1950)). Louis Hawes challenged Badt's thesis, citing Constable's early experience as a miller trained to read the sky for signs of approaching storms. See his 'Constable's sky sketches', *Journal of the Warburg and Courtauld Institutes*, 32 (1969), pp. 351–8. In 1960, E. H. Gombrich, in his classic study of mimesis in Western art, *Art and illusion* (Princeton), demonstrated the extent to which Constable's cloud studies derive from the schemata for clouds developed by Alexander Cozens which Constable modified and naturalised by 'matching' them against nature. Most recently, John Thornes, on the evidence of the published contents of Constable's library, has attempted to set out a complete account of Constable's meteorological understanding. See his 'Constable's clouds', *Burlington Magazine*, 121 (November 1979), pp. 697–9.

14 Constable, *Discourses*, p. 39.

15 Ibid., p. 40.

16 Ibid., p. 58.

17 Ibid., p. 51.

18 Ibid., p. 53.

19 Ibid., p. 61.

20 Ibid., p. 62.

21 Ibid., p. 64.

22 Ibid., p. 60.

E

23 Ibid., p. 52.
24 For a thorough discussion of the development of Constable's six-foot exhibition paintings, see Graham Reynolds's *The later paintings and drawings of John Constable*, 2 vols. (New Haven, Conn. and London, 1984). For an important essay on Constable's early works and in particular his plein-air oil sketches, see Michael Kitson, 'John Constable, 1810–1816: a chronological study', *Journal of the Warburg and Courtauld Institutes*, XX, (1957), pp. 345–57.
25 Constable, *Correspondence*, vol. 4, p. 77.
26 Quoted in William Whitley, *Art in England*, 2 vols. (New York, 1973), vol. 2, pp. 7–8.
27 Ibid., p. 8.
28 Michael Rosenthal has identified his critic as Robert Hunt. For a general overview of Constable's relationship to the press see Conal Shields's 'Constable and the critics', in the Tate catalogue by Leslie Parris, Ian Fleming-Williams and Conal Shields, *Constable: paintings, watercolours and drawings* (London, 1976), pp. 13–28.
29 Whitley, vol. 1, pp. 244–5.
30 Ibid., p. 258.
31 Ibid., p. 269.
32 Ibid., p. 300.
33 Sir Joshua Reynolds, *Discourses on art*, ed. Robert Wark (New Haven and London, 1975), p. 253.
34 Whitley, vol. 1, p. 317.
35 Reynolds, p. 249.
36 Constable, *Correspondence*, vol. 4, p. 74.
37 Ibid., pp. 76–7.
38 Reynolds, p. 237.
39 Constable, *Correspondence*, vol. 4, p. 78.
40 Philip Thicknesse, *A sketch of the life and paintings of Thomas Gainsborough, Esq.* (London, 1788), pp. 5–6. Constable possessed a copy of Thicknesse's account which Allan Cunningham tried to borrow in 1829. Rosenthal (p. 244) notes that Constable first referred to this passage in 1799–1800. For the contents of Constable's library see the *Correspondence*, vol. 7, pp. 25–52.
41 Constable, *Correspondence*, vol. 2, p. 16.
42 Constable, *Discourses*, p. 67.
43 T. J. Clark, *The painting of modern life: Paris in the art of Manet and his followers* (New York, 1985), p. 255.
44 Constable, *Correspondence*, vol. 4, p. 78.
45 Whitley, vol. 3, p. 23.
46 Constable, *Discourses*, p. 48.
47 Constable, *Correspondence*, vol. 4, p. 157.
48 This subject has been penetratingly discussed by John Barrell in his article, 'The functions of art in a commercial society: the writings of James Barry', *Eighteenth-Century Studies*, 25 (1984), pp. 117–40, and in his essay in this volume (pp. 19–40). It has also been taken up in a persuasive essay by Carol Fabricant, 'The aesthetics and politics of landscape in the eighteenth century', in Ralph Cohen, ed., *Studies in eighteenth-century British art and aesthetics* (Berkeley, Los Angeles, London, 1985), pp. 49–81, and is addressed by me in *Landscape and ideology: the English rustic tradition, 1740–1860* (Berkeley, Los Angeles and London, 1986).
49 Constable, *Discourses*, p. 69.
50 The idea of the simulacrum might be useful to apply to Constable's *esquisse*-like handling. To use the words of Gilles Deleuze, the simulacrum is an 'image without resemblance'. The *esquisse*-like finish we find in Constable's late works is a simulacrum of emotion because it suggests emotion without either copying it or being it. See Giles Deleuze, 'Plato and the simulacrum', trans. Rosalind Krauss, *October*, 27 (winter 1983), pp. 45–56.
51 Constable, *Correspondence*, vol. 4, p. 258.

# 8

# A villa in Arcadia
## John Murdoch

The three most famous houses in the Lake District are arguably Dove Cottage, Brantwood and Hill Top. They were the houses of Wordsworth, Ruskin and Beatrix Potter, all of whom adapted traditional local buildings to their special needs or taste. They are not the subject of this essay,[1] which is, rather, the houses built by those who came as tourists or residents, sometimes in retirement, and built from the ground up during the nineteenth century. They transformed the appearance and the social structure of the whole historic centre of the District, especially from Windermere to Grasmere. These developments caused controversy in which the famous literary residents joined energetically. Put very simply, the problem was to identify an architecture suitable for what was seen as one of Europe's great landscapes. Although they themselves lived in converted houses, Wordsworth, Ruskin and Potter all confronted the architectural issues of new building: Wordsworth as a client when he hired George Webster to design him a new house in 1826[2] and as a theorist in successive editions of the *Guide to the lakes*,[3] Beatrix Potter as a tenant through successive family holidays in at least four of the great new villas – Wray Castle, Lingholm, Fawe Park and Holehird. Her decision in 1905 to purchase a working farm at Sawrey can be seen as a reaction against the artfulness of her father's architectural preference and in favour of the prevailing Gimson–Barnsley aesthetic of her own generation. Ruskin, like Wordsworth, not only encountered the problem but discussed it at length in his first published work, *The poetry of architecture* (1837–38). Reacting against the neo-classical villas of the Lake District such as the round house on Belle Isle in Windermere or the Pocklington houses at Derwentwater, he wrote:

The house must *not* be a noun – substantive, it must not stand by itself, it must be part and parcel of a proportioned whole ... [He who sees it should be] impressed with a feeling of universal energy, pervading with its beauty of unanimity, all life and all inanimation, all forces of stillness or motion, all presences of silence or sound.

But unlike Wordsworth, he seems never to have considered the possibility of commissioning a new building for himself:

Nature has set aside her sublime bits for us to feel and think in . . . all that we ought to do in the hill villa is, to adapt it for the habitation of a man of the highest faculties of perception and feeling . . .

For these reasons, the cottage–villa, rather than the mansion is to be preferred among our hills.

In September 1871 he became a permanent resident of Brantwood on Coniston: 'a bit of steep hillside, facing west', he told Thomas Carlyle. 'The slope is half copse, half moor and rock – a pretty field beneath, less steep – a white two-storied cottage and a bank of turf in front of it; – then a narrow mountain road and on the other side of that . . . my neighbour's field, to the water's edge'.[4]

The idea of the cottage was fundamental in the motivation of incomers to the district. In the Pastoral tradition the cottage was a locus of virtuous simplicity and frugality, a place of retirement from the turmoils of urban political life, in which the possibility existed of redemption and the recovery of innocence. There can be no doubt that Brantwood represented such a possibility for Ruskin, a rural vantage point from which he could survey industrial capitalism and survive his own terrible depression. 'Retirement' thus meant the recruitment of new energies and a deeper involvement in the politics of industrial society. Similarly, Wordsworth's return to Grasmere in 1799 was a 'retirement' into heightened consciousness and a more active creativity, and was intended to bring him closer to the babble of common life, not to separate him from it. For the rest of the nineteenth century, and certainly now, the Wordsworthian achievement was, in a significant sense, contained at Dove Cottage. A Christian culture, accustomed to the placing of the supreme instant of its religious myth in a stable by an inn, no doubt found especially rich the image of the poet discovering the birth of his mind in a cottage that had been an inn, the name of which recalled God's promise of redemption. Certainly the humility proper to the enactment of great creative endeavour was to later tourists better symbolised at Dove Cottage and in Goethe's sparse rooms at Weimar than in Scott's carved library at Abbotsford; a moral and aesthetic judgement deriving from the same values that identified Wordsworth with Dove Cottage rather than with Rydal Mount, and that had made the cottage as an architectural and moral ideal, a touchstone of virtue in our culture.

It was Wordsworth's example that brought John Wilson to the Lake District. In 1802, at the age of seventeen, he had read the *Lyrical ballads* and written at length to Wordsworth; in 1805, he bought Elleray, a statesman house and a farm on the eastern slopes of Windermere; in 1807, bearing the laurels of the Newdigate Poetry Prize from Oxford, he moved north to set up house as a poet near Wordsworth. At a time when most young men ambitious for a career in letters moved from the country to London, it is interesting that Wilson, with his sharp journalistic eye for a trend, took himself off to a cottage in the Lake District; and it is interesting too that the word 'cottage' first became applied to this modest but characteristic statesman house at the point in its history when it became part of the cultural aspirations of a young poet. Other changes suitable to the new role of the house involved the addition of a room, with double-height windows, nearly as large again as the main part of the existing structure. The junction of old and new was masked by a sycamore growing a few yards from the front door, and the whole was duly absorbed into Wilson's aesthetic consciousness and made ready for its appearance as literature: 'True, 'tis but a cottage – a Westmoreland Cottage –. . . But then it has several roofs shelving away there in the lustre of loveliest lichens . . . Each roof with its assortment of doves and pigeons preening their plumage in the morning pleasance. . . O sweetest and shadiest of all Sycamores – . . . we love thee beyond all other Trees. . . .'[5]

The reliance on the Picturesque in Wilson's taste is evident in this eulogy. Of course Wilson, who was a very big man, needed another room to his house, and in any age the necessary addition would no doubt have been made. In Picturesque doctrine, however, the very fact of the architecture being a series of responses to changing needs, rather than a single conception, was of aesthetic significance. The changing roof-lines along the facade, the three clear building stages, were thus deliberate and desired, to be looked for like the lichens and doves by those of educated taste.

Wilson valued the character of Elleray as a 'cottage' both in the moral and the Picturesque sense, but above all for its views, which comprehend virtually the whole range of desiderata in post-Burkeian English aesthetics. Wilson's friend de Quincey enumerated the virtues of the site in the language of the Picturesque:

Seated on such an eminence, but yet surrounded by foregrounds of such quiet beauty, and settling downwards towards the lake by such tranquil steps as to take away every feeling of precipitous or dangerous elevation, Elleray possesses a double character of beauty, rarely found in connexion; and yet each, by singular good fortune, in this case absolute and unrivalled in its kind. Within a bow-shot of each other may be found stations of the deepest seclusion, fenced in by verdurous walls of insuperable forest heights, and presenting a limited scene of beauty – deep, solemn, noiseless, severely sequestered – and other stations of a magnificence so gorgeous as few estates in this island can boast, and of those few perhaps none in such close connexion with a dwelling-house. Stepping out from the very windows of the drawing-room, you find yourself on a terrace which gives you the feeling of a 'specular height', such as you might expect on Ararat, or might appropriately conceive on 'Athos seen from Samothrace'. The whole course of a noble lake, about eleven miles long, lies subject to your view, with many of its islands, and its two opposite shores so different in character: the one stern, precipitous, and gloomy; the other (and luckily the hither one) by the mere bounty of nature and of accident – by the happy disposition of the ground originally, and by the fortunate equilibrium between the sylvan tracts, meandering irregularly through the whole district, and the proportion left to verdant fields and meadows, – wearing the character of the richest park scenery: except indeed that this character is here and there a little modified by a quiet hedge-row or the stealing smoke which betrays the embowered cottage of a labourer. But the sublime, peculiar, and not-to-be-forgotten feature of the scene is the great system of mountains which unite about five miles off at the head of the lake to lock in and inclose this noble landscape. The several ranges of mountains which stand at various distances within six or seven miles of the little town of Ambleside, all separately various in their forms and all eminently picturesque, when seen from Elleray appear to blend and group as parts of one connected whole; and, when their usual drapery of clouds happens to take a fortunate arrangement, and the sunlights are properly broken and thrown from the most suitable quarter of the heavens, I cannot recollect any spectacle in England or Wales, or the many hundreds I have seen bearing a local, if not a national, reputation for magnificence of prospect, which so much dilates the heart with a sense of power and aerial sublimity as this terrace view from Elleray.[6]

It was in recognition of this prospect, this exceptional command that Elleray had of all that was finest in the potentialities of landscape, that Wilson decided within his first months at Elleray to advance his viewpoint to the knoll, perhaps fifty feet higher than the cottage, and forming a slight buttress to the hillside a couple of hundred yards away from it. Here he began a house[7] that was radically different from the cottage and of which the guiding architectural principle was to take advantage of the site and to use the house, as it were, as a camera to take and present the views.

Wilson was his own designer, but he followed precedent in the Lake District and was also presumably aware of the design principles discussed by members of the Picturesque elite for houses in such places.

The case of Uvedale Price, who bought a piece of land by the sea at Aberystwyth in 1796, is instructive. He too chose the site for the views:

the waves breaking against the near rocks, and . . . the long chain of distant mountains with their monarch Snowdon at their head . . . we thought how charming it would be to look at it comfortably from our own windows in all weathers, instead of being driven away 'when the strong winds do blow' just when the waves are the most magnificent . . .

At first I thought merely of running up two or three nutshells of rooms, and got a plan from a common welch carpenter: then Nash was mentioned to me, & he had a mind to build me a larger house indeed, but a square bit of architecture. I told him however that I must have, not only some of the *windows*, but some of the *rooms* turned to particular points, and that he must arrange it in his best manner; I explained to him the reasons, why I built it so close to the rock, showed him the effect of the broken foreground & its varied line, & how by that means the foreground was connected with the rocks in the second ground; all which would be lost by placing the house further back. He was excessively struck with these reasons, which he said he had never thought of before in the most distant degree, and he has I think continued the house most admirably for the intimation, & the form of it is certainly extremely varied from my having obliged him to turn the rooms to different aspects. At first, as I told you, I meant only to have nutshells, but I now thought I would have one good room; & so I magnificently ordered one of 30 by 20; a charming room it is. . .[8].

Price's attempt here to describe (in fact to sell) his Welsh house to Beaumont helps us to understand the peculiar form of Lord William Gordon's single-storey house on Derwentwater,[9] a product surely of the same aesthetic, and seeking similarly to unite a very close-up view of water over a broken line of beach foreground, with the distant line of hills above Barrow Cascade, Watendlath and round to the jaws of Borrowdale. Price's house sounds very like a single-storey affair, and Nash's talent for the spreading silhouette and the fringed veranda would have eased his task of realising Price's brief, wrapping the house into the long horizontals of its beach site. The effect was probably similar to that of the Gordon house at Derwent Bay, which contrasts sharply with the Pocklington houses around the lake in that it is not itself part of the view from anywhere. It does not stand up nor make a monumental presence in the landscape, but rather hugs the ground and looks outward. Its axes are varied, and appear to point the whole room that lies behind the window either up, across or down the lake. Structurally, it has the character of a 'nutshell' run up in stuccoed brick (a bizarrely non-local material) and appliqué neo-classical internal joinery.

Unlike Derwent Bay House, Elleray had an elevated site, one that might have challenged the designer to make the building an ornament to this gentle, 'beautiful' bank of Windermere as viewed perhaps from the Claife Station.[10] Wilson's decision to build low therefore seems to indicate a conscious aesthetic option. His decision to erect what was, in most accounts, 'a rambling building forming three sides of a square', suggests that he was, like Price and Gordon, probably pointing the rooms to the three main lines of vision. We know from de Quincey's account that the drawing-room had full-length windows opening on to the terrace, and that the natural view thence was across the lake to Claife Heights. The northern side of the square must accordingly have faced the view to the head of the lake and the Langdale Pikes. The third side presumably faced either the southward view to the islands, or conceivably the Picturesque close-up view of the cottage and the hillside behind, which probably, however, was the open side of the square with the entrance in it. At the same time as managing the views of the world outside, the house, with its irregularity, its terraces, creeper-covered walls and flower beds, would itself have been a discreetly Picturesque object, not glaring conspicuously out of its site but holding the visual attention of those that were close to it. It would serve the self-contained aesthetic interests of a proprietor whose relation to the landscape was not seigneurial, and who came to the place to see it as little changed by his coming as possible.

It seems clear that these single-storey houses were not seriously intended for permanent residence, having space for entertainment and hospitality rather than for work. As the ideal manner of life associated with the cottage was one of retirement and creativity, so the main association of the low house was of festival, of the Regency elite on holiday. Wilson's capacity for fun and sport became legendary. He swam, fished, wrestled, climbed the hills, organised cock-fights, chased bulls, kept a fleet of seven sailing boats and a ten-oared Oxford barge on the lake. In 1825 he at last put the finishing touches to the low house at Elleray when he came down from Edinburgh for the summer vacation, and took a leading part as Admiral of the Regatta to celebrate the presence of George Canning and Walter Scott on Windermere. Lockhart's description, poignant with retrospective foreboding over the economic crisis of 1825–26 which brought down Scott, and over Canning's imminent death, shows the extent to which Windermere had been assimilated to the status of an Italian lake by these well-travelled neo-classical intellectuals, assimilated not only as a Claudean prospect but as a site for southern festival:

reaching that lake, we spent a pleasant day with Professor Wilson at Elleray, and he then conducted us to Storrs. A large company had been assembled there in honour of the Minister – among others was Mr. Wordsworth . . .

There was 'high discourse', intermingled with as gay flashings of courtly wit as ever Canning displayed; and a plentiful allowance, on all sides, of those airy transient pleasantries, in which the fancy of poets, however wise and grave, delights to run riot when they are sure not to be misunderstood. There were beautiful and accomplished women to adorn and enjoy this circle. The weather was as Elysian as the scenery. There were brilliant cavalcades through the woods in the mornings, and delicious boatings on the lake by moonlight; and the last day, 'the Admiral of the Lake' presided over one of the most splendid regattas that ever enlivened Windermere. Perhaps there were not fewer than fifty barges following in the Professor's radiant procession, when it paused at the point of Storrs to admit into the place of honour the vessel that carried kind and happy Mr. Bolton and his guests. The bards of the Lakes led the cheers that hailed Scott and Canning; and music and sunshine, flags, streamers, and gay dresses, the merry hum of voices, and the rapid splashing of innumerable oars, made up a dazzling mixture of sensations as the flotilla wound its way among the richly-foliaged islands, and along bays and promontories peopled with enthusiastic spectators.[11]

The impluse behind settlement and building such as Wilson's, Gordon's and that of William Gell of Grasmere was therefore both scenic and participatory. The house, in its situation and design, presented the landscape, drawing people out to enjoy the scene both as a picture and as a place of activity and social enjoyment. The house, as it were, pushes its people outwards. The contrast, in architectural manners but not necessarily in the actual behaviour of the occupants, would be with those houses that draw aesthetic interest in to themselves. Barrow Cascade House,[12] one of Pocklington's carefully posed houses on Derwentwater, thus contrasts with Gordon's Derwent Bay; Barrow Cascade is an important motif of the central view from Derwent Bay, but not vice versa, and Barrow Cascade is also a regular ingredient of paintings of Derwentwater, like the Curwen house on Belle Isle[13] and like Storrs with its temple on Windermere. Brathay Hall was placed similarly in the landscape, carefully sculpted in the pre-Picturesque Brownian mode, as itself a conspicuous ornament to the head of the lake, and frequently therefore included in the paintings. Similarly Belmount, visible intermittently from Esthwaite on the Hawkshead road, dominates the landscape, classicising it by the force of its presence and style. At Brathay and Belmount, as at the lake houses, the aesthetic character aimed at in the landscape was the Burkean Beautiful, the shaved lawns, clumps of trees, smoothed hillocks and bare-banked water combining with evidence of a rich pastoral land economy to produce the characteristic sensations of pleasure and security. No doubt the near-availability of genuinely Sublime landscape increased the attractions of the Brownian-Beautiful style of landscape architecture in the Lake District, and even Wordsworth, while he scathingly reviewed the Pocklington and Curwen island houses, allowed the aptitude of gentlemen's houses as a 'principal feature in the landscape . . . where the mountains subside into hills of moderate elevation, or in an undulating or flat country'.[14]

Wordsworth, though he covered his tracks somewhat by depreciating contemporary aesthetics as a deep influence on his mental growth, was himself a persistent advocate of Picturesque values in the treatment of actual landscape. These values effected a reformation in the placing of buildings in the Lake District as they did in other parts of the country, offering another way forward, less negative than the self-effacing structures of Gordon, Wilson and Gell. Antiquarianism and the Gothic revival, more particularly perhaps, after about 1820, an enthusiasm for Tudor–Renaissance architecture, were fed into the equation, together with a respect for the random growth of trees in the natural landscape. Wordsworth accordingly wrote:

The rule is simple; with respect to grounds – work, when you can, in the spirit of Nature, with an invisible hand of art. Planting, and a removal of wood, may thus, and thus only, be carried on with good effect; and the like may be said of building, if Antiquity, who may be styled the co-partner and sister of Nature, be not denied the respect to which she is entitled. I have already spoken of the beautiful forms of the ancient mansions of this country, and of the happy manner in which they harmonize with the forms of Nature. Why cannot such be taken as a model?[15]

Pressure such as this, and the sense that historicism gave a way forward for architecture in general, had already brought buildings like Lyulph's Tower[16] (1780) to the side of Ullswater. This, an exercise in Walpolian Gothic and as such an unexceptional house for a metropolitan aristocrat to erect, was significant in the Lake District as the first example of the historicising manner. Significantly, it was thought to be on the site of an older tower, its name derived from that of Ulf – L'Ulf – the first Baron of Greystock. The antiquarianism may have been imaginative, but such imaginative effort was essential to the aesthetic rationale of such designs, which proclaimed the rightness of building a castle where a castle had stood, in a Border region, part of the estate of a Marcher lord, where the historically active imagination would sense the risk of incursions and value the appearance of security in a castellated structure. The sense of dangers averted would also effect appreciation of the house viewed from the lake against the threatening backdrop of the Helvellyn range, and the continuity of the house into a gentler age would be expressed in the ancient trees of the Glencoyne and Gowbarrow woods. Aesthetic endorsement of Lyulph's Tower was still strong fifty years and more after its building; Wordsworth's praise of castellated buildings as specially suitable for mountainous regions could be extended sympathetically to include Lyulph's Tower:

[It] may not want, whether deserted or inhabited, sufficient majesty to preside for a moment in the spectator's thoughts over the high mountains among which it is embosomed; but its titles are from antiquity, – a power readily submitted to upon occasion as the viceregent of Nature: it is respected as having owed its existence to the necessities of things, as a monument of security in times of disturbance and danger long passed away, – as a record of the pomp and violence of passion, and a symbol of the wisdom of law; – it bears countenance of authority, which is not impaired by decay.

    Child of loud throated war, the mountain stream
    Roars in thy hearing; but thy hour of rest
    Is come, and thou art silent in thy age![17]

The encomium applies more closely to Lyulph's Tower with Aira Force behind it than to the greatest of the Cumbrian neo-Gothic castles, Lowther, a few miles to the east on the fringes of the hills. Lowther, with its great central tower, is far more learnedly derived from the Border tower-house tradition, and owes its existence in fact quite directly to the proponents of the doctrines discussed here. It was Robert Smirke's first commission, and he was recommended for the job to Sir William Lowther (created Earl of Lonsdale in 1807) by Sir George Beaumont, then at the height of correspondence with Wordsworth on the treatment of the grounds at Coleorton, and still deeply embroiled with Uvedale Price. But Lowther, whatever the magnificence of its situation, does not represent an attempt at the problem of building suitably in the mountains or in an already famous beauty-spot, which was what concerned Wordsworth.

More nearly influenced in terms of date by the architectural neo-feudalism of the 1820s, which saw Abbotsford completed in 1825, was Croft Lodge (1828),[18] rebuilt with West Indian sugar money by the Liverpool merchant James Brancker. The house forms part of the Brathay group, dominated as we have seen by the Brownian composition of Brathay Hall, with the church on the knoll behind it: further back, under Loughrigg and overlooking the junction of the Brathay and the Rothay, was Croft (Fig. 6). The point is that Croft forms part of the important view to

**6** The Croft, Ambleside (photo David Lyons, Trustees of Dove Cottage).

the fells of Rydal and Ambleside from the north-eastern wing of Brathay Hall, and against this magnificent and famous backdrop it adopts a transitional castellated-Tudor idiom calculated to harmonise with its setting. Not that Croft is a particularly good building nor an apt interpretation of the historic building tradition of the district, but the approach to the problem of building conspicuously in the Lake District, of adding if possible to the imaginative effect of the landscape rather than simply providing a proprietorial view of it, was made with an educated and up-to-date sense of aesthetic proprieties.

By the 1840s the resolution of the problem by the use of castellation and other decorative devices applied superficially to a conventionally Augustan structure seemed inadequate to scholars and architects. Croft indeed is surprisingly little learned for its date, surprising in a district which had Waterhead House at Coniston (c. 1820–22) to point the way to a richer and more detailed antiquarianism. The 1840s, however, saw easily the most significant attempt to build properly in the grandest location. Wray Castle,[19] by H. P. Horner for Dr James Dawson, forms part of all the classic views of the head of Windermere, critically sited on a wooded eminence forming a promontory at Watbarrow Point, and providing the unmistakable motif of the view to the Langdale Pikes. Behind it, set back above a system of intricately wooded hills, is the arc of the Coniston fells, from Wetherlam to the Old Man. More than two generations of the intellectual and artistic elite of Britain had by this time travelled to the Lakes to look at this view of the head of Windermere. It was a staggeringly bold enterprise to place a building, of such innate gestural power, in such a sacred situation.

The views from Wray Castle are of course part of the house's overall rhetoric. The woodland, pressing quite closely on the lawns and terraces and allowing glimpses across the Lake to the Troutbeck and Ambleside fells, was evidently carefully preserved and interplanted when the house was built in order to encourage the historical illusionism. The interior, both architecturally and in its furnishings, had much of the lavish eclecticism associated with the Great Exhibition style, but in that was equally part of the address to the inhabitants' sense of themselves as inheritors of a significant past. Wray, in the photographs taken by Rupert Potter of his family as tenants of the house, was clearly comfortable in that profounder way of providing right spaces to inhabit and move through, and exciting in the close-up drama of its top-heavy towers rearing over terraces ornamented with additional fanciful ruins. But Wray must always have been primarily a house to be looked at, seen from the classic

distances that allowed its scale a proper relation to the landscape around
it. In that context of immemorial hills, a prompt to the active imagination
to reflect on the great issues of transience – of war and peace, of stress
and security, the whole process that connects the present with the past –
was introduced, and became part of the famous view.

As a matter of design, Wray, with its great central tower, seems like
Lowther to have been loosely adapted from the northern tower-house
tradition, clearly influenced by Lowther itself and, with less local
legitimacy perhaps, by memories of the great Edwardian castles of north
Wales. Wordsworth, who had doubted precisely on this point of dignity
whether a house could hold its own among the hills, pronounced that
Wray 'added a dignified feature to the interesting scenery in the midst of
which it stands'. By 1855, when Harriet Martineau wrote, the general
sense that buildings could contribute thus powerfully to the effect of
landscape had been greatly reinforced by the brilliant efflorescence of
British architecture in the central decades of the century. Her Guide
shows a developed sense of the importance of the human presence in
the landscape, and her observations are almost as much of houses and
the amenity of particular sites as they are of the 'natural' landscape.
Inescapably perhaps, but repeatedly, she notices Wray as she goes round
Windermere – 'Wray Castle stands forth well above the promontory
opposite', 'On the opposite shore is Wray Castle . . . – a most defensible-
looking place for so peaceful a region; but an enviable residence, both
from its interior beauty and the views it commands.'[20] Martineau herself,
in a building idiom that was very different from Wray, but which can
now be seen as one of the characteristic and brilliant inventions of
mid-nineteenth-century bourgeois domestic architecture, placed her
own bay-windowed Italianate villa The Knoll (built in winter 1845–46)[21]
in a prominent place outside Ambleside and used an engraving of it to
herald the contents on the title page of her Guide.

The distribution therefore of buildings in the central Lake District – in
the sanctified heartland where the landscape had attained a supreme
cultural importance – was governed either by the wish to see, or, while
seeing, to endow the view for others with an evocative architectural
presence. The weight of Picturesque aesthetics, authoritatively wielded
by Wordsworth, operated against the classicising shaved lawns and open
prospect school, castigating the settler houses 'with their craving for
prospect . . . rising as they do from the summits of naked hills in staring
contrast to the snugness and privacy of the ancient houses'. It was to
avoid such a charge that the sensitive developed the self-effacing

single-storey design, and it was in accordance also with the Picturesque advocacy of historical architecture in conserved or regenerated woodland that the brave and the wealthy began dreaming of castles. Either way, their houses tended to be distributed round the lakes, looking at specific views, looking occasionally at each other, but still, despite anti-prospect doctrine, selecting long and extensive views. Except perhaps in the Rothay suburb under Loughrigg, or where, in Ambleside, Rydal, or Grasmere, a village provided a stronger planning motive, the result was that houses were relatively isolated from one another, connected only by a common interest in the landscape and by the ready availability of transport by road or water to maintain the pattern of visiting customary for the leisured classes. Windermere began to resemble more thoroughly the Italian and Swiss lakes, its development organised on an aesthetic rather than a communal principle.

An additional planning impetus came from the railway which in 1847 reached Windermere, overcoming the residual protection afforded to the Lake District by its remoteness from the economic springs of the would-be settler. Perhaps too much in the development of housing in the Lake District is attributed to the railway's actual arrival at Windermere, rather than to the existence, through railway and other industrial investments, of an enlarged capital-owning and leisured bourgeoisie in the golden decade of the 1850s. The local presence, too, of an exceptionally energetic developer, Abraham Pattinson, must have been instrumental, as was the local availability of a banking system sufficiently flexible to finance both the land purchases and the development costs of his enterprise. That said, however, it is difficult to think of Windermere without its railway: difficult to explain the shift in the centre of gravity from Bowness, the historic town, to the new town up the hill at Birthwaite; plausible to note that the string of great houses along the Windermere – Ambleside road was largely developed after the railway came and emphasised the importance of that road as the main line of access to the central and the northern area of the district.

In the 1830s Bowness began spreading up the hill, and in 1838 the Pattinsons built The Craig for Lord Decies.[22] This house commanded the northerly views of the head of Windermere, with the Langdale Pikes presenting their classic profile and the circle of hills from Bow Fell and Scafell round to the Coniston fells rising above the line of Claife Heights seen obliquely across the water. The house was an exercise in the bay-windowed, gabled villa style, and was surrounded by terraced gardens set amongst feral coppice and standing timber. In the area it was one of the earliest of the adapted Italinate compositions, a sensitive response to the Picturesque admiration for terrace gardening, picked up by Price at the Italian lakes.

On the gently rising slopes towards Post Knott, it represented an alternative solution to the problem of building in a beauty spot. Words-worth's preference was for historic styles, but

> should an aversion to old fashions unfortunately exist, accompanied with a desire to transplant into the cold and stormy North, the elegancies of a villa formed upon a model taken from countries with a milder climate, I will adduce a passage [from Spenser] which will show in what manner such a plan may be realized without injury to the native beauty of these scenes.[23]

The operative Spenserian phrases italicised in Wordsworth's quotation refer to the *enclosed shadow* of the trees surrounding a house which is *scarcely to be seen*. When he himself confronted the problem of building at Rydal Mount[24] he did not in fact opt for total seclusion, but rather for a much more subtly Picturesque composition of terraces and trees. Rydal Mount and The Craig show in their different ways and at their different social levels the more discreet and fully naturalised use of the Italianate inspiration.

The Craig, which has now disappeared, was earlier and arguably more distinguished as a Picturesque composition than the far better known and extant Belsfield (Fig. 7). Belsfield,[25] attributed to the Kendal architect George Webster and again built by Pattinsons, is in terms of its architecture a more uncompromisingly Italianate design, perhaps the most distin-guished example of the style in the district. The first stage of its building for the Baron de Sternberg dates from about 1840, but successive exten-sions both for the Sternbergs and for H. W. Schneider after 1869 made it grow almost as fast as the boom town at its feet. Belsfield has little of the subtlety of setting that The Craig once had, and is extravagantly and obviously a rich man's house, dominating the waterside over a sloping system of lawns that increase rather than disguise the perceived emi-nence of the establishment. In a sense it repeated the 'error' of Belle Isle, towards which it looks, but crucially it lacks the character of a retreat and all sense of privacy. It was away from the ethos of Belsfield and Bowness, with their increasing orientation towards Barrow-in-Furness and the flow of tourists by steamboat from Lakeside, that the developers of Windermere pushed north along the Ambleside road.[26]

Before the railway, Elleray, the beginning of the chain, was in place together with a 'cottage ornée' further round on the northward slope of

Orrest Head on the St Catherine's estate. The railway station itself was under way during the period 1845–47, and the hotel, of which the architect was Miles Thompson of Kendal, was completed for opening in time for the 1847 season on 12 May. Between 1847 and 1854, financed either by or more probably through the Revd John Addison, was the St Mary's Church complex, the church itself (1847–54), the vicarage (1847), abbey, cottage and school. A contributor to the cost was John Braithwaite, who was building at Orrest Head in the years 1853–54; by 1855 his house was occupied by George Holt Esq. At this time the social preponderance of Windermere over Bowness, on the crude but dramatic measure of identifiable gentry listed in Harriet Martineau's *Directory*, was clear. Windermere had at least forty-two household heads listed as either Revd or Esq., or with some clear female status indicator. Bowness, far stronger in tradespeople, had nine. There was certainly a tendency to list houses which physically seem part of Bowness[27] in the Windermere

7 Belsfield Hotel, Windermere (photo David Lyons, Trustees of Dove Cottage).

section – for example William Greg renting The Craig, Admiral Sir
Thomas Pasley at Craig Foot and the Revd Thomas Staniforth at Storrs all
appear for Windermere – but if this indicates a preference, it reinforces
the point. Apart from the old-established Curwens at Belle Isle and
George Marwood who was still at Old England, few of the other listed
gentry are at addresses of much status. Bowness was already a tourist
town, with no less than sixteen households, hotels or lodging-houses,
explicitly dependent on the passing trade. In 1869 Marwood's house was
pulled down and the first (central) section of the new hotel was put up by
the Pattinsons: proof of change and a marker for the future.

In 1854 John Wilson died and his house – the 'new' single-storey house
which had been let more often than lived in since the great regatta of 1825
and was probably neglected – came on the market and was bought in
1855 by William Eastted. Eastted was alive to the heritage and seems to
have quickly concentrated his energies on improving its picturesque
amenity. Harriet Martineau writes already in the *Guide* that the estate is
'now so much improved' and refers to the 'new drive'. The grounds of
Elleray, by this drive, were open to the public on Monday and Friday,
and the proceeds of ticket sales were directed to Addison's new school at
St Mary's. Martineau prefers the Elleray view to that from Orrest Head
via the Windermere Hotel access point and records (usefully for us)
the changing foreground of the Wilson–de Quincey view:

All below are woods, with houses peeping out; on a height of the opposite shore,
Wray Castle; further north, the little Brathay Chapel . . . the little white house of
Clappersgate, with the chateau-like mansion of Croft Lodge conspicuous above
the rest . . . The village of Windermere is like nothing that is to be seen anywhere
else. The new buildings (and all are new) are of the dark grey stone of the region,
and are for the most part of a medieval style of architecture. The Rev. J. A.
Addison, late of Windermere, had a passion for ecclesiastical architecture; and his
example has been a good deal followed. There is the little church of St Mary, and
there are the schools belonging to it, with their steep roofs of curiously shaped
slates: and there is St Mary's Abbey . . . and St Mary's Cottage. And there is the new
college of St Mary, standing in a fine position, between the main road and the
descent to the lake . . . The large house, on the hill and amidst the woods of the
Elleray estate . . . is [Oakland] the property of John Gandy, Esq., who has chosen a
charming site for his abode: and a little further, on the same side of the road, is the
pretty villa-residence [The Wood] of Miss Yates . . .

There is a new house, built just below the ridge at Miller Brow by William
Sheldon [Highfield], which we have thought, from the time the foundation was
laid, the most enviable abode in the country . . . Cook's House has only just
disappeared, and a new residence, built by Peter Kennedy Esq., [Cook's Hall] has
taken its place.

Martineau's great strength as a commentator perhaps lay in her open-ness to change, and her vivid 'sociological' grasp of the landscape as a living, peopled object of aesthetic pleasure. There is no strain of lament in her description of the Pattinson urbanisation programme: 'There are villas on either side of the road, on almost every favourable spot, all the way to Bowness . . . We pass rows of lodging-houses . . . Further on is the Hydropathic Establishment, conducted by Mr. E. L. Hudson, F.R.C.S.' Her testimony in general as to the effect of the arrival of the railways has the clear ring of doctrinaire liberalism:

We have no fear of injury, moral or economical, from the great recent change, – the introduction of the railways. The morals of rural districts are usually such as cannot well be made worse by any change. Drinking and kindred vices abound wherever, in our day, intellectual resources are absent: and nowhere is drunken-ness a more prevalent and desperate curse than in the Lake District . . . Under the old seclusion, the material comfort of the inhabitants had long been dwindling; and the best chance of recovery is clearly the widest possible intercourse with classes which, parallel in social rank, are more intelligent and better informed than themselves.

Such belief in the healthy influence of the urban working class was rare in mid-nineteenth-century tourist literature, and forms an interesting corollary of the more usual view that it was the trippers from the indus-trial cities who would (unless drunk when they looked upon Helvellyn) be the net beneficiaries of tourism.

It was on this side of the balance that the weight of Martineau's *Guide* certainly fell. She was an enthusiast for tourism of all kinds, and there is an unhesitant generosity in her references to the strings of lodging-houses lining the approach to Bowness that sets her apart from any other commentator. Her real love however was hotels rather than boarding houses, and she wrote close to the outset of the great age of hotels when, in Bowness, Thomas Ullock's Royal, making up its 70–80 beds, ruled in conspicuous splendour on its 'garden platform . . . overlooking the gardens that slope down to the shore'. Ullock, Rigg, and William Bownass, the rising star of the trade who took over the Royal in about 1855, followed a decidedly up-market policy. The Royal acquired its name in honour of Queen Adelaide's visit of 1840, and complaints against the high prices charged at these establishments were sufficiently common to merit rebuttal by Martineau: '. . . these inns are extremely well-managed'.

In Grasmere, the small but perfectly placed hotel, now The Hollens, had proved too small, and Edward Brown had moved to a new site at

Town End, beside the lake, where he built the enormous Prince Of Wales,[28] so called, he informed his patrons, after the stay by the Prince and his Suite during the 'greater part of the time they were in the Lake District'. The fact of Royal visits, so proudly proclaimed and memorialised in names, was actually of far less lasting (or immediate) significance even for the proprietors than the flow of relatively ordinary people who came, not in imitation of royalty but in search of the authentic Lake District experience. This, by the mid-nineteenth century, had largely ceased to be that which Ruskin and his parents had enjoyed thirty years earlier, as coach-borne travellers putting up at roadside inns like the Lowwood. The experience offered by the new hotels was richer, depending less on the quality of the food and drink (for which the visitor to Grasmere might still prefer to go to the Red Lion) and convenience of access, than on a more thorough illusion of belonging in the landscape. Unlike the old inn, with its rudimentary public facilities, the new hotels offered grand public rooms with great windows commanding views managed with all the art of the villa architect, as in the private house there was the opportunity to walk out into the gardens, passing terraces and through shrubberies, with the sense of enclosure and privacy on small lawns, with flower beds contrasting with the grandeur of the surroundings. In the sixties, even the Lowwood dragged itself into this idiom – Manchester-fashion – vastly extending its accommodation and surrounding itself with formal gardens and shrubberies and increasingly it was the hotel, rather than the house that seemed to offer the more thorough illusion of belonging in the landscape.

The equivalence between the private house and the hotel was evident early, with Rothay Manor making the change from one to the other as early as the 1830s; the Hollens going the other way and enjoying a short spell as a private house in about 1852. Moss Head House, built for the Earl of Cadogan in 1871–72, lasted ten years before conversion into the Rothay Hotel by R. Hudson, who emphasised the facilities for 'gentry sports' – croquet, archery, and bowls on the lawn – and in the conservatory the availability of exotic fruit. The demolition of Marwood's house at Bowness to make room for the Old England was in that way exceptional, since both economy and the borrowed prestige of the former owner's life-style made conversion advantageous. The important historical principle was that the moneyed, mobile class of the employed and economically active took over the emplacements of the *rentiers*: the buildings, the gardens and their prospects being valued precisely because they gave access without commitment to the esoteric culture of the previous residents.

The process was not simply one of replacement in time – the houses did not as a genre come first to be taken over by the relatively enlarged hotel market. Hotels and houses are contemporary phenomena of the bourgeois landscape culture, and the very pricing policy of the great hoteliers, together with the state visits of queens, princes and Kaisers, show that the distinction between house and hotel was not one of relative expense nor of old as against new money. Like the houses, hotels not only manage and present the landscape but are part of it themselves, listed and criticised in the guidebooks, drawn, painted and photographed as part of the general pictorialisation of the District. The Francis Frith photographs, sold to tourists as a prime record of the landscape experience, are rich in views of hotels – Bowness's Ullswater Hotel punctuating the long slope of Glenridding down to the water's edge; the Prince of Wales in Grasmere, wrapped in trees, and no longer standing starkly above its stone-built boat station, but mellowed in perhaps thirty years to a rich pattern of fretted gables, compositionally answering the spare outline of Helm Crag. By this time the Royal in Bowness, upstaged on the waterfront by the Old England, was pictured as part of a town view, with Atkinson's Stationer and Draper, agent for the Kendal Bank and the Circulating Library claiming the foreground. There is sure evidence here of an influence in photographic aesthetics from the town view drawings that began appearing as part of Boningtonism in the 1820s, a sort of proto-Realism evident also in the truncation of the horse-drawn bus in front of the Queen's Hotel in Ambleside, and in the calculated banality of the announcement 'Barrow's Lodging Hot and Cold Baths' in the foreground of the otherwise exemplary modern Picturesque of In the Village, Ambleside. Photography being an art of selection, the inclusion of such details is not random, or rather the randomness is highly calculated.

The emergence of such demotic elements in mid-nineteenth-century imagery is probably a function of the process of popularisation in landscape enjoyment. Frith thus has an image of the boat-station at Bowness, with the paddle-steamer Rothay at the pier and groups of (presumably) company officials and boatmen holding their pose and watching the camera attentively. A high view over Windermere with, apparently, the island Rough Holme, shows a jumble of generically Pattinsonian terraces and semis spreading up the hill: a picture as demotic, as intriguingly non-compositional and calculatedly unbeautiful in its aesthetics, as anything in the Realist tradition.

Just as the Windermere semis did not displace, but marked an adaptation and popularisation of the high bourgeois villa style, the 'Realist' Frith photograph did not displace either from his own list or from the market in general the more conservative view. The aesthetic pluralism of the later nineteenth century was reflected in the currency of painted views by Messrs A. & G. Pettitt of Keswick, who continued the tradition of the authoritarian Picturesque and advised their clients to inspect their products *before* visiting the sites, in order to pre-condition their response to them; and by Mr and Mrs Lindsay Aspland of Bowness, who traded on an adapted neo-pastoralism similar to that of Birket Foster. The London firm M. & N. Hanhart advertised separately mounted and framed lithographs after artists with a national reputation, T. L. Rowbotham and T. M. Richardson: priced at 42s they were far up-market of Harwood's *Splendid Views in the Lake District*, sold by the quire as letter paper (3s 6d) and notepaper (1s 9d), intended 'to convey some idea of the locality and charm of the place of residence (especially if temporary); for then there is generally a freshness of feeling to appreciate the surrounding beauties . . .'. The emphasis on the sentiment of landscape here contrasts with the intention behind the *Stereoscopic Views of the Lake District* of Thomas Edge, which made available the hyper-scientific vision of the Ruskinians: the wonder and beauty emerging in proportion to the verisimilitude of the image. In 1881, Maysons of Keswick were advertising 'A very large selection of Photographic Views by Payne, Jennings, Frith, Pettitt, Ferguson, &c', still up-market, but Maysons became the great local postcard company, and translated many of the images (of Pettitt especially) which had already done service as fine prints into cheap cards for the mass market. The Barrow-in-Furness railway company evidently had a contract with Alfred Heaton Cooper (1864–1929) to reproduce his watercolour views, from about 1890 and they remained in currency well into this century, sold alongside photographs of the Furness Abbey Hotel, its great rooms and gardens, and the adjoining station. In a sense the postcard, because it was cheap to produce and buy, could please everyone, and it therefore seems to maintain in currency virtually the entire range of traditional landscape while being ever ready to include the new.

Though one may wish to insist that the culture of landscape, at least of the Lake District landscape, is accumulative – holding every element in consciousness – there is a principle of renewal, replacement and actual change running through it as well. Thus houses have become hotels; houses and hotels have become schools; some schools have been turned into apartment houses for retirement or holiday lets, and others have been demolished, their sites cleared and densely built over. The history of buildings is almost always a history of continuous change and adaptation. The northern push out of Windermere established by the 1880s a colony of some of the richest and, as far as consciousness of landscape amenity was concerned, the most vociferous householders anywhere in the country. When a proposal to extend the railway from Windermere to Ambleside came before Parliament in 1887 the owners of the houses affected, mostly those highest on the slopes above the lake, formed a lobby to resist the bill. Robert Dunlop of Holehird (c. 1869)[29] petitioned individually, on the grounds that a fifty-foot high embankment was planned to run below his house, severing his drive and cutting off the entrance lodge. He went on:

Property in the district of Windermere Lake is all but worthless if the views of the lake and surrounding country are interfered with. The views from your Petitioner's residence and estate generally will, by the proposed embankment and roadway, be interfered with very materially, the views of the lake and mountains from the residence being practically shut out by the said embankment.

Other owners submitted a collective petition, objecting in similar terms to the compulsory purchase powers in the bill: Frances Turrill of Browhead pointing out that the line would pass along the steep bank directly above the entrance to the house on which a special garden of evergreens was laid out; Edward Gibson at Chapel Ridding, whose grounds 'have been very carefully laid out', was also set to lose his garden, and John Bore and William Lister, joint trustees of Dove Nest, pointed out that the estate 'celebrated in the district for the beauty of its situation and surroundings' would be split along its length, two houses and a cottage on the land ruined by the line within sixty yards of them. The hardest case was that of John Rigg, proprietor and manager of the Windermere Hotel. The proposal there was to pass the line in a shallow tunnel through the front garden of the hotel, ten yards from the door and underneath the coach-houses: Rigg pointed out that the 'annoyance and discomfort' of trains passing so close would ruin his business. Had the line been built it would now be valued as the most stunningly ambitious example of engineering and landscape architecture, perhaps comparable with Brunel's Cornwall line, but the petitioners (their case reinforced by economic factors) were victorious, and the houses survived as desirable entities. But of that group of houses, Browhead and Chapel Ridding, together with Elleray, now make up the campus of a girls' boarding school: the millionaire view along the length of Windermere to the peaks of Langdale spreads sweetness and light amongst the daughters of the northern bourgeoisie. Above Bowness, Annisgarth, a girls' preparatory school after the war, became an apartment block after a period of dereliction in the late 1950s. Below it, The Craig, which had become a boys' preparatory school soon after the First World War, and from which at midsummer midnight a party of boys would set out to watch the sun rise from the top of Helvellyn, was sold by its proprietor and headmaster to be developed as a housing estate. Instead of children, elderly free-holders lift up their eyes to the hills. The anxiety, the pressing question, which faced Lord Decies about building to enhance the landscape in harmony with its architectural and natural history, had passed by 1960 to the official planners. It is interesting that the modern custodians of taste turned back in this case to the Pricean resort of the 'bungalow', as though it were wise to intrude on the eye as little as possible, to hug the ground with light nutshell structures. But they created on this estate a convoluted layout that actually seems to turn inward, away from the majestic view.

The modest, tentative quality of the building at The Craig, bizarrely symbolised in preserved relics of its former gardens, technically accords with the conservationist principles of the historic Picturesque. In con-trast, perhaps, the Greenbank estate at Ambleside sweeps boldly up the fellside on the south bank of the Scandale back, arranged in great sweep-ing curves with the odd isolated tree rising out of smoothed turf and mown lawns: a culverted beck follows the serpentine line of the main access road. Aesthetically the estate seems to look back to the classicising Brownian idiom so well entrenched at this northern end of Windermere at Rydal Hall, Rothay Hall and nearby at Belmount: self-confident public enterprise, more certain of the virtue of housing those qualified from the list, handles the greenfield site with radical panache. There is not the slightest attempt at creating or imposing 'community', no hint of the village, nor of planting for enriched close-up effects. Each house commands a view across the Rothay valley to the shoulder of Loughrigg, and has its share of the lawns and serpentine beck; each house, and the estate in general, is a presence in the landscape: neo-classical, neo-Whig in its imagery of harmonious individualism.

## Notes

1  This essay was originally drafted as a contribution to a book planned by Robert Woof and
myself to accompany the exhibition *The discovery of the Lake District*, held at the Victoria &
Albert Museum in 1984 (accompanied finally by a catalogue, hereafter referred to as

V&A 1984). During this work I had the privilege of long conversations with Robert Woof and had access to his researches. Together we visited many of the houses referred to here and enjoyed the generous hospitality of their present owners. In my pocket I carried Geoffrey Beard's brilliant short book *The greater house in Cumbria* and G. H. Pattinson's privately printed booklet on his family firm, *Pattinsons Builders, of Windermere, 1573–1973* (Liverpool, 1973). My debt to these several sources of information has proved too pervasive to acknowledge in detail: my gratitude is the greater. The text presented here has been only lightly revised and remains as a largely descriptive piece. Indications of the more reflective and analytic aspects of the work appeared in the catalogue of the exhibition and in the volume of essays, *The Lake District: a sort of national property* (Countryside Commission, 1986).

2　The date is on the plan. *V&A* 1984, no. 221, Trustees of Dove Cottage.

3　The printing history of the text generally referred to as the *Guide* is complicated. It appeared first as anonymous letterpress to accompany Joseph Wilkinson's *Select views in Cumberland, Westmorland and Lancashire* (Ackerman, London, 1810) and was subsequently published separately as *A descriptive survey of the lakes in the north of England*, nominally a third edition with considerable enlargements, in 1822. Wordsworth himself supervised five editions, culminating in the definitive edition of 1835, *A guide through the district of the lakes*. Much more than a guidebook, it represents Wordsworth's main statement on the aesthetic issues arising from settlement in the Lake District and is an attempt to establish rules of 'taste' for those intending to develop or improve the locality. The edition used here is that of E. de Selincourt (Oxford, 1906), based on the text of 1835, hereafter referred to as *Guide*.

4　*Works of John Ruskin*, ed. E. T. Cook and A. Wedderburn (1903), I, pp. 167, 182, 187.

5　*Noctes Ambrosianae* in *Works* . . . ed. Professor Ferri (Edinburgh and London, 1855–57), IV, pp. 2–4. John Wilson: b. 1785; moved to Edinburgh from the Lake District in 1815, contributed to the Tory *Blackwood's Magazine* and in it adopted the pseudonym 'Christopher North' as the author of the occasional papers *Noctes Ambrosianae*. In 1820 Walter Scott promoted him as the Tory candidate for the vacant Chair of Moral Philosophy at the University of Edinburgh and he was elected. From then on he was always known as Professor Wilson. He was a summer-only visitor to the Lake District from 1813 to his death in 1854.

6　T. de Quincey (1829); quoted from B. L. Thompson, *Professor Wilson of Elleray* (1875), p. 14.

7　See *V&A* 1984, 70.

8　Ms. letter, Uvedale Price to Sir George Beaumont Foxley, 18 March 1798. I am indebted to Felicity Owen for a sight of the text of this letter.

9　Derwent Bay House, *V&A* 1984, 69.

10　Claife Station, *V&A* 1984, 50.

11　J. G. Lockhart, *Narrative of the life of Sir Walter Scott* . . . (Edinburgh, 1838), quoted from the compact edition of 1848 (Everyman, 1931), pp. 478–9.

12　Barrow Cascade House and other Pocklington buildings, *V&A* 1984, 63–8.

13　Belle Isle, *V&A* 1984, 38–45; Storrs Hall, 46–9; Brathay Hall, 56–60.

14　*Guide*, p. 77.

15　*Guide*, p. 74.

16　Lyulph's Tower, *V&A* 1984, 73.

17　*Guide*, pp. 76–7.

18　Croft Lodge: *V&A* 1984, 248–9.

19　Wray Castle, *V&A* 1984, 250–2. The house is now in poor condition, but the illustrated particulars of sale from Messrs Capes, Dunn and Co., 14 July 1920 (Lancashire Record Office, DDN3) give a good idea of it at the height of its prosperity.

20　H. Martineau, *A complete guide to the English Lakes* (Windermere and London, 1855).

21　The Knoll, *V&A* 1984, 254.

22　The building is demolished – the date here is given from my memory of the inscription

on the western façade.
23  *Guide*, p. 75.
24  Rydal Mount, *V&A* 1984, 212–22.
25  Belsfield, *V&A* 1984, 253.
26  Windermere, *V&A* 1984, 256–66.
27  Bowness, *V&A* 1984, 262–7.
28  Prince of Wales, Grasmere, *V&A* 1984, 283.
29  *V&A* 1984: Holehird, 285; Browhead, 287; Chapel Ridding, 288.

# 9

# Loitering with intent:
# from Arcadia to the arcades
### Simon Pugh

## I

Short of Halesowen, turn into a green lane. Descend a valley, past a root house ('in cool grot and mossy cell we rural fays and faeries dwell tho' rarely seen by mortal eyes . . .'), the Priory Gate and seat (lines from Virgil), a seat beneath oaks (lines from the 7th Eclogue), a piping faunus, and an urn. Walk through forest ground 'fit for the pencil of Salvator Rosa', past a bench (lines from Horace), and a Gothic seat ('shepherd, would'st thou here obtain pleasure unalloy'ed with pain . . .'). Climb a 'circular green hill' to an octagonal seat inscribed with 'an old Shropshire health' ('To all friends round the Wrekin') and a view divided into 'compart-ments' of hill and vale, plain and woodland, mountains and hills, hamlets and villages, a serpentine stream. Ascend to a Gothic Alcove (inscribed 'O you that bathe in courtly blysse . . . do too rashly deeme amysse of him that bydes contented here . . .') and a seat under a beech (lines from Horace's 6th Satire). Walk along Lover's Walk to an Assignation Seat (lines from the 7th Eclogue), by an urn inscribed to 'puellarum elegantissima' Maria Dolman and a bench (line from Pope's Eloisa, 'divine oblivion of low-thoughted care') and a seat 'alluding to the rural scene before it' ('hic frigida Tempe', from the Georgics), and a rustic Temple of Pan (lines from the 2nd Eclogue). A high terrace with a seat commemorates 'Divini gloria ruris!' and a view of Clee Hills, the Wrekin, Caer Caradoc and the Welsh Mountains. Descend to a 'beautiful gloomy scene', designated Virgil's Grove, and pass an obelisk (to Virgil), a seat (to Thomson, with lines from 5th Eclogue), and a seat inscribed 'O let me haunt this peaceful shade . . . &c'. Finally pass a 'chalybeat spring with an iron bowl chained to it' and a stone seat (lines from Virgil), seats to friends Richards Graves and Jago, and a Venus de Medici 'beside a bason of gold fish' inscribed with Shenstone's poem, 'Semi-reducta Venus'.[1]

Souvenirs, relics, emblems, monuments, commodities. The souvenir, says Walter Benjamin, is the complement of the experience through which the self-alienation of the collector who inventories the past as a dead possession is distilled.[2] The souvenir is the relic secularised, but whereas the relic derives from the corpse, a presence, the souvenir is 'dead' experience – Adorno argues that representations of nature seem to be authentic only as *nature morte*, as an 'encoded historical message'. The souvenir's meaning is always elsewhere, an absence. The garden souvenir (seat, inscription, object) is a prototype of the commodity, self-referential and esoteric. As an embodiment of an experience a souvenir preserves memory from time, against time. The tourist 'rediscovers' a site through the photograph or the guidebook, both of which hold the experience immobile in time; the garden spectator discerns the 'reality' of the landscape through souvenirs, mostly literary, prescribed by classical tradition. The indigenous human life of the countryside disappears in favour of the monument (the hamlet, the root house, the seat, Virgil's Grove, Venus).[3] The garden becomes a commodity and the garden walk a museum corridor.

William Shenstone, the Columella of Halesowen, was born in November 1714, died of putrid fever in February 1763 and was sometime of Oxford, London, Bath or 'any other place of public resort' (for a time he 'wandered about to acquaint himself with life'). The Leasowes is an ersatz farm for 'the improvement of beauty rather than the increase of produce', a 'sport' rather than a 'business', a one-way street up hill and down dale, a pastoral excursion, a blind alley past old horizons on the path from Pope to Wordsworth, where he walked to disacquaint himself with life.

As a child, he had an obsessive need for fresh entertainment and demanded a new book whenever the family went to market, 'in fondness carried to bed and laid by him'. Otherwise a piece of wood wrapped up to simulate a book would do to pacify him at night. His mind, said Dr Johnson, was not very comprehensive nor his curiosity active, his life 'unstained by any crime'. Even the unpleasant elegy, a tale of Jesse's pregnancy and her suicide through shame, supposedly a 'criminal amour' of his, was symptomatically 'suggested' by Richardson's *Pamela* just as his groves were by Virgil's *Eclogues*.[4] He even arraigned pigs for trampling his periwinkles with 'a faggot stick in one hand and a *book* in the other' (Fig. 8).[5]

An idler, he felt uneasy about rural retirement, 'against his will', as Gray pointed out, in a place 'only enjoyed when people of note came to see and commend it', although he corresponded 'about nothing else but this place [The Leasowes] and his own writings'.[6] Of limited intelligence ('had his mind been better stored with knowledge . . .'), mocked as 'a little fellow trying to make himself admired', his poems 'want variety', his elegies have 'too much resemblance of each other', his pleasure was 'all in his eye' (Johnson), and he was 'too indolent to be more than a

8 C. W. Bampfylde, Frontispiece of Richard Graves, *Columella or the Distressed Anchoret* (London, 1779), vol. 1.

speculative farmer' (Graves). He concealed rather than described life, living life out of books. Beauty might embellish business but his expenses, said Johnson, 'overpowered the lamb's bleat and the linnet's song and his groves were haunted by beings very different from fauns and fairies'.

Shenstone collects Nature as a commodity ('collecting, or collecting into smaller compass, and then disposing without crowding the several varieties of nature', he wrote).[7] He is the precursor of the flâneur, the weekender, the tourist. For Shenstone, the pastoral is not about real life as it is lived, which is found perhaps in 'any other place of public resort', nor is it Lotus-eating, the touch of Circe's wand nor the song of the Sirens, a surrender of the will, 'picking the lotus and forgetting the homeland' (*Odyssey*, 9.94ff), addiction. His pastoral is not mannered regression to picking the fruits of the earth, a period the pastoral purports to invoke, but merely echoes that is older than all production, older than agriculture or even hunting. Shenstone's pastoral is a manner, a style, like arranging Dresden china on the mantel or playing the apache on the streets of Paris. Johnson says the pastoral 'exhibits' a life of 'peace, and leisure, and innocence', that 'drives away cares and perturbations . . . *without resistance . . . transported to elysian regions*'.[8] Life is not Arcadia but *acedia* – for Pope, 'Ambition and Avarice employs Mens Thoughts' but these are 'uneasie Habits' indulged not out of 'Choice but from some Necessity, real or imaginary' (*The Guardian*, 22). The pastoral offers freedom from necessity, the illusion that life can be fairyland, but only for delimited periods (two weeks in the summer, a Sunday outing, *déjeuner sur l'herbe*). Life is not, can never be, 'peace, leisure and innocence', but the *promesse de bonheur* allays the fear of the permanent state of emergency we live in (Benjamin), 'objective despair' (Adorno), in a blotting out of everything known about the later course of history. Such a pastoralist merely pretends, along with Pope, that thought is 'too hard for rustic apprehension' (*The Rambler*, 36), disavowing thought in an attempt to escape 'civilisation'. Sadness is a thorn in the foot, a lover's rejection, a wistful inscription. The magic of enjoyment can only be rediscovered in a dream which releases the pressure of work, releases the bond which binds the individual to social function and ultimately self, a dream which leads back to the pastoral 'elysian regions' (Pope's 'Fairy-Land') without masters and discipline.[9] For Johnson, the pastoral is Nature-as-home-land, regression to childhood ('we recur to it in old age as a port of rest'), to the pre-Oedipal:

> We have seen fields, and meadows, and groves, from the time that our eyes opened upon life; and are pleased with birds, and brooks, and breezes, much earlier than we engage among the actions and passions of mankind. We are therefore delighted with rural pictures, because we know the original at an age when our curiosity can be very little awakened, by descriptions of courts which we never beheld, or representations of passion which we never felt. (*The Rambler*, 36)

By mid-century, nature is already a spontaneous after-image of mercantilism and industrialism. Pastoral pleasure is social, not natural. It is from the 'courts and passions' that the pastoral inclination seeks the return to nature. The form of Shenstone's pastoral is less festival, more farce, 'the same images in the same combinations . . . incapable of much variety of description', with 'small augmentations from time to time' (*The Rambler*, 36). This is its charm, mindless pleasure made rational and administered sparingly (a fortnight a year, a coach trip, or even after 'retirement'), an entertainment: holidays have replaced festivals. Just as the holiday site is purged of all association with real life (a poor wine harvest may intrude, a 'petty enormity', but not an Ethiopian famine), the pastoral is a partial truth, 'half an image', so that 'the Mind is so dextrously deluded that it doth not readily perceive that the other half is concealed'. Give 'what is agreeable in that Scene and hide what is wretched'; give not 'the whole Truth, but that Part which only is delightful'; 'cover misery' (*The Guardian*, 22).

Shenstone the idler. Idleness is a parody of self-generating nature that seemingly requires no labour, for the more dependent the rulers are on the work of others the more work is despised and idleness becomes a virtue.[10] But to be the idler, Johnson wrote in the first number of his eponymous journal, is the ultimate purpose of the busy. Who can be more idle than the reader . . . sacrificing duty to the love of ease? The idler has no rivals or enemies, forgotten by the businessman, despised by the entrepreneur, welcomed by those equally idle. Those who attempt nothing think everything easily performed, the unsuccessful as criminal. Satisfied by what can most easily be obtained, the idler sometimes succeeds better than those who despise all that is within reach and think everything the more valuable as it is harder to be acquired.[11] But Johnson is merely playing with idleness: his idler is not the indolent, the lotus-eater, whom Odysseus must remove by force and drag back to the galleys.

Shenstone is also the hermit, the 'distressed anchoret', a gentleman amateur, rather than Sir Humphrey Whimwham's 'professional' (in Graves's 1772 satirical novel on Shenstone) employed to do his idling for him. This 'professional' performed poorly and was dismissed for 'getting the dairy maid with child' and preferring a pipe and a jug of ale to a book and a crucifix when he sat on a stone outside the hermitage on visiting days. Himself his own hermit, Shenstone had no need to employ one who 'rather than be out of *business* and live *idle*' would work for less than twenty pounds per annum to be employed idly in the landscape. This is paradigmatic of the class system under capitalism: what is labour for the labouring class (however much that rural labour is crudely parodied) is transformed into leisure which is 'the ultimate purpose of the busy' rulers. As Whimwham's fashionable accoutrement, 'keeping an hermit may be cheaper than keeping a wh-re, or . . . a pack of dogs'.[12] Rhetorically linked, worker, whore and dogs are adornment and amusement. Labour finds no role in landscape. Gilpin's 'lazy cowherd resting on a pole' is permissible, but hard graft has no place in representations of Shenstone's Arcadian landscape however much graft must pay for it and make it. Tidy landscapes make tidy profits, but picturesque hedges are as much to keep the game high off the ground and provide adequate jumps for hunting. The 'wh-re's' function in landscape was more complex. Contradictory things were expected from both women and nature,[13] yet the rhetoric employed to represent both coalesces. Women are, says Addison, 'lovely pieces of human nature' (*Spectator*, 477) and Nature should be both productive yet 'yield satisfaction' and 'entertain the sight every moment';[14] it should be 'most rude uncultivated' (*Spectator*, 414) and 'promiscuous' (Switzer) and yet the landscapist's skill lay in 'contracting Nature's beauties' (Shenstone to Thomson, 1746). Hogarth's line of beauty is well exemplified by stays ('by their bulging too much in their curvature [they] become gross and clumsy and as they straighten become mean and poor'), demonstrating how, with appropriate curves, 'the form of a woman's body surpasses in beauty that of the man'.[15] Set against the stay is the pleasure of 'roving uncontrollably' (Switzer) in the 'pudenda of nature' (Charles Cotton). The mean way is Shenstone's 'thoughts by decency controlled' (inscribed on the back of a Gothic seat) or Pope's treatment of nature as a goddess but 'like', that is *as if* she were but is not (what 'wh-re' could be?), a 'modest fair'.

> Nor over-dress, nor leave her wholly bear;
> Let not each beauty ev'ry where be spy'd,
> Where half the skill is decently to hide. ('Epistle to Lord Burlington', 11. 51–4).

The landscapist wished both to 'live alone with Nature and view her in her inmost recesses' (Shaftesbury), but to constrain, control and possess those recesses, the promiscuous unboundedness (Nature 'spreads unbounded beauty to the roving eye' ('Spring', 11. 506–7)), in the tight stays of boundaries and circuits. Landscape is like 'the imperfections of a wife's Humour' that the man can claim the credit for softening 'by degrees . . . those very Imperfections into Beauties' (*Spectator*, 261).

But Shenstone kept no hermit, whore or dog: his books and his landscape were apparently more than enough though he might, says Johnson, have 'obtained', as if she were a commodity, land or a work of art, 'the lady, *whoever she was*, to whom his "Pastoral Ballad" was addressed'.[16] He had his pastoral 'mistresses', equally anonymous, the literary Delias, the Camillas, the Cynthias, shepherdesses all, sublimated pleasures, the rural fays and fairies that resided in cool grots 'rarely seen by mortal eye', naiads and dryads of landscape, and Maria Dolman ('Ah Maria Puellarum Elegantissima'), who died of smallpox at twenty-one years of age, commemorated on an urn that 'terminated' (Dodsley), an expedient euphemism, Lover's Walk. Above all, he had the mute, the naked, the frigid *semi-reducta* Venus, nature monumentalised in lead: 'half withdrawn she seems to hide, and half reveals, her charms'. The boundary, the ha-ha, is like the stay: it contains the expansiveness of nature within accepted lines, yet it emphasises and imposes structure, 'contracts'. By opening out and yet protecting the landscape, like a beautiful woman a commodity, a public adornment of wealth, ownership is advertised and privacy against intrusion and theft is secured.[17] Beauties, natural and female, should be open to the unrestricted gaze of the owner and those he chooses to display his possession to, but concealed from the vulgar. Pope's garden had 'Hedges with a thick Shade, which prevents all prying from without, and preserves the privacy of the interior Parts',[18] a privacy that could be made 'naked and exposed by that ruffian winter [the 'vulgar' as a force of nature] to universal observation' (Dodsley on Shenstone's nymphs). What could be seen was enticing ('seems to hide'), but exposure of property to others was carefully controlled ('half reveals her charms'). The display of the landscape is as circumscribed by rules and conventions as precise as the striptease: Addison ('Mr Spectator') referred to the 'Secret Satisfaction' derived from looking at landscape which lies 'so conveniently under the Eye of the Beholder' (*Spectator*, 477). This was supported by a rhetoric that warned off (in the semi-legal language of 'trespassers will be prosecuted') the 'uninitiated'. 'Procol este profani' [profane, keep out!] was carved above the portal of the first temple at Stourhead (the sybil's admonishing words to Aeneas, and Julius II's to the visitor of the Belvedere *giardino segreto*.) In less terse language, Shenstone admonishes:

> And tread with awe these favour'd bowers,
> Nor wound the shrubs, nor bruise the flowers; . . .
> But harm betide the wayward swain,
> Who dares our hallow'ed haunts profane! (Root House inscription)

At other strategic parts of the garden, moral homilies order the 'swain' to 'learn to relish calm delight' and 'hear what Reason seems to say, hear attentive and obey'.

Defiance and infatuation are two sides of the same coin. Adorno and Horkheimer tell that Odysseus does not take another route to avoid the Sirens but struggles in his bonds at the mast: he is both in control and seduced, the binding becomes a condition of the pleasure, and by eluding he is fulfilled, 'just as later the burghers would deny themselves happiness all the more doggedly as it drew closer to them with the growth of their own power'.[19] The pleasure of nature, a devitalised beauty, has to be experienced and controlled. For Shenstone, the Sirens' song is no longer fatal but already art and, as Kant insisted, art 'declines' to pass as cognition and separated from social practice it is tolerated as mere pleasure, harmless and under control. Both Shenstone's 'semi-reducta Venus' and nature 'sovereign rule decline' so that 'sight unveils a part' of the landscape, like Venus's body, for fancy to 'paint the rest'.[20] Landscape has sex appeal; it is both fleshy and elusive. Prototypical commodities, landscape and Venus are both untouchable Madonnas and mythic 'wh-res'.

Taken in (in both senses of the word) by culture, nature is absorbed, commodified. Setting foot in nature, taking nature by the hand and leading her an irregular dance (as Shenstone so charmingly puts it), must be done clandestinely, at night, an assignation, set in a garden like the last act of Mozart's *Marriage of Figaro*, so the reversion to basic impulse may be disguised by the dark. Both Venus and nature are courtesans, seductive, irresistible, to be both violated and repressed. In the eighteenth century, sexuality is at the crossroads between understanding and control: emancipation and repression lead each other a circuitous dance. The invading pigs that Columella chastises with faggot stick and book for trampling his periwinkles (Odysseus's sacred moly flower against Circe's enchantment perhaps) are neither emancipated nor repressed, not wild beasts but unclean domestic animals. Like 'ruffian winter' and obtrusive rural worker, they are an unhealthy, untidy and artless intrusion of nature (there are no accounts in Gilpin of picturesque pigs), quasi-human, fat and naked, swine with an instinct for brute pleasure, charmed and made as nature by the enchantress–courtesan Circe, victims of a ritual they willingly subject themselves to, a ritual to which patriarchy repeatedly subjects the woman.

The journey round the garden is a commodification of the body, the equivalent of the pornographer's journey round the female figure, dimensions, angles, postures, views, zones, absurd unnatural contortions of the landscape (such as the emphasis on bub-like hilliness) to secure the best shots, odd styles of dress thrown together for effect to emphasise or to conceal a feature. The sexiness of a commodity is how it is 'dressed up' for sale. 'You have nothing to do,' said Thomson to Shenstone at the Leasowes, 'but to dress Nature . . . to caress her; love her; kiss her; and then – descend into the valley'. He described two hills as 'the two bubbies of Nature . . . observed the nipple, and then the fringe of Uphmore wood'.[21] Just as the poet takes control of the woman's body, a passive commodity, through division into parts, through inventory and itemisation,[22] likewise the landscape should be 'composed,' says Gilpin, 'as the artist composed his celebrated Venus, but selecting accordant beauties from different originals'.[23] The rhetorical tradition of 'division' and 'partition' both divides up matter to 'increase and multiply' but also opens it up and opens it up to view, to 'enlightenment', by uncovering something hidden. Epistemologically, this is the rhetoric of scientific knowledge, but it is also the rhetoric of acquisition, wealth and ownership (Bacon's 'a way to amplifie anything is to break it and to make an anatomie of it in several parts'), and leads through the emphasis on the gaze to an 'eroticised, even potentially prurient and voyeuristic, looking' (Parker).

The excitement is the journey through the terrain, the succession of views, the sequence of carefully arranged shots. Shenstone designates a scenic route indicated by direction indicators, travel notes, guidebooks, letters, poems. It is indicative that nature as landscape is known first through writing, legitimated at each turn of the corner by an inscription or a poem on a seat, an urn, a tablet, that the spectator must read before looking at the landscape. The cruellest trick is to break the sequence by 'conducting visitants perversely to inconvenient points of view, and introducing them at the wrong ends of a walk to detect a deception' (Johnson, 1792), as if the circuit is all and the views merely narrative incidents or assembly-line production that make no sense out of order. The accretion of freedom, that there is such an abundance open to the gaze, is circumscribed by sets of laws, regulations and directions. Shenstone's circuit anticipates the tour, the excursion, the vacation, controlled entertainment with an expected response. Like Odysseus, the tourist is bound helplessly to the mast, unable to take the initiative, to *engage*. There are speed limits (instructions to 'stay awhile', to look here, to look there), orders to stay in lane (go here, go there, guidebooks, descriptive poems, topographical illustrations), diagrams showing the shape of the road ahead (maps), and an obligation to keep the eyes on the road ahead (to see everything, never to miss a thing, spotting the view). Our spontaneity has been replaced by a frame of mind which compels us to discard every emotion or idea that might impair our alertness to the impersonal demands assailing us.[24]

## II

Benjamin's work schedule: arriving from the Left Bank by subway, he would have surfaced at rue 4. Septembre through the still-standing art nouveau portal. In bad weather he would have sought the shelter of the Passage Choiseul (built in 1825) with its clothing and stationery stores catering to office workers; he would have turned left through its still-moribund extension towards the rue Sainte-Anne, exiting a block from the small, lush-green Square de Louvois, the quiet peace of which ends abruptly at the rue de Richelieu. Crossing its speeding lines of traffic, he would reach the safety of the entry courtyard of the Bibliothèque Nationale . . . The themes of the *Passagen-Werk* can be mapped out typographically on a small section of Paris, with the Bibliothèque Nationale at its hub . . . the surviving arcades which ring the Bibliothèque National: Choiseul, Vivienne, Colbert, Puteaux, Havre, Panoramas, Jouffroy, Verdeau, Prices, Caire, Grand-Cerf, Vero-Dodat . . .[25]

Shenstone's circuit, authenticated by objects inscribed at strategic points, is a literary experience. A prototypical picturesque tour, it can, like all tours, be read about: the walking comes last if at all. All tours are first *texts*, whatever they may become afterwards ('lived experience'?). William Combe's appropriately named Dr Syntax, searching for the picturesque, for its *grammar*, does it on ponyback, always book in hand, writing but reading as well for the route has been mapped out in advance: his writing merely confirms what he had already read. In nineteenth-century Paris, the city is discovered through the *feuilleton*: Poe's Dupin never needs to leave his room to solve his crimes. The *flâneur*, solitary, walks alone through the *passages*, the arcades: like Shenstone's loitering, Baudelaire's illustrates his poetry. Shenstone's garden marked the extension of private interior space into the public countryside – furniture (the inscribed seats), rooms (the *giardino segreto*), corridors (alleys), balconies (high views) – and his circuit proposed a way to take command of the landscape from within an enclosed landscape space. Shenstone's country walk from text to inscribed text becomes the arcade, reprivatised social space, the new Arcadians' habitat, a cross between a street and an *intérieur*, where 'every pedestrian is able to pass through the entire city without having to go outside', an intoxicating fusion of street and dwelling, of 'countryside and living room' (Benjamin). It was no longer possible to be protected from the social forces of production, from the collective, from 'nature': the bourgeois interior or its extension into the garden was no longer adequate defence. The city had to be appropriated in a different way: furniture becomes the benches, corridors the arcades, balconies the café terraces: 'to the collective, shining enamelled signs of a store or a company are as a good as or better than the decorative oil paintings on the wall of the bourgeois salon . . . walls the collective's writing desk, newspaper stands its libraries . . .'.[26] This is 'democratisation' of public space, but just as the rural poor have little interest in sentient quotes from Virgil, the *flâneur* loiters differently than those for whom, says Benjamin, 'poverty and vice turn the city into a landscape in which they stray from dark till sunrise',[27] the successors of the rural dispossessed. Proudhon once said that Paris is a democratic city for both the rich and the poor can sleep under the arches of the Pont Neuf. For the *flâneur*, the city is a 'show-place': in the streets, 'the product surrounded by a flow of customers' (Benjamin) gives the illusion of reconcilliation with the wilderness of the big city, just as the privatised spaces of the garden tramped by a succession of visitors make nature into a side-show. Both are landscapes, the unknowable made domestic, controllable, 'reconciled' (Benjamin). An arcade is 'a city, even a world in miniature' (according to a Paris guide of 1852); a 'safe, if not cramped, promenade', says Benjamin. In the early 1840s it was even fashionable, he recounts, to take turtles for walks in the arcades to 'set the pace',[28] to regulate movement according to the supposed tempo of the country walk (traffic did the flâneur in or, at least, changed the parameters-Adorno described radio channel-switching as 'aural flânerie'). The flâneur strolls and contemplates not country views but shop windows although both are the scene of commodities, the bought and the for sale. If the man who loiters is the flâneur the loitering woman is a street-walker, 'la grande horizontale', the 'landscape', signifier of the 'virgin forest' of the city, the 'body' of nature, although more public than Shenstone's privileged views of Nature's 'bubbies'. The whore is the commodity: 'under the domination of commodity fetishism, the sex appeal of woman is tinged with the appeal of the commodity'. But the whore is also the seller for 'her trade brings with it the fiction that she is selling her capacity for pleasure' (Benjamin). The pleasure of Shenstone's nature is equally fictive. His Venus and invisible naiads become the lifeless mannequins used to display the latest fashion or even the present-day Parisian stripper who performs behind a glass shop-front. If, Benjamin says, the department store is the flâneur's last haunt, in flânerie 'we can recognise our own consumerist mode of being-in-the-world,'[29] for like the pastoralist who does not work the flâneur does not trade. Both protest with 'ostentatious languor against the process of production'.[30] In the garden, the stuff of nature is laid out at the end of vistas like windows, in blind alleys like corridors, in green cabinets like rooms, as if in shop windows, fetished. In the garden, the pastoral is the always-the-same, a restitution of the archaic as the ideological re-reading of the modern. In his Arcades Project, Benjamin used the Parisian arcades as a point of departure to demonstrate that the modern, an endless stream of consumer goods, manifests itself as the always-the-same,[31] free from the traces of their production in the same way that the pastoral landscape is absolved from any contact with the workers who made it. Both are seemingly ensconced in that archaic world where nothing that is made has had to be produced. Pastoral idler shares with the urban loiterer 'the delights of possessing unpossessed and seeing unseen, of tasting transiently so as to remain self-composed', for what is perused, a commodity, 'promises permanent possession without aban-doning its secretive isolation'.[32]

Circuits, both country and city, imply detachment, odysseys from one place to another without ever belonging. Both are rhetorical experiences: in the city, Baudelaire's poetry, the novels of Balzac, Hugo and Sue, detective fiction, latterly even Benjamin's stroll to and from the BN to read, and then write, about what he had walked through. The circuit walker can experience an aloof, detached pleasure, remain almost invisible and apart from life as it is lived. In the country landscape, the working labourer is invisible (except as indolent adornment), the better to preserve the illusion of unproduced nature. In the city, 'les profon-deurs sont des multitudes'.[33] Writing of Haussmann but with Speer's schemes in mind, Benjamin was also writing of the Paris of the first bourgeois dictator but during the rise of Hitler. He points out that the crowd the flâneur observes is the mould into which the *Volksgemeinschaft* was poured some seventy years later, the flâneur the first to fall victim to what has since blinded millions. Columella, the flâneur and a race of healthy peasants: whether extolling the virtues of rustic life or of blood and soil, all promote imperalist propaganda. The crowd is Columella's pigs, kept at bay with stick and book, for here in the city the crowd cannot be written out and, like boundless nature, is there for the explorer to discover. The crowd is the landscape. The city is encountered as wild nature at a time when poets and painters were discovering the sublimity of the natural world. As a crowd, 'nature exercises her funda-mental right on the city', for 'what happened on the street would not have astonished a forest.'[34]

> Foule sans nom! chaos! des voix, des yeux, des pas.
> Ceux qu'on n'a jamais vu, ceux qu'on ne conaît pas.
> Tous les vivants! – cités bourdonnantes aux oreilles
> Plus qu'un bois d'Amérique ou une rouche d'abeilles.[35]

The flâneur in the open streets becomes the pioneer, the city a circuit for 'Mohicans in spencer jackets and Hurons in frock coats',[36] a prairie for the apache. The flâneur 'goes botanising on the asphalt' (Benjamin), discovering 'a tropical forest in the Rue d'Enfer' (the title of the fronti-spiece for *Mohicans de Paris*); Balzac used Fenimore Cooper as his model ('the poetry of terror of which the American woods with their hostile tribes on the war-path encountering each other are so full . . . attaches in the same way to the smallest details of Parisian life'); Féval's redskin Tovah managed during a ride in a fiacre to scalp his four white companions in such a way that the coachman noticed nothing.[37] To be part of the surging crowd, yet apart from it as an observer, is to be an urban pastoralist, part of and apart from nature: to be *outside* so as to be *inside* is to view the world and still to remain hidden from it, the commanding view from an 'eminence' leaving the viewer invisible from below. 'Virgin' nature is mechanical, uniform nature, the 'man of the crowd' in the eponymous story by Poe, 'the type and genius of deep crime [as a detective, says Benjamin, the *flâneur* acquires new social legitimation] . . . It will be in vain to follow; for I shall learn no more of him, nor of his deeds . . . perhaps it is but one of the great mercies of God that *es laesst sich nicht lesen* [it does not permit itself to be read].' The pursued, like nature, is an empty moment: neither have anything to teach, they 'cannot be read'. Of course, Poe's Dupin did not follow: he did all his *flâneuring* hermit-like and unseen in the armchair by reading about the city in the *feuilletons*: the daily newspaper recorded the living, he simply read about the 'asphalt jungle'. The detective *flâneur* is like Kierkegaard's philosophical subject who (says Adorno) goes for a walk without ever leaving his room. Programmed for the unique event, 'the man in the crowd' is the Sphinx, a closed book after the riddle has been answered, a solved crime. This reciprocity between text and reader has no place in nature where the differentiation between a force and how that force is acted out is not delineated. The circuit is one way to learn more of 'the type and genius' of nature, to put it under the microscope, or to discover that there is nothing to be learnt, and to solve its 'crime'.

In important respects, the *flâneur* grew out of the pastoralist. Both attempted to privatise social space by arguing that passive and aloof observation was adequate for a knowledge of social reality, rhapsodising their illusory view of life. Constructed images of paradise or Arcadia purport to offer a subversive reading of capitalism by protesting with 'ostentatious composure' (Benjamin) against the production process and against social control. But Arcadian idleness is a mockery rather than a critique of exploitative labour and redundancy, both of which are a necessary feature of capitalism. It seems absence of work is offered as the purpose of capitalism, the *promesse de bonheur*, while it is instead the threat that keeps people under control. In perpetrating this lie, pastoralist and *flâneur* developed a life-style that looked back to leisured 'unemployment' as a sign of class isolation and dominance but which concealed the social relations of class. In the end the Marie Antoinette role as a shepherdess and the bourgeois indolent are one and the same – both play with idleness as if work were not an essential feature of capitalism.

Both turned 'the class struggle against misery into an object of consumption',[38] picturesque squalor an adornment of the landscape. Neither represented the real conditions of country or city but provided instead small diversions from their tedium. It is fitting that, like other gentlemen 'amateurs' who established the country house syndrome, Shenstone's epigone markets the heritage industry and the theme park. The *flâneur* is the prototype of the employee of the 'entertainment industry' (advertising, journals, sex magazines with the maxim 'you can look but you'd better not touch') as well as the loiterer in the shopping mall who buys to escape the pressures of social life. All have an appropriate place in an enterprise culture, trading on imaginary gratification as a substitute for social reality.

# Notes

1  This description of the Leasowes is abstracted primarily from Dodsley's lengthy description in [R. and J. Dodsley] 'A description of the Leasowes', *The works in verse and prose of William Shenstone*, 2nd edn (London, 1765), vol. 2, pp. 287–320, henceforth referred to in the text as 'Dodsley'.

2  Walter Benjamin, 'Central park', *New German Critique*, 34 (winter 1985), pp. 48–9.

3  See Roland Barthes, *Mythologies*, trans. Annette Lavers (Paladin, St Albans, 1972), pp. 74–5.

4  Comments are from Samuel Johnson's 'William Shenstone', in his 'The lives of the English poets', from *The works of Samuel Johnson* (London, 1792), vol. 11, pp. 276–85. 'He had no value for those parts of knowledge which he had himself not cultivated' (p. 281).

5  See Richard Graves, *Columella or the distressed anchoret* (London, 1779), vol. 1, p. 45 (emphasis added).

6  From Gray's letters and quoted Johnson, p. 282.

7  See John Dixon Hunt and Peter Willis, *The genius of the place, the English landscape garden 1620–1820* (Paul Elek, London, 1975), p. 245.

8  *The Rambler*, 36 (July 1750) (emphasis added). *The Guardian*, 22 and 23 and *The Rambler*, 36 and 37, consecutive issues devoted to the Pastoral by Pope and Johnson respectively, follow similar forms: the first numbers address general issues, the second the form of the poetry.

9  See Theodor W. Adorno and Max Horkheimer, *Dialectic of enlightenment* trans. John Cumming (Allen Lane, London 1973), p. 105.

10  *Ibid.*, p. 231.

11  See the first number of *The Idler* (15 April 1758).

12  The incident of the 'professional' hermit in search of employment in Columella's service is recounted by Graves, vol. 2, pp. 121–4.

13  For an elaboration of this argument, see Carole Fabricant's article, 'Binding and dressing nature's loose tresses: the ideology of Augustan landscape design', *Studies in Eighteenth-Century Culture*, 8 (1979), pp. 109–35, esp. pp. 131ff.

14  Stephen Switzer, *Ichnographia rustica*, 2nd edn (1742), vol. 3, p. 5.

15  *Analysis of beauty* (1772 edn), pp. 49–50.

16  Johnson, p. 281, emphasis added. More accurately, William Shenstone never married, although as Columella, the protagonist of Graves's novel, he eventually married his maid, thus securing his creature comforts.

17  For an extensive critique of this argument, see 'Rhetorics of property: exploration, inventory, blazon', in Patricia Parker's collection of essays, *Literary fat ladies. Rhetoric, gender, property* (Methuen, London and New York, 1988):

> The interrelations that enabled a wife to be spoken of as 'high-priced Commoditie' which might, through adultery or sexual theft, 'light into some other merchants' hands' or as 'our private Inclosure' which might prove 'to be a Common for others', reveal in their very language the articulation of a discourse which, beyond the enclosures of the patriarchal family in the [eighteenth-century], accompanied the increasing consolidation of the modern state and the increasingly enforced gentlemanly 'enclosure' of land. (p. 154)

18  Quoted from Fabricant, p. 118.

19  'A presentient allegory of the dialectic of enlightenment . . .', Adorno and Horkheimer, pp. 32–4, 58–60.

20  From the poetic inscription that 'illustrated' The Leasowes Venus, see Dodsley, p. 319.

21  Thomson to Shenstone (1746), quoted from Hunt and Willis, p. 244.

22  See Parker. To illustrate this argument, she cites Shakespeare's Sonnet 106: 'the blazon of sweet beauty's best. / Of hand, of foot, of lip, of eye, of brow.'

23  William Gilpin, *Observations relative chiefly to picturesque beauty, made in the year 1772, on several parts of England, particularly the mountains, and the lakes of Cumberland, and Westmorland*, 2nd edn, vol. 1 (London, 1788), pp. 128–9. According to Nicolas Penny, the Venus he has in mind exists only in literature. Zeuxis, according to Cicero (*De inventione*, 2, 1, 1) and Pliny (*Natural history*, XXXV, 64), made a painting of Helen or Venus taking as his model not one but a whole group of women from Croton.

24  Max Horkheimer, 'The revolt of nature', from *The eclipse of reason* (The Seabury Press, New York, 1974), p. 98.

25  Abstracted from Susan Buck-Morss, 'The flâneur, the sandwichman and the whore: the politics of loitering', *New German Critique*, 39 (fall 1986), pp. 129–30.

26  Benjamin, quoted in Burkhardt Lindner, 'The *Passagen-Werk*, the *Berliner Kindheit*, and the archaeology of the "recent past" ', *New German Critique*, 39 (fall 1986), p. 45.

27  Walter Benjamin, 'A Berlin chronicle', in *One-way street and other writings*, trans. Jephcott and Shorter (New Left Books, London, 1979), p. 316.

28  Walter Benjamin, *Charles Baudelaire: a lyric poet in the era of high capitalism*, trans. Harry Zohn (New Left Books, London, 1973), p. 54.

29  Quoted from Benjamin's 'Passagen-Werk' in Buck-Morss, pp. 121, 124, 105.

30  Benjamin, 'Central Park', p. 40.

31  This argument is developed by Richard Wolin (1981), 'From messianism to materialism: the later aesthetics of Walter Benjamin', *New German Critique*, 22 (winter 1981), p. 101ff.

32  The flâneur's

> solitary dispossession reflects the commodity's existence as fragment [Benjamin speaks of the commodity as 'abandoned' in the crowd], and his meanderings are as magically free of physical traces as the commodity is absolved from the traces of its production. Yet at the same time his painstaking production of himself as "personality", his genteel–amateur distaste for the industrial labour through which he glides, signifies the protest of a fading aura in the face of commodity production – just as the commodity itself, that glamorous, eternally self-possessed "subject", offers itself as compensation for the very drab vision of labour of which it is the product. Both the flâneur and commodity tart themselves up in dandyish dress. The flâneur at once spiritually pre-dates commodity production – he strays through the bazaar but prices nothing – and is himself the prototypical commodity, not least because his relationship to the masses is one of simultaneous complicity and contempt.

> See Terry Eagleton, *Walter Benjamin or towards a revolutionary criticism* (Verso, London, 1981), pp. 25–6, 27.

33  Victor Hugo, quoted from Benjamin, *Baudelaire*, p. 61. For Baudelaire,

> they do not stand for classes or any sort of collective; rather, they are nothing but the amorphous crowd of passers-by, the people in the street. . . . If he succumbed to the force by which he was drawn to them and, as a flâneur, was made one of them, he was nevertheless unable to rid himself of a sense of their essentially inhuman make-up.

> Walter Benjamin, 'On some motifs in Baudelaire', *Illuminations*, ed. Hannah Arendt (Schocken Books, New York, 1969), pp. 165, 172.

34  From *Les misérables*, quoted Benjamin, *Baudelaire*, p. 62.

35 From 'Les orientales, les feuilles d'automne', quoted Benjamin, *Baudelaire*, p. 62. 'Nameless mob! chaos! voices, eyes, steps. Those one has never seen, those no one knows. All the living! – cities buzzing in our ears louder than an American forest or a beehive.'

36 From André Le Breton, *Balzac* (Paris, 1905), p. 83, quoted Benjamin, *Baudelaire*, p. 42.

37 Benjamin, *Baudelaire*, pp. 36, 41–2.

38 Benjamin, 'The author as producer', in *Understanding Brecht*, trans. Anna Bostock (NLB, London, 1973), p. 96. Brecht is talking here of 'the New Objectivity [in Germany in the 1920s] as a literary movement . . . converting revolutionary reflexes into themes of entertainment and amusement which can be fitted without much difficulty into the cabaret life of a large city'.

# 10

# Rustic retreats: visions of the countryside in mid-nineteenth-century France
## Nicholas Green

very lovely rural residence, twelve hectares of *jardins anglais*, cover and grounds . . . magnificent view over the Seine, ten minutes from Paris by railway.[1]

Coach, boat or train to Paris; ornamental grounds or kitchen gardens; fishpond or safe enclosure of walls; the charms of situation – the *view*. In 1840s France notaries' adverts like this were more than commonplace. And they were not all for massive estates catering for the extremely wealthy; small cottages with perhaps only two rooms were also on offer as desirable rustic retreats. The litany of marketing imagery may seem surprisingly familiar to a British audience today. Access to civilisation was repeatedly yoked to the benefits of solitude, security, *and* to the pictorial delights of panoramas and views. But then 'getting away from it all' into the countryside, taking pleasure in spectacular viewpoints, picnicking among hayfields, renting or buying a property for weekend or occasional use; all these apparently familiar activities had a potent appeal for a broad Parisian public in the 1840s.

For a more caustic appraisal of the phenomenon let us turn to the cartoon series by Honoré Daumier on *Les Bons bourgeois* from the same decade. Several prints work the theme of the Parisian trip out into the country: respectable, though modest couples trudging wearily across a barren wasteland towards a distant train station, or failing to grow flowers on their infertile little plot, or dallying clumsily in the hay.[2] In one of the best, the usual rather hard-worked urban couple – shopkeepers or small business people – he with a suspiciously bloated red nose, are sitting on the grass watching a butterfly. A rural idyll! The punchline runs: 'Don't frighten him, Eudoxie . . . he's going to land . . . he thinks my nose is a rose!'[3] If the joke ridiculed *other* people's unself-consciousness, their absurdity, it also played on structures of recognition, nudging the audience's familiarity with escaping from the city into the flowery outskirts.

Daumier's cartoons, their humour still fresh, were part of a massive proliferation of visual imagery – prints, pictures, illustrations – on 'natural' landscape in the first half of the nineteenth century. Landscape imagery cropped up everywhere, from improving educational magazines for artisans like Le Magasin pittoresque to the elite artistic journal, L'Artiste, from the shop windows of dealer galleries and diorama spectaculars to the walls of the prestigious Salon. Yet, paradoxically, much of the painting (rather misleadingly reduced to the rubric of the so-called Barbizon school), far from stimulating our interest in the nature of the nineteenth century, no longer signifies to a modern audience. Despite successive attempts at revival in recent books and exhibitions, these often rather blackened crusts depicting trees, cows, ponds and sunsets signally fail to make sense, to connect with our own feeling for the countryside.

That failure of communication generates some of the questions running through this essay. What, in this context, do we mean by nature? The first thing to say is that we cannot simply presume that what is designated by the term has remained static from one historical moment to another. Nor that landscape speaks to and for the same social constituencies now as then. This is to push further than the view that it is the 'imagery' that has changed according to 'style' and 'taste'; that there is, after all, some topographical and geographical sub-stratum 'out there' interpreted and reinterpreted according to the 'ethos' of changing historical periods. The problem with such a stance is that while gesturing to historical change, there is still a separation out of some physical – and supposedly transhistorical – essence of nature from representations of it! In other words, enshrined is a lurking idealism whereby the reality of nature as a set of objects and structures is abstracted from the rough cut and thrust of social relations. I want to argue for a greater historical relativism. For the physical, quite as much as the textual, has its own representational order. The geographical perception of natural space is already socially constituted and, as any geographer will tell us, carries distinct registers of cultural meaning. My point is, then, that in unpicking historical formations of nature we need to approach it as an entity whose physical and spatial as much as cultural form is moulded by the conditions and power relations of the period in question. So, what are we really talking about here – the representation of space in landscape painting, or the representation in space of landscape structures? The answer is both, and in 1840s Paris a kind of curious productive tension between the two. At the heart of the argument is the power of forms of visual perception in framing the experience of the metropolitan public, whether walking through the forest of Fontainebleau or admiring pictures of landscape. We are not just dealing with a series of constructed objects and themes but with historically produced *ways of seeing*.

This marks something of a departure from existing treatments of space and the visual. Analyses of landscape fall usually into two separate camps. On the one hand, there are those sociologies and geographies that fix on the patterns and structures played out in space, from the geographical disposition of capitalist production to the shape of town planning, from tourist development to geo-politics and environmentalism. As early as Durkheim and Simmel sociologists were correlating certain social and psychological effects with forms of urban development.[4] *Anomie* or alienation were the results of dense concentrations in huge, uniform cities. Implicitly there was a sense in which space became a marker for levels of social advancement and disintegration. More recently investigations by Marxist geographers and urban planners have stressed the complex autonomy of the spatial, recognising it as a potential site for struggle over dominant power relations.[5] Yet in many senses it still remains difficult to grasp how the cultural materiality of space and its effects are to be understood, except as the condensate of complex chains of external determinations – economic and social. In the standard contrast, for instance, between suburbs and inner city, different spatial arrangements carry clear class connotations, but they do so because of the imprint of factors whose rationality lies elsewhere: the play of market forces, the way capital shapes land-use, the political and cultural battles over social segregation or integration. Consequently, there is little illumination here on the way spatial forms, in their historical specificity, affect and modify the experience of inhabitants or visitors.

In the other camp line up the accounts of landscape *painting*. These are of course absolutely committed to the visual as a modality of social expression, though from a very precise stance. Leaving aside the old and relatively discredited tradition that dealt in stylistic evolution judged by the criteria of Modernism, let us focus on the newer and more radical 'social art histories'. Even in the best of these, as with T. J. Clark and John Barrell, the visual imagery of art retains its central niche as the object of explanation.[6] The implications are twofold. The privilege accorded to such cultural texts lifts them out of the texture of history and (shades of the Frankfurt school) sets them up in an expressive or reflexive relation to forms of social power. For Clark art imagery *is* qualitatively different

from other modes of cultural representation and Impressionist landscapes do catch something of bourgeois anxieties about class dislocations
in the suburbs. For all the wealth of social evidence brought to bear, this
remains a black on white, figure on ground approach that treats art more
as a commentary on history than a component complicit within it.
Second, and perhaps more germane to the current argument, radical art
histories still shadow the assumptions of the traditional approach in
identifying the role of the visual with discussion of pictures. The call to
respect the specificity of the visual is often repeated. Yet why is it that this
invocation turns out to be a justification for talking about art, as if there
were not a thousand and one other historically pertinent visual
structures, from clothes to domestic decor to public space, on which
they could turn their analytic gaze? Such defensiveness suggests that
there is too much at stake – the particular professional expertise of the
discipline. Yet we would do ourselves little harm in casting the net wider
and tapping into 'ways of seeing' in a more intradiscursive and
interdisciplinary fashion.

Looking both to urban sociologies and radical art histories the
following essay aims to bridge the gap. It examines landscape imagery
not as the mediated reflex of contemporary interest in the countryside
but as part of the vocabulary from which that interest was put together. It
seeks to demonstrate how in this experience of nature the reading of
three-dimensional space and of pictures became elided and even
confused. The social significance of nature in terms of cultural power lay
along the intersection of these two representational axes. All of which
brings us back to the substance of our story.

## To forget Paris in the centre of Paris

Looking back from the 1890s Jules Simon, moderate republican and
educationalist, reminisced on the events of his long life. He recalled
student leisure hours of the 1840s spent not in the fashionable crush of
the Tuileries, but away from the crowd in the solitude of the Luxembourg's jardin anglais. Here, he mused: 'in certain corners you could
almost believe yourself in the countryside. There was nothing more
delicious, after a wearying day, than to find yourself hidden among these
great trees, to forget Paris in the centre of Paris, to smell the invigorating
scents of earth and vegetation . . .'[7] Simon's vision – an old man's
nostalgic dream – was of course coloured by the glass of memory. Yet
the selective distillations of the past, filtered through the fine gauze of

personal experience, also provide illuminating insight into some of the recurring themes of early nineteenth-century nature. For a start, the Luxembourg was one of Paris's few public gardens in the first half of the century to sport a picturesque landscape park in the so-called English style. Dating back to the 1790s, this was considerably enlarged and replanted around 1801.[8] It soon gained a reputation for meditative students (like Simon), poets and lovers. As the blind poet, the Marquis d'Avèze, thrilled in 1818, everyone mingled easily here, for 'in the Luxembourg it is just like in the countryside'.[9]

It is just like in the countryside! What are the resonances written into that exclamation? Something may be gleaned from Simon's choice of imagery. For him too the garden was to be read as if it really were the countryside. The displacement was engineered through hiding, finding seclusion under the trees, getting close, physically, sensually, to the sights, sounds and smells of the undergrowth. Thus cocooned, Simon could cast off the weary cares of the city; he was invigorated and refreshed. And yet equally central to the structure was a self-consciousness about the illusory, even artificial quality of the experience; some recognition that pleasure was generated by forgetting Paris in the centre of Paris. There was, it seems, a slippage between being inside and outside the frame.

That is one starting point. Another would be to listen in on a young man whose talents, hopes and fears were invested in the Paris of the 1830s and 1840s. A man young enough and new enough to the capital to be simultaneously sincere and disingenuous in his invocation of this type of nature. Here is Théophile Thoré writing to his mother in 1837:

I will ask of you only a bed in the countryside and some provisions. For the rest I will make my arrangements to live with the peasants, particularly as I want to work among them.

Our Parisian life is utterly abnormal. We have given over too much energy to developing intellectual life and none to natural life. All equilibrium is broken, that is one of the reasons we suffer so. Thus it is my resolve to try out, for a time, a life that is simple, restful and primitive . . .[10]

Scurrying between political projects, a popular dictionary of phrenology and art journalism, Thoré was typical of many trying to build fortunes in the city on pluck and perseverance. While pathologising Paris as abnormal and out of joint, his attitude bristled with excitement and self-congratulation. It was, for this ex-provincial, our Parisian life that was so sick. There was a deliciousness to the suffering he felt. Consequently, his projected return to nature did not just mean going home to relatives in the provinces; it was altogether more exotic and literary (he evoked the name of the romantic Senancour) – altogether more constructed. As with Simon, the fantasy was of complete immersion which would restore the mental balance ruptured by urban frenzy. Yet the very desire for natural refreshment was also transient and temporary, depending as it did on a massive investment in the city.

In Thoré's journalism of the next ten years these private equations were converted into a more public rhetoric. In 1847, musing before landscape paintings by Narcisse Díaz de la Peña at the annual art exhibition, he came up with the following powerful, if carefully contrived formula:

We have quite enough worries in our political and private lives to forgive the arts for reminding us of natural nature, *natura naturans* as the ancients called it, that nature eternally fecund and luxuriant which contrasts so cruelly with our artificial ways and all the grievous inventions of a topsy turvy world.[11]

This was in part political critique, using the supposedly innocuous domain of art criticism to mount a coded republican attack on the decaying Louis-Philippe regime. But it also touched on something of the representational slippages intrinsic to nature. For if the obvious feature here was the polarity between civilisation and nature, an equally structural undercurrent was the oscillation between looking at pictures and being in the countryside.

Such narratives give some flavour of the objects, themes, relations and processes from which the dominant discourse on nature as the countryside, Thoré's *natura naturans*, was put together in early nineteenth-century France. One striking hallmark is the constancy of Paris as the major point of reference. Nature was in a sense a *Parisian* obsession, the property of those with access to metropolitan culture. Now it may come as no surprise to link the framing of a rural idyll with reactions to city life, but in fact by the Parisian connection I mean something quite specific. It was, I shall argue, the conditions and developments peculiar to the capital that generated the *vocabularies of looking* capable of bringing nature into visibility as a mode of social activity.

## Environmental anxiety

One crucial dimension feeding into the visualisation of nature was a heightened awareness of the urban *environment*. Here the role of official knowledges put to work by the state (within the Prefecture of the Seine and the Prefecture of Police) was paramount. From the 1820s state intervention into both 'policing' and improving the city was under-pinned by the crystallisation of statistical methods and the growing hegemony of medical discourse. Symptomatic was the statistical report of 1828 by Louis Daubanton, general inspector of highways, into the recent crisis affecting the building industry.[12] Setting up the new quarters north-west of the centre (of which more later) as a standard of progress and comparison, his survey drew out a series of shocking contrasts with the old and decaying centre:

> the harvest of death is far greater in those narrow quarters than in areas where the air circulates easily and which benefit from the nourishing rays of the sun [but] . . . poverty, the privations which it causes, the absence of personal hygienics and the immorality of a part of the labouring classes . . . these are also the causes of high mortality.[13]

The vocabulary for conceptualising and tackling 'poor' Paris here was predominantly medical. It plundered the hygienist approach promoted by the *Annales d'hygiène publique et de la médecine légale* from 1829 (of which the prostitution reformer Parent-Duchâtelet was a leading light) and institu-tionalised in the *Conseil de Salubrité* within the police department. Hygienics advanced an environmentalist thesis to the problems of conta-gion and epidemic disease – and especially cholera in 1832.[14] That is, disease was claimed to result from local environmental conditions rather than infection carried in water or air. What constituted environmental factors were highly fluid – witness the Daubanton quote – sliding from the physical to the moral, the material to the social. In the 1830s and 1840s riot and political uprisings as well as vice and crime were frequently constructed in terms of environmental threat; what Hugo in the June days of 1848 excoriated as the 'insurrectionary virus' oozing out the 'entrails of the city'.[15]

Environmentalism furnished a powerful language – rapidly circulated in the press and popular literature – that for all classes of 'respectable' Parisians condensed a range of urban anxieties. Crucially, its expansive logic was written into the perception of the city's topography. Vice and sedition could be seen to be lurking in narrow, stinking alleyways or even, like cholera and prostitution, to be infiltrating the healthy spaces of the capital. As a corollary, official initiatives were concerned to preserve and create safe and healthy space in and around the city. As the Prefect of the Seine, the Comte de Chabrol, worried in the 1820s: 'The fields and gardens which used to exist within the vast enclosure of the capital are being transformed into streets. Soon we shall have no other well-aired open space apart from the public places which have long existed.'[16] Medics too insisted on the need for gardens 'planted with trees and surrounded by a rail where the children of all classes could . . . enjoy the games and exercise appropriate to their age, and where the inhabitants of all ages could feel the benefit of the sun and breathe air far fresher than in their homes'.[17] The imagery projected was of a sensual immersion secure from the incursions of disease or evil. Gardens were imagined as concentrated enclosures of wholesomeness – moral as well as physical – breathing-holes punctuating the dense skin of metropolitan space.

Similar imagery surfaced in the demands of the utopian planner Hippolyte Meynadier in the early 1840s.[18] while applauding the many piecemeal improvements initiated by the current Prefect, Charles Rambuteau, he polemicised for a huge park at the heart of the city, something like London's Hyde Park, that would be 'a real countryside in the town'.[19] His identification of healthy space with the *countryside* – the landscape outside the city – registered a turning point in the construction of nature. As in other areas of sanitary policy, Rambuteau's tight grip on the exchequer and administrative caution put paid to any grandiose projects for parks and gardens. That would have to await the bold interventions of the Haussmann era.[20] It was up to civil society to take up the challenge of nature!

In fact, well before the 1840s the individualised search for safe enclosures had turned outwards to the outskirts, the suburbs and beyond. It was a Parisian invasion that took many forms. On the one hand there was the mushrooming of *maisons de campagne* or country houses. These extended from Belleville and Passy, villages on the footstep of the city to the heights of the Seine or the primitive Fontainebleau forest. On the other hand there was a proliferation of excursions and trips – what might be called the beginnings of nature tourism. Jules Janin, like Daumier, pinpointed the 'popular' end of the spectrum in his evocation of the jaunt to the lush valleys and forests of Montmorency. On Sundays the crowds would arrive by hackney coach, carriage or even cart. Hardly had their feet touched the ground when cries of delight rang through the air: 'The grand young men, the best behaved and most unaffected girls are at once seized with the sweet folly that consists in shouting, running, climbing, lying upon the grass, mounting on horseback and galloping through the hilly and venerable forest.'[21] The vision of different classes of Parisian liberated into a childlike freedom by the plunge into the countryside echoes the medics' urban garden where children could play in health and safety.

Of course neither the rural excursion out of Paris nor the *maison de campagne* were in themselves particularly new phenomena. Country houses had been advertised back in the 1760s while the writings of Jean-Jacques Rousseau and the vogue for 'natural mediation' they inspired stimulated a whole genre of guidebooks.[22] But to point up the continuities is to miss more fundamental differences. There is no neces-sary identity of meaning between apparently similar cultural practices at distinct historical moments. Taking the excursion as an example, there was a qualitative transformation in the construction of what travellers went to see and how their experience was organised. In the late eighteenth century trips were organised around renowned landscape parks and the favourite haunts of cult figures like Rousseau.[23] A passing view may have seized the attention of the guide, but the real aim was to peruse the charms of nature as ordered by human hands (and often to productive as much as picturesque effect). Connected with this, guides posed as educational or philosophical reveries in the manner of Rousseau, setting up the natural as the medium for the education of a refined sensibility. By the late 1820s the emphasis was shifting to the very different kinds of pleasures – running, walking, riding – conjured up by Janin. The new case for nature was eloquently put by Julien Lemer's guide to Montmorency of 1847.[24] Castigating existing publications for their 'literary preoccupations' and for forgetting 'nature, landscape, everything except to dream about Rousseau', he described his promenades as a series of views, spaces, sensual experiences. What he loved most was 'solitude and walking through the woods and fields, I love specially the spectacle of nature's changing apparel in spring, the tender green of young shoots in the first days of May, and the wonder-fully sweet scents exuded by the early blossoms'.[25] Leaving aside for the moment the richly pictorial cast of his imagery, what is clear is that the pleasures of this trip are not to do with Rousseauesque meditation. They are steeped in a sensual and individualised response to sights, textures and smells (remember Simon in the Luxembourg). Nature was staked out as a total environment, and to step inside it was to move into a peculiarly individualising structure of perception; one that seemed made for and by you alone!

Finally, the environmental dimension to nature was pulled into sharp focus by a complex of material developments specific to the early 1840s. A nascent industrial hinterland beyond the existing tax barrier, factories belching out noxious pollutants, was one factor.[26] Even more dramatic was the effect of the massive fortifications constructed around the capital between 1841 and 1845, which destroyed many of the areas traditionally used as a playground by the 'poorer' classes of Paris.[27] The implications were twofold. First, the outskirts now registered a transitional *rite de passage* into nature, dramatising the symbolic distance of natural regeneration. Second, with the dispersion of working-class pleasures from the suburbs, this area became both literally and metaphorically a class barrier, restricting the benefits of the 'real' countryside to those with the resources to travel further out.

Travelling further, though, did become a real option for many bourgeois Parisians with the opening-up of the railway network from the mid-1840s.[28] In cultural terms train travel involved a double dynamic. If the obvious advantage was the opportunity to explore 'unsullied nature' distant from the capital, there was also the facility to bridge or close up distances. In other words, as important as the move out across the suburbs through geographical space was the possibility of remaining in the same spatial continuum. That counterpoint between moving (physically) away from the city and yet staying (psychologically) in touch with it encouraged some of the representational slippages between the experience of being in and looking at the countryside.

For while taking its cue from environmental equations, the trip to the country was never solely that. It was never simply dictated by the pressures of health – moral as well as physical. Whether in the form of the tourist guide, the *maison de campagne*, or even a railway ticket, it was simultaneously projected as a leisure commodity on offer to the urban consumer. By which I do not just mean that to be satisfactorily experienced nature had now to be bought, that it was only available to those with time and money to lavish on rustic pleasures, but that its instrinsic appeal was built on being a visual, a pictorial commodity. It fed off and into the range of images and entertainments marketing a spectacle of nature within the city. Being in the country and viewing images of nature in paint or print were equally set up as a pictorial treat, to be pleasurably consumed with the eyes.

## The urban consumption of nature

Against traditional accounts which tied the modernisation of Paris to Haussmannisation, it is being increasingly recognised that an ideology of metropolitan modernity was already in place in the early nineteenth-century city. Once again the 1820s was a formative moment. During that decade a particular complex of material and social factors coalesced to generate a distinctive structure of self-consciously modern urban life. Indeed, it could be argued that this formation set the conditions for large-scale urban interventions later. Physically, the modern city was located to the north and south of the grand boulevards and especially around the boulevard des Italiens. To the north and west were clusters of new streets and luxury housing, much of it still in the process of construction. Here private enterprise worked hand in hand with innovative guidelines laid down by the state, the latter regulating road width, gaslighting and bitumen pavements.[29] To the south was the Stock Exchange and nearby the nexus of banking houses that supplied speculative investment capital for the recent land and building boom. On the boulevard and adjacent streets thronged a concentration of entertainments (like the Opéra on the rue Lepelletier), cafés (such as Tortoni's, also notorious as a black market in shares) and luxury goods businesses. The silk industry, complained one anxious town councillor, was deserting its base in the old commercial centre, hypnotically drawn by the wealth and glamour of the new quarters.[30] A similar phenomenon could be observed among art dealers. These traders in fancy goods, who marketed a wide spectrum of luxury novelties – paperweights, dolls and stationery as well as pictures and prints – crept insidiously towards Bourse and boulevard.[31]

Behind the logic of physical displacement lay the recognition of a dramatic reshaping of the economic and cultural topography of the city. At the same time, commercial initiatives did not simply follow and express forms of urban development, they brought to bear ideologies of personal consumption. These operated through precise cultural rituals and were integral to the experience of the modern city. For a graphic example, turn to the arcades, full, enthused contemporaries, of 'scintillating shops' and a 'coquettish public'.[32] These elegantly covered walkways, public yet free from the nuisance of traffic or beggars, were lined with enticing shop-window displays (exploiting the large glass window which was in itself a recent innovation). Visual allure was intensified by strips of mirror, often decorated, set to either side of the window, which cast flattering reflections back on the strolling viewer/flâneur. It was a visual-cum-spatial arrangement that engendered a series of linkages between promenading, looking, displaying and consuming. The mutual display of leisurely shoppers, especially women in the most up-to-date fashions, became integrated into the objectified spectacle of luxury consumption.

Across an expansive range of texts and commentaries addressing the city – guidebooks, anecdotal histories and sociologies, comic cuts, gossip columns – new building and urban pleasures, dynamic speculation and luxury commerce formed a signifying chain that delineated a unique cultural 'topography'.[33] In the eyes of these 'guides' to city life, what mattered for the initiated was a mode of spectatorship that could single out, sift and reassemble the meanings of public space. The emphasis, insistently, was on the surface of things, whether the gleam of gaslight or fancy building detail, whether the latest fashion in hats or alluring *articles de luxe* in the dealer window, as if the experience of modernity was written into the flow of visual objectifications. This Paris, dynamic yet unstable, was a rapid sequence of spectacles; to be grasped in the pleasure of a gaze that structured the ebb and flow between promenade and café, theatre and arcade.

How did the spectacle of nature fit into all of this? In fact landscape images were a recurrent feature of the luxury commodities and entertainments on offer in the city. They were a dominant item among the fancy goods and stationery of the dealer shops, a frequent accompaniment to illustrated books, ubiquitous in the scenery of the Opéra and diorama. To put it another way, for the Parisian stroller of the 1840s the picture of nature was a taken-for-granted component of urban existence. But how were such images consumed? The answer is complex, involving a number of overlapping strands. At one level certain elite responses were framed by the official ideologies of landscape perception and composition laid down in art manuals by Valenciennes and the like.[34] This was the response of the connoisseur and art professional. More generally, the reading of nature imagery was inflected both by metropolitan codes of consumption and those structures of environmental experience we have already discussed.

Take the diorama. A 'novelty' entertainment pioneered by Louis Daguerre from the early 1820s, the diorama involved large painted canvases radically transformed by the passage of different light effects.[35] Landscapes – storms, volcanoes, earthquakes – were very much to the fore in an 'event' that twinned reality and magic. On one occasion Daguerre incorporated real objects like a goat nibbling grass in front of a painted mountain panorama, and to his invited guests he offered a genuine Swiss breakfast.[36] Here was a play on illusionism whereby the experience of reality was set off against and disrupted by the recognition of a clever counterfeit. Such sensations were materially enhanced by the very brevity of the performance (each scene lasted only ten to fifteen minutes) and the spatial set-up, with a mysterious entrance to the auditorium via a darkened passage. In other words, the entertainment capitalised on the modes of visual consumption played out on the streets of the modern city, setting up the 'reality' of nature as the material for cunning transformations, scintillating surprises.

Related themes surface in the art reviews of the press. The significance or otherwise of art criticism is a contentious area. Certainly it gained notoriety in the early 1830s for vitriolic and politically coded attacks on the official institutions of art like the Academy and Salon jury. And quantitatively, its growth and its spread into the most unlikely places (children's revues, professional journals) was phenomenal. Having said that, it may well be that art reviews were historically less important as commentaries on art than as a form of 'popular' literary leisure that initiated a broad reading public into codes of Parisian 'taste' and culture. On landscape, topographical and picturesque, critics were deeply ambiguous. The genre was both discussed and dismissed, much liked as spectacle or event, yet, following the dictates of official aesthetic hierarchies, downgraded as art.[37] In tune with such assessments, analysis was rarely posed at an intellectual level; instead it consisted of long, bland and literal descriptions of the scene and how well it was depicted. ·The literalness, though, is rather misleading, for here as in the diorama there was a complex tension between the *artifice* of the object, its surface workmanship as a luxury commodity and the fantasy of immersion in the reality of its contents. Viewers were always being invited to step inside the picture, to test the solidity of the ground, the luminosity of the horizon, the shimmer of the leaves, against the benchmark of their own experience. The stategy of course relied upon an existing common sense of walks in the suburbs, trips to the fresh air and green valleys of Meudon or Montmorency. Thus criticism oscillated between the glossy surface of the well-crafted commodity and the 'realist' evocation of natural space. It activated an illusionistic rhetoric that plugged landscape as luxury consumption into the pleasures of getting out into the countryside.

To turn full circle. When guidebooks like Lemer's to Montomorency were lavish in painting word-pictures of the country, when country-house adverts insisted on views and panoramas, quite obviously they were tapping analogies with contemporary pictures of nature. They were, in part, making appeal to a pictorial vocabulary concerning composition and focus. But pictures of landscape, as we have seen, were never consumed in a vacuum, and in early nineteenth-century France were rarely consumed as art pictures as such. Instead they took their cue from the broader cultural circuit of metropolitan spectacle. In that sense, guidebooks and adverts were referencing less the picture as text than those structures of looking, those languages of perception precipitated within the modern city.

In conclusion, Thoré's *natura naturans* described not merely a set of objects to be admired and enjoyed, nor even a repertoire of social values. Rather, it described a structured mode of apprehension, both of the world and of oneself. Communing with nature could transcend in an urban garden – as with Simon in the picturesque Luxembourg – as well as in the wilds; it might involve a metaphorical excursion into the heart of a painting as much as a train ride out into the country. And though solitary, indeed private as an experience, this was a profoundly *social* relationship; shaped by conditions which placed the spectator in a particular relation to the dynamics of class and gender. Finally, on a less historical note, landscape here has been the metaphor for a more general analytical message; a message about the way we handle looking and its conditions of formation. It is time to have done with a commonsense that claims the visual as the primary property of pictures. In breaking the chains of that particular restrictive practice, we can turn our attention to all those other 'ways of seeing' that structure the experience of space and through which space structures social relations.

## Notes

1  *Journal Général d'Affiches, annonces judiciaires, légales et avis divers* (31 January 1840), p. 9.
2  Honoré Daumier. *Das Lithographische Werk*, ed. K. Schrenk, 2 vols. (Munich, 1977).
3  *Ibid.*, vol. 1, p. 509, from *Le Charivari* (30 May 1846).
4  G. Simmel, 'The metropolis and mental life', in P. K. Hatt and A. Riess, eds., *Cities and societies* (Glencoe, NY, 1961), pp. 635–46; and E. Durkheim, *Selected writings*, ed. and trans. A. Giddens (London, 1972), pp. 150–4.
5  See, for example, M. Castells, *The urban question. A Marxist approach*, trans. A. Sheridan (London, 1977), or more recently N. Smith, *Urban development: nature, capital and the production of space* (Oxford, 1984), or D. Massey, *Spatial divisions of labour: social structures and the geography of production* (London, 1984).
6  If anything, this central focus was reasserted in T. J. Clark's recent book, *The painting of modern life. Paris in the art of Manet and his followers* (London, 1984).
7  J. Simon, 'Souvenirs de jeunesse', in P. Audebrand, ed., *Faisons la chaîne* (Paris, 1890), pp. 3–4.
8  L. Marin, *L'Art des jardins et les mouvements de l'esprit humain* (Paris, 1970), p. 162.
9  Marquis d'Avèze (J. B. D. Mazade), *Distractions ou passetemps de l'aveugle de Luxembourg* (Paris, 1818), p. 6.
10  P. Cottin, *Thoré-Bürger peint par lui-même* (Paris, 1900), p. 36.
11  T. Thoré, *Salon de 1847* (Paris, 1847), pp. 80–1.
12  L. Daubanton, 'Rapport relatif aux entreprises de construction à Paris et à l'interruption des travaux depuis cette année', in *Mémoires statistiques de la ville de Paris* (Paris, 1829), vol. 4.
13  *Ibid.*, p. 39.

14   E. A. Ackerknecht, 'Anti-contagionism between 1821–1867', *Bulletin of the History of Medicine*, no. 5 (September–October 1948), pp. 562–93; L. Chevalier, ed., *Le Choléra, la première epidémie collective du XIX siècle* (Paris, 1958).

15   J. Gaillard, *Paris, la ville 1852–1870* (Paris, 1977), p. 561.

16   J. Pronteau, *Construction et aménagement des nouveaux quartiers à Paris 1820–1826*, extract from *Histoire des entreprises* (Paris, 1958), p. 15.

17   Trébuchet, 'Rapports généraux des travaux du Conseil de Salubrité depuis 1829 jusqu'en 1839', *Annales d'Hygiène publique et de la médecine légale*, (Paris, 1841) vol. 25, p. 75.

18   H. Meynadier, *Paris pittoresque et monumental* (Paris, 1843).

19   *Ibid.*, pp. 105–7.

20   In his *Mémoires* (Paris, 1905), pp. 368–9 and 399, Rambuteau maintained proudly that he had resisted all attempts to extend the city's tax barrier and that he had left the municipal budget well balanced (unlike his famous successor!). The parks designed or revised by Alphand under Haussmann (Buttes Chaumont, the Bois de Boulogne, etc.) were precise attempts to invent a countryside in the town, cunningly twinning artifice with reality. See A. Alphand, *L'Art des jardins* (Paris, 1885).

21   J. Janin, *The American in Paris or Heath's picturesque annual for 1843* (Paris, 1843), p. 241.

22   D. Mornet in *Le Sentiment de la nature de J. J. Rousseau à Bernardin de Saint-Pierre* (Paris, 1907), marshalled an impressive dossier of evidence to show the emergence of a 'modern feeling' for nature from the mid-eighteenth century, but his argument was underpinned by an entirely idealist conception of nature.

23   See, for example, the anonymous *Promenade ou itinéraire des jardins d'Ermenonville* (Paris, 1788); A. Thiébaut, *Voyage à l'île des peupliers* (Paris, 1799); M. le Normand, *Lettres à Sophie ou Itinéraire de Paris à Montmorency, à l'hermitage et à l'île des peupliers en passant par Chantilly* (Paris, 1813).

24   J. Lemer, *La Vallée de Montmorency – promenades sentimentales, histoire, paysages, monuments, moeurs et chroniques* (Paris, 1847).

25   *Ibid.*, préface, p. viii.

26   For one account of the growing industrial belt round Paris and its pollutant effect on the suburbs, see F. Bernard, *Fontainebleau et ses environs* (Paris, 1853), p. 3.

27   Le Roux de Luncy, 'Les fortifications', in L. Lurine, ed., *Les rues de Paris*, (Paris, 1844), vol. 2, p. 407 ff., and P. Lavedan, *Histoire de l'urbanisme (nouvelle histoire de Paris)* (Paris, 1975), p. 376.

28   K. A. Doukas, *The French railroads and the state* (New York, 1976), pp. 18–23.

29   Pronteau, *Construction et aménagement*; F. Loyer, *Paris XIXe siècle. L'Immeuble et la rue* (Paris, 1987), pp. 67–99.

30   P. Lavedan, *La Question du déplacement de Paris* (Paris, 1969), p. 19.

31   Dealers mainly developed out of artisanal trades like framing, gilding, restoring and stationery suppliers into traders in prints, pictures and all kinds of fancy goods. Susse brothers, one of the leaders in the field and located just opposite the Bourse, marketed a sumptuous range from paintings – for sale or hire – to engravings, lithographs, bronzes, religious books, keepsakes, artists' models and daguerrotypes. By 1842 about a quarter of the dealers listed in the commercial almanacs were orientated towards the new quarters.

32   E. Berthet, 'Rue et passage du Caire', in Lurine, ed., *Rues de Paris*, vol. 1, p. 250, and A. Cler, 'Rue Lepelletier', *Rues de Paris* vol. 1, p. 382. Also see W. Benjamin, *Charles Baudelaire. A lyric poet in the high era of capitalism*, trans. H. Zohn (London, 1973), pp. 36–7, 157–9.

33   These texts include Chevalier Jacob-Kolb, *Le Frondeur ou observations sur les moeurs de Paris et des provinces au commencement du XIX siècle* (Paris, 1829); A. Luchet, *Esquisses dediées au peuple parisien* (Paris, 1830); Pluchonneau aîné, *Paris aujourd'hui. Poème historique des monuments érigés, achevés ou embellis de la capitale* (Paris, 1844); Meynadier, *Paris pittoresque et monumental*; Lurine, ed., *Les rues de Paris*, and perhaps most influential, D. Gay (pseud. Vicomte de Launay), *Les Lettres Parisiennes 1836–1848*, vols. 4 and 5 of *Oeuvres complètes* (Paris, 1860–61).

34   P. H. de Valenciennes, *Elémens de perspective pratique à l'usage des artistes suivis de Refléxions et Conseils à un Elève sur la peinture et particulièrement le Paysage* (Paris, 1800). Many of Valenciennes's injunctions were implemented in the official training programme for a *Grand prix du paysage*

historique set up in 1816.

35 A. and H. Gernsheim, *L.-J.-M. Daguerre. The history of the diorama and the daguerreotype* (New York, 1968), pp. 14–38.

36 *Ibid.*, pp. 30–1.

37 See, for example, *Journal des Artistes* (31 August 1828), p. 133, or C. Lenormant, *Salon de 1831* (Paris, 1831), p. 77, for an attack on landscape as a genre for the incompetent; or G. Planche, *Etudes sur l'école française* (Paris, 1855), vol. 1, pp. 189–90. The descriptive approach to landscape can be found in the reviews of Decamps, Janin, Laviron, Gautier, Planche, Haussard and Thoré, among others.

# 11

# The alphabetic universe: photography and the picturesque landscape
## John Taylor

## Introduction

It is illusory to develop beliefs and responses to landscape photography: it does not exist. This assertion does not contest that people walk about the land and sometimes take photographs or look at them. What it does contest is that there is an underlying reality to either landscape or photography and that we can know them by studying them directly or in isolation. Photographs do not offer a simple window on to the world 'out there'; nor is landscape anything and everything seen from the top of a hill. To imagine their relationship in landscape photography we have to study *practices*.[1]

What follows is an examination of the conditions for the meaning of landscape photography within new relations of commodity, class and leisure in the period *c*. 1885–1925. Firstly, there is the currency of the photograph as the small change of the growing tourist industry. This involved the combination of machines (railways, bicycles and cameras) with variable increases in leisure for different sectors or classes of society which may be subdivided into fractions. The countryside as a play-ground for holidaymakers came under increasing pressure from the newly mobile fractions of class. This pressure meant new meanings and importance for who could see the ideal of the landscape; who could 'take' it; who should protect it and what should be preserved.

Secondly, the essay looks at the attempts of two art photographers, H. P. Robinson (1830–1901) and P. H. Emerson (1856–1936), to save the paradigm of the ideal in their work. They demonstrated individualistic, class-based responses to the threat of trade.

Thirdly, there is a brief mention of the organised and quasi-scientific approach to preserving the ideal against the encroachments of commerce by the photographic survey groups.

Fourthly, there is an account of the pressure group known as SCAPA

– The Society for Checking the Abuses of Public Advertising – which was founded in 1893 and lasted until the beginning of the Second World War. SCAPA is an example of how the combination of middle-class people was able to establish a legal framework for the valuation of the aesthetic ideal of landscape. This lobbying and the effective but loose support of other pressure groups who were also active at the local and national levels produced legislation that benefited the art and record photographers. They themselves tended to be locked in the discourses on art and science, and did not understand the limitations this placed upon their practice.

And finally there is a section on landscape and patriotism. Both the organised groups and individual photographers believed there was a close link between the English landscape and the sense of the whole nation. As a factor of nationalism, the concept of landscape seems to be beyond sectional interest and to be unbound by time. The purpose here is to show that neither is the case: the idea of landscape remains a powerful tool in the struggle for cultural hegemony amongst the class fractions.

## Landscape, trade and tourism

In the 1870s, during the period of wet plates, it had been difficult to 'take' a landscape. Photographers had to be strong to carry the bulk of the equipment – a dark tent, a camera stand, a box of chemicals, another for the camera, developing gear and attachments, and another for glass plates. The photographer had also to be thick-skinned, because of the interest the activity aroused in the countryside, the commotion of sending a lad to fetch water, and the 'terror' to 'well regulated establishments and innocent people' of seeing the 'dreadful' photographer 'steeped in strange odours and stained with spots'. No irony was intended in describing this as a 'campaign'.[2]

The photographer had also to be relatively wealthy. In the 1880s a complete photography outfit could easily cost more than £40, which was as much as a farm labourer earned in a whole year. Even someone in the lower middle classes, such as a clerk, would be well paid on £200 a year.[3] Photography was still the hobby of the better-off, the middle classes with professional incomes or private means. In 1878 the introduction of the dry plate freed the photographer from so much work in the field – but there remained still the cost and bulk of stand cameras. It is only with the mass production of hand cameras, particularly the Kodak of 1888 which separated the snapshooter from the technology of developing and printing, that a new market for photography was invented.

It was at this time that photography changed from being a 'cottage industry' into one of the 'ordinary' enterprises of the day, organised along factory lines.[4] Three measures of the growth of the industry and the hobby are the census figures for those people employed in photography; the numbers of firms selling photographic goods, and the growth of the photographic societies.

The first entry for photographers is in the census of 1851, when there were just fifty-one professionals. By 1861 this number had grown to 2,534, which would have served the small community of patrons. The business expanded gradually till 1881 when there were 6,661 employees, with a large increase by 1901 when the number stood at 14,999. The number levelled off somewhat by 1911 when there were 16,915 employees. In addition, there were numerous dependent trades and occupations.

Another indication of the change in the industry is the percentage number of women employees. In 1861 this was 6.6 per cent of the work-force. Once photography was industrialised, more women were employed to pack, label and despatch, act as receptionists, and perform low-level jobs in developing and printing. Because of the concentration of industry in factories the percentage of women workers there would have been much higher than in the High Street portrait studios. As a total of the labour force in 1901, women workers made up 26 per cent, and nearly 70 per cent in 1911.

The growth in number of firms can be seen in the index of advertisers in the British Journal Photographic Almanac. There were 142 firms in 1881, and 246 in 1891. A decade later the number fell back to 225 because during the 1890s there had been bankruptcies forced upon the industry by its own success.

The expansion in trade had reduced profits at a time of rising expenses and costs of production. The market also shifted away from professional portraiture towards the amateurs.

In 1881 there were only twenty photographic societies listed in the Almanac (though this list was not exhaustive), and they were in the large cities. By 1891 the number had increased to 172 and ten years later increased again to 229. Noticeable also is the diffusion into the towns and suburbs, with a marked shift away from the title of 'society' or 'association' to the less exclusive title of 'photographic club' or even 'camera club'.

It seemed to the privileged middle-classes that this mass market had suddenly sprung up. It seemed to be spreading everywhere owing to the combination of extended railway networks, cheap fares, increased income and leisure in half-days, bank holidays and even, for some, annual summer holidays of a week or more.[5]

The mobility of people, and so the pressure on the countryside, was greatly increased by the bicycle. In 1887 there were at least 300,000 machines in use, twenty cycling publications and hundreds of local clubs in various parts of the country.[6] The Cyclists' Touring Club offered the travelling photographer information not only about moderately priced hotels but also advice on hotels that would provide darkrooms and 'a candle lamp to change plates as well'.[7] The CTC had built up a membership of 22,000 in ten years, and had 1,000 hotels under contract. It claimed to be a better alliance for photographers than the Pedestrian and General Tourists' Club, which was newly established and already had 700 hotels under contract. It was only the CTC which offered the benefits of conjoining two machines.[8]

The mass market did not destroy the elite market. On the contrary, the proliferation of goods allowed minute differences in class fractions. Status could still be signalled through the purchase of an object that was predicated upon relatively more income as well as time and education for its use. In the 1890s an enthusiast for hand-cameras warned buyers not to expect a half-guinea camera to produce a landscape worthy of an art photographer.[9] Such a camera probably lacked even a shutter – and the photographer was advised to spend money on the best quality lens for the 'natty' camera, just as he would for the field camera, if he had any serious expectation of 'taking' a landscape. The message was clear. New commodities did not bring higher status. Indeed, their relatively low technology might exclude their owners from the landscape, and so it was important to keep going 'up market'.

After all, even the half-educated had some sense of the picturesque; but this was supposed by their superiors in class and education to be so feeble that it was the subject of ridicule, using dialect as a mark of lower-class tradesmen. These people were supposed to have so little sense of the value of the picturesque landscape that they would casually destroy it for profit. One fictional character, Silas Lapham, 'rose' by means of paint which was used by advertisers to daub signs all over the country. Silas is made to say, 'There ain't any man enjoys a sightly bit of nature – a smooth piece of interval with half-a-dozen good-sized wine-glass elms in it – more than I do. But I ain't a-going to stand up for any ugly rock I come across, as if we were all a set of dumn Druids.'[10]

Those who could see 'beauty spots' or picturesque 'bits' often described them in florid prose, but at the same time seemed to draw upon a standard set of types that could be pictorial or picturesque. In 1884 it was said that suburbia might be growing but within five or six miles of every photographer's door there were abbeys, ancient places, birches, brooks, canals, cattle, churches, cottages, crags, crosses, dingles, farms, ferns, foxgloves, gables, ivy, lanes, locks, oaks, ponds, rustic bridges, rustics at work, tombs, watermills, windmills, walls and woods.[11]

The pace of destruction was relentless, but not catastrophic. By 1899 the photographer had to search for the picturesque, but it was still possible to find 'a few villages and hamlets which seem to belong to past centuries – fresh looking plaster and stucco are there unknown; fashion has not quite ousted primitive dress, nor has the din of factories disturbed the sleepy aspect of the surroundings'.[12] There follows a description of the flora at the heart of England: the luxuriant growth of trees, creepers, hedges and mosses; the special mix of light and shade; the typology of meadows, banks, gates, a moated ruin, an orchard, and a quaint old duck house amongst the 'score more unnamed objects' that made up the 'photographic paradise'.

But the relentless destruction of this world was alarming. The 'happy' and 'contented' villages were now stripped of their trees, and cut up into roads, railways and building plots.[13] The picturesque lanes and cottages of Kent and Surrey had been knocked down, and in their place were built 'regular, ugly houses . . . monuments to perpetuate the confidence of capitalists in "jerry" builders'. Photographers had a duty to picture this world before it disappeared beneath sprawling villas.

Photographers had long practised the salvation of the picturesque. In the 1860s tourists were said to be satisfied if they could see a beauty spot 'tolerably well' from the road.[14] It was the business of the photographer to 'scramble' for the 'superb' view – which might then be turned into a picture-postcard. The idle tourists would buy this not because it represented their view but because it was the ideal view.

The Edenic landscape could be saved in pictures, so it was possible to avoid the countryside altogether, and still celebrate that aspect of national life. It seemed enough that someone had witnessed the scene at some time, and taken a photograph of it. These pictures then became talismans or touchstones, evidence that landscape really did exist. The viewers could stay at home, and still be incorporated in the array of feelings that would be evoked by landscape. In a photographic book of 1902 entitled *One hundred gems of English scenery*, we read, 'those whose tastes or means do not allow such visits may be in a position to surround themselves, at merely nominal costs, with faithful presentments of quiet scenic beauty, such as can never be excelled by any country in the world'.[15]

## The art photographers

Before we can look at the practice of Robinson and Emerson as case studies in relation to the threat to the landscape, there are three general conditions that have to be outlined. Firstly the discourse on photography in the nineteenth century was borrowed from those of art and science. Everything that was significant had to be said in one or other language, or else be consigned to the level of trivial speech. Emerson wrote, 'we in the photographic world should be either scientists or artists', aiming to increase the number of facts or to give aesthetic pleasure.[16] The journals of the period are full of speech in one mode or the other; they are rarely mixed and are lightened only by journalistic chatter. The discourses of science and the arts were those of the professions, and so the voice of the journals also preserves the elite public voice of professionals.

This leads into the second point: running through the journals are different sets of fears. The professional man, or gentleman, or the man of leisure who at one time was proud to be called on amateur (and therefore free of the taint of trade) was now anxious not to associate himself with the new mass market of amateurs, or 'dabblers' as Emerson called them.

The gentleman photographer also felt threatened by the attempts of the trade to organise itself as a profession – but he was probably not as nervous as the tradesmen themselves who expended a lot of energy in speaking out against amateurs who damaged business in the High Street. Professional photographers complained, but were relatively slow to organise – emerging as a Qualifying Association as late as 1901. They were many years behind other bureaucratic, financial and manufacturing groups: for instance, the accountants were organised in 1880, clerks-of-works in 1882, auctioneers and estate agents in 1886, secretaries in 1891, decorators and interior designers in 1899.[17]

Their complaints were mostly to do with loss of business, but their income also depended upon status. It was galling that the photographer could have a wide range of knowledge and yet be ranked no more than a 'butterman or a butcher . . . Local lawyers and doctors exlude him from the professional class, while society generally turns up its aesthetic nose and regards him simply as a shopkeeper.'[18]

Thirdly, the class status of the photographer could be measured through the speciality of the objects he produced. Emerson, again, put this most succinctly. He said that the order of rank for pictorial representation was 'an oil painting, then a photogravure, and finally a good photograph, one which is a picture, and which is printed in platinotype' – a permanent and relatively expensive process.[19] He believed that uneducated and inartistic people were spoiling photography: 'nine-tenths of photographs are no more works of Art than the chromos, lithos and bad paintings which adorn the numerous shops and galleries'. What offended Emerson so much was the abundance of cheap goods. He went to great lengths to produce his own work in books of photogravures, and in limited editions of 500 to 750 copies or de-luxe editions of 50 to 150 copies.[20]

We have to see the position of landscape photography within this interlocked regime that is derived from the discourses on art and science, the struggle for status between trades, professions and amateurs, and the determination to maintain a hierachy within picture-making as a proof against the mass market.

In their different ways, Robinson and Emerson were both engaged in this project. They were opposed to each other's methods and theories, but their disagreements about art now seem less interesting than their strategies to sustain the differences between class fractions. The idea was always to preserve the landscape from incursion by the lower middle class.

H. P. Robinson was a specialist in photography by rule and the combination of negatives to build up a picture. He favoured landscape scenes with figures, and was certain about the need to study the 'masters'. He said, 'study art if you want to make pictures; you cannot learn by studying nature alone . . . Anyone who has not studied from books and pictures does not see ten per cent of the beauties of nature; he does not know how to see them.'[21]

He wrote eleven books on photography, many of which were revised and went through several editions. The most popular, *Pictorial effect in photography*, was published four times in England from 1869–93, twice in the USA (1881 and 1892) and once in France (1885) and Germany (1886). It is written in the tradition of venerable treatises on art, and quotes extensively from eighteenth-century writers on the Picturesque and the Grand Tradition in fine art, and also from mid-nineteenth-century authors of handbooks for art students, as well as John Ruskin.[22]

This work was dismissed by Emerson as 'a senseless jargon of quotations from literary writers on Art matters, a confused bundle of lines'.[23] The difficulty may have been that his references were relatively old-fashioned. They were so steeped in art that they failed to notice that poets and artists, and critics such as Ruskin, had complained bitterly about industry. In *Pictorial effect* Robinson never once used Wordsworth who was later said to have been the common father of all those who 'squealed' about the desecration of the landscape because he addressed the problem of the railways.[24] Robinson, on the contrary, showed a complete lack of interest in the quickened commercial life of his times.

For him, the countryside was always and already Arcadia. It was peopled with 'folk' who were in harmony with nature. It was a countryside easily imagined from the drawing-room, a view of nature in harness, the conjunction of husbandry and idyll. In Arcadia there was no work to be done, only a rustic life to be lived. And because 'rusticity' was a concept that was only ordinary to the educated classes, Robinson never used 'peasant girls' in his pictures. For his idealisations he chose to dress up the daughters of the gentry. This once caused an embarrassing scene – not for Robinson, but for the gamekeeper who failed to recognise the daughter of his employer dressed up as a country girl, and roughly ordered her off the 'sacred precincts of real property'.[25] For Robinson the incident was a measure of his success at the art of 'travesty'. What Robinson achieved was an imaginative retreat into the conventional landscape picture.

In contrast, what Emerson did was travel rather like an explorer into the unconventional, unpicturesque landscape of the Norfolk and Suffolk Broads.[26] And yet, as we shall see, this strategy was quite like Robinson's; it was still a retreat, moving away from the exigencies of the modern world to a place where they as yet scarcely signified. He removed himself from the scene of the struggle over the countryside to a boat on the Broads, where he lived at one stretch for over a year, and where it was possible to keep up a (bohemian) middle-class life and keep it distinct from any other.

Settled on board a fishing smack, Emerson and his friends settled down to 'drink to the Arts in bumpers of claret.'[27] He noted that during the afternoon 'natives' came down to watch them: 'they stared at us as if we, not they, were the "heathen"'. An exotic place, the Broads; and a place for the internal migration of the wealthy who could cruise the waterways, and pass by the incredulous 'natives' when it suited them. For Emerson, the world beyond the Broads meant not only 'civilisation' but 'boredom'.

Near contemporaries thought Emerson's photographs were 'ugly'.[28] But this aesthetic assessment of the work – how far away it stands from the ideal of the picturesque – fails to acknowledge that Emerson did behave like a wealthy tourist. What was unusual was his pleasure in the link between tourism and underdevelopment.

On the Broads, the differences between the classes were sharp. In Norfolk conditions for the labourers were the worst in the country, and in 1899 it was the third most pauperised county in England; in Suffolk the wages for labourers were the worst in the country.[29] It was easy for Emerson to meet 'paupers' and buy food for next to nothing. At the same time, East Anglia was an enormous game reserve: two out of every three country seats were let out for game, and in 1911 the county was the most densely keepered in the land.[30] Between these extremes, the tourists could find places that suited them, and avoid the others. The working class on day excursions stayed in Yarmouth; the middle-class families who wanted a seaside holiday went further north; adventurous young men – 'bent on fishing, shooting, sailing and photographing' could hire cheap boats for the day; the businessman could relax there for two or three weeks.[31] Emerson's lengthy visits made him no less of a tourist – he maintained that economic relation and mobility with his exotic surroundings.

Both Robinson's and Emerson's responses to the commercial pressures on the land were no doubt personally satisfying. What is unusual about them is not that they retreated – the whole enthusiasm for the picturesque testifies to the desirability of this – only that they were able to do it so fully: Robinson into a version of pastoral and Emerson into the wilderness. And though both wrote about photographic theory, it is not surprising that both were unable to conceptualise their practice as no more than consumer choice amongst the touristic resorts. They wanted to make their marks as *individual* art-photographers, and they succeeded in this – partly because much of our own understanding of photographic history derives from the art of discourses of their times.

## The photographic survey

It was this discourse on science that underlay the record work of the

many photographers who banded together to photograph in a systematic way the buildings and customs of their counties. The ways in which
the surveys interlaced with other groups, or interested individuals, is
perhaps difficult to know – but the results of their work were always
intended to be deposited in reference libraries – guardians of public
knowledge. Moreover, the survey work was definitely local; and as we
shall see shortly, some people had the idea to create a complete network
of local groups which could be persuaded to add weight to the movement to save the countryside. The local groups would combine into a
national network, and the appeal of the countryside was also made at this
level. It was not a matter of local interest only – the picturesque landscape
was a national ideal and a national asset.

The extent of national wealth was so wide that the survey groups were
in danger of working under the burden of trying to record everything. The
most complete expression of this plan was made in 1889 before any of
the County surveys had begun, and the necessary limits placed on what
would be practically possible. It was proposed that a 'Society should
keep a library of great albums containing a record as complete as can be
made . . . of the present state of the world.'[32] The society would not be
the resting home for art photographs, or anything that smacked of
personal interpretation. The photographs would 'carry a guarantee of a
real scientific knowledge of photography instead of being a sort of charm
or fetish bought for money'.[33] The records would be kept by 'one of its
highest and most trusted officials, a keeper of the albums', who would
look after the photographs, see them mounted and labelled, with every
precatuion taken for their preservation.[34]

The subjects to be photographed would be all 'social states'; all types of
faces; all aspects of work; all beasts; all flora; measurements of exact rates
of all growth; the present aspect of all buildings and all natural objects, for
even 'rocks are not eternal'.

Undeterred, and perhaps even inspired by this plan, the first Photographic Survey was established in Warwickshire in 1890.[35] The photographs of ancient and notable buildings, as well as customs, were deposited in the Birmingham City Reference Library. However, the emphasis
here cannot be upon the history of this group, or this movement, but
upon the connections that were made between the methodical survey
workers and other groups which were more active in local propaganda
and politics. The case of the Photographic Survey of Surrey is instructive.
It was founded in 1902 with the aim 'to snatch from oblivion the monuments of a whole county', as well as faces, manners, amusements and

ceremonies of local people. The programme was set out in alphabetical order: to preserve 'Records of Antiquity, Anthropology, Buildings of Interest, Geology, Natural History, Passing Events of local and historical importance, Portraits of Notable Persons, Old Documents, Rare Books, Prints, Maps and Scenery, so as to give a comprehensive Survey of what is valuable and representative of the County of Surrey'.[36] They seem to have had some success: by 1909 3,000 prints had been deposited in the Public Library at Croydon, and 7,000 people a year were consulting them. It seemed that photography could be the dispassionate record of data, free from the bias of taste and trade, since (it was asserted) the process 'nothing extenuated, nor aught put down in malice'. In principle, photography could measure the world.

In 1906 some of the photographs were used in an 'Old and Picturesque Wimbledon' Exhibition which was organised by the John Evelyn Club.[37] This was a pressure group founded in 1903 for the preservation of local sites. The Club was the first group organised along the lines of the Local Amenities Association proposed by the 1898 Parliamentary group for Concerted Action in Defence of the Picturesque and Romantic Elements in Our National life.[38] The group proposed in general to protect rural scenery, landscape and town prospects from 'disfigurement'; establish commons and parks; preserve buildings and places which were of interest because of their age, beauty or historical and literary association; save wild animals and flowers; and to 'assert the importance on the broad grounds of public policy of maintaining beauty, simplicity, dignity and interest in the aspect of out-of-door Britain'.

In particular they drew up a draft proposal for local societies to be known as Local Amenities Associations. The purpose was to create a seamless and impregnable web of interested parties – not centrally controlled, but all impelled by the same patriotic urge and with the same set of standards:

the fabric which we contemplated (in the John Evelyn Club) has its base in the village green and its apex in Westminster. Midway would lie the great Societies (such as The Commons and Footpaths Preservation Society etc).[39] A network of District Associations would represent locally the various aims and interests with which these central societies have several concerns, while a Parliamentary Amenities Party in each branch of the Legislature would always be ready to aid in those cases where State action is requisite.[40]

So the grass-roots John Evelyn Club, with its intellectual origins and support in Westminster, set out to co-opt other active groups, such as the Photographic Survey of Surrey, in the salvation of the countryside. In this way the positivists' methods were put to use by utilitarians at the local and national levels of politics. It did not matter at all that in 1889 photography had been misrecognised as an unbiased tool that could map the visible universe. The belief had set the Survey groups in motion, and little more than a decade later the civic-minded were impressively mobilised to put that body of work to use.

## The Society for Checking the Abuses of Public Advertising (SCAPA)

The different groups did not need to be formally linked. Their interests overlapped, and they held the picturesque landscape as common coin amongst them. They were also averse to what someone in SCAPA called 'the catchpenny alphabetification of the visible universe'.[41] A train journey into the countryside was an affront because of the advertising billboards. In 'Impressions of English Landscape' as seen from the railway the author Stephen Crane wrote, 'after passing through a patent mucilage, some hams, a South African Investment Company, a Parisian millinary firm, and a comic journal, I alighted at a new and original kind of corset. On my return journey the road almost continuously ran through soap.'[42]

In response, some culturally and civically active people combined to create legal restrictions upon 'disfigurement' of the landscape by 'spectacular' advertisements. The need to mobilise these people was recognised by the Member of Parliament Phipson Beale, who was precise in identifying their class interests: he suggested sticking a little pill advertisement in the centre of every landscape-painting in the Royal Academy.[43] The intention was to awaken people to the need to save the scenery from 'a limited class' which was destroying sensibilities and architectural effects paid for by public money.[44] Advertisements had to be curbed 'to protect and promote the picturesque simplicity of rural and river scenes and the dignity and propriety of our towns'.[45] Phipson Beale had known whom he could rely upon: the first President of SCAPA from 1893 to 1901 was the Royal Acadamician, Alfred Waterhouse.

We can see from the various names that were suggested for SCAPA that the members were not certain about the best tactics – whether to foreground the elusive quality of beauty or the more legislative 'checking abuse'. The first suggestion had been 'The Society for the Protection of the Picturesque'.[46] Other similar names were 'The Society for the Protection of Natural Beauties' and 'The Beautiful World Society'. At the other extreme was the title 'The Society for Controlling Advertisements and

Protecting Amenities'.[47]

The key to the success of SCAPA was the ability of its members to see the landscape not as the subject of artistic whim, but as an *amenity* that was being wrecked precisely by the flowing of the lower classes.

In Black's *Handbook of Sussex* the author described a beauty spot near Brighton as ruined by the *apparatus* of holidaymaking – 'a switchback railway and such like tea-garden apparatus, and a glaring display of hideous and mendacious advertisements' turning the 'noble scene' into a 'Cockney Brocken Haus'.[48] To combat this destruction was not a question of sentiment, but one of utility: 'It should be discussed in a business like spirit as if the particular utility in question could be bought over the counter or priced in Trade Lists.'[49]

Treating the landscape as a commodity was pragmatic and philosophic. As the President of the Royal Academy, Sir Frederic Leighton, recognised it was fruitless to blame the barbarism upon the tradesmen when manufacturers, landowners and farmers were all benefiting from it.[50]

The intimate link between powerful interests and despoliation was always recognised by SCAPA, and was something of a moral paradox. Manufacturers who were responsible for 'the systematic attacks on beauty and repose' were also men of taste, art collectors, lovers of picturesque travel and philanthropists. But in the morning they would sign cheques for thousands of pounds for the Garden City Movement, and in the afternoon, in another chequebook, would sign drafts just as large for the advertising industry.[51]

In 1893, however, it was the advertising trade itself which felt under threat. At a meeting of The United Bill-Posters Association, SCAPA members were called 'busybodies' who, like their master John Ruskin, would abolish the railways because they did not harmonise with their idea of the beautiful: 'these people have no sympathy with the bitter cry of the poor, but their feelings are lacerated at the sight of an ordinary letter pillar and lamp post'.[52]

SCAPA was seeking to bring the advertisers within the law, impose taxes and rates upon them, to have Parliament and Local Authorities control them in the same way they controlled butchers, bakers, cabbies, publicans and theatre managers. It had the support of the political philosopher W. E. H. Lecky who, in his *Democracy and liberty*, claimed that the state had a duty to protect its citizens against the defacement by advertisements of 'the beauty of a quarter', in the same way that there was pressure to act against noise by the Association for the Suppression of

Street Noises, and against smoke by The Coal Smoke Abatement Association.[53] The most telling pressure from all these groups was for the protection of amenities, and SCAPA's novel contribution was to seek the protection of the amenity of sight. This ran counter to the current position: in 1987 it was said, 'the law is well settled that a mere amenity such as that of a view cannot be protected'.[54] But twenty years later the activities of the pressure groups made themselves felt, and Parliament passed the first Advertisements Regulation Act, the first public statute that recognised the claim of the 'seeing eye', and treated scenery as a national asset.[55]

The Act sought to regulate advertisements that would 'affect injuriously the amenities of a public park or pleasure promenade, or to disfigure the natural beauty of a landscape'.[56] However, when Local Authorities tried to frame by-laws under the Act, this last phrase proved to be a stumbling block. Either 'a landscape' was too wide in extent, or it was too narrow and did not protect roadsides and rail embankments.[57] The Act was amended in 1910, and the indefinite article removed – but this change was still not enough for the framing of precise by-laws, and so the act was altered again in 1925.[58] The final version banned advertisements that would injuriously affect

a) the amenities of a public park or pleasure promenade; or
b) the natural beauty of a landscape; or so as to disfigure or injuriously affect
c) the view of rural scenery from a highway or railway or from any public place or water; or
d) the amenities of any village within the district of a rural district council; or
e) the amenities of any historic or public building or monument or any place frequented by the public solely and chiefly on account of its beauty or historic interest.

Under the Act 'rural scenery' meant exactly that; any fields, hedgerows, woods, streams, downs and farms and other 'familiar things'. It did not mean 'beauty spots'. Indeed, the law made no attempt to define the terms 'natural beauty', 'landscape', 'amenities', 'disfigure' or 'injuriously affect'.[59] The meaning of the words were left to the 'understanding of ordinary reasonable folk and, in the last resort, to the decision of magistrates'. It was said that there is nothing 'artistic' or 'highbrow' about any of these terms, and though opinions might differ, 'we most of us know what kind of out-door scenery is pleasant to the eye'.

The Acts were not as fierce as SCAPA might have wished in the 1890s. By 1907 the cities were effectively given up as a lost cause; though 'many' would defend the beauty and dignity of town scenery, 'all are agreed that the defacement of the rural landscape is a public wrong'.[60] By 1932 only around 20 per cent of municipal boroughs, district and county boroughs had been able to frame by-laws precisely enough for the Home Office. In contrast, the counties of England and Wales made their by-laws in the terms of the Act, and so by 1933 more than 93 per cent of counties had by-laws in place.[61] The validity of the Act was tested in 1926 by the United Billposting Company which took Somerset County Council to court, and lost. The judgement said it was possible for the by-law to apply to the whole of a county because 'the very subject of the by-laws involved aesthetic consideration on which greater precision was not to be expected'.[62]

SCAPA had helped to establish in law protection for things or concepts such as amenities and landscapes which remained ill-defined but which nonetheless would be understood by reasonable people, or if not, then by magistrates. The class basis of the understanding exists in SCAPA's language – terms such as 'dignity', 'decency', 'comeliness', 'property', 'congruity', and 'repose'.[63] But SCAPA was at pains to say that its tastes existed in all classes and leapt over class differences about use and access to the land by declaring and establishing in law that the protection of the 'beauty and dignity of aspect' was a 'patriotic duty', since 'the best part of the wealth of the country is the goodliness of its aspect'.

The shift from the local to the national is not at all surprising, since they are coterminous. SCAPA made this explicit:

It is absurd to talk of English freedom and prosperity and the greatness of our Imperial mission, if no regard be paid to the beauty of the landscape, to dignity and propriety in the common round. We are proud of our fatherland, we care for our countrymen, and wish to make the national domain pleasant and worthy of a great people.[64]

SCAPA had successfully appealed for landscape as more than a subject for those of an artistic temperament: it had appealed for the landscape at the nebulous but potent level of patriotism.

## Landscape and patriotism

The extraordinary activity of building and defending an empire seemed possible and worthwhile because of the tranquility of England – for that was how it was perceived. The Rev P. H. Ditchfield, who was a prolific and popular antiquarian, enthused about 'the delicious calm and quietude of an Old English Village'.[65] In 1897 he wrote:

History tells us of the past glories of our race . . . We are the inheritors of all the conquests which they have achieved: and we are bound to hand down to future generations, unsullied and intact, the country and the Empire, and the national character commited to our keeping. Our land is the land of patriots, martyrs, sages and bards.[66]

Twenty years before, Henry James, on a visit to Kenilworth Castle in Warwickshire, had noticed something similar, though he had concept-ualised it more fully. From a distance Kenilworth had looked like a 'perfect picture', but on approaching he had found hawkers, paupers and beer shops.[67] Inside the Castle, things were no better: 'The very echoes of the beautiful ruin seemed to have dropped all their h's', susceptible, as most romantic sites in England, to 'constant cockneyfi-cation'. Here were tourists pushing, eating from newspapers and reading aloud from guidebooks; but even so 'there was still a good deal of old England in the scene'. Nearby was 'a quaintish village' and 'dark, fat meadows'. It seemed to James that in this 'richly complex English world', with ancient pictorial cottages and its tourists and trade, the present was always seen 'in profile,' and it was only the past that showed itself 'full face'. He looked about for the village stocks, was ready to take the modern vagrants for Shakespearian clowns, and was on the point of 'going into one of the ale-houses to ask Mrs. Quickly for a cup of sack'.

Shakespeare had become an industry. There were photographic books such as James Walter's *Shakespeare's home and rural life* (1874) and James Leon Williams's *The homes and haunts of Shakespeare* (1894). This book managed the contemporary scene so that it looked older than it was, using for instance old-timers in smocks – so keeping the modern world in profile and the theatrical representation of the past full-face. Through the choice of scenery and actors, a landscape could signify the past without the expectation of precision. Old buildings, old meadows, old men and old customs could all be photographed and reproduced, often expen-sively, in the latest reprographic techniques and still continue to stand for the past. It was as if the modern printing, and the artful faking of scenes, posing and other stage-like effects counted for nothing against the magical link made by the photographs with this imagined past. As long as there were no signs of modernity to spoil the effect of distance, the photographs seemed the perfect vehicles for time-travel. There had to be a necessary distance to suggest the pre-modern world, but there really was no need for it to be very great. The past of England pushed right up into the present, and that was one of her glories.

The eruption of the past into the present was carefully nurtured by the many local associations whose interests overlapped with those of SCAPA. Besides the naturalists' field clubs, natural science and scientific societies, there were antiquarian societies, archaeological societies, architectural associations, historical societies, Ruskin societies, various trusts and preservation societies for specific villages, moorlands, monuments and old towns and their neighbourhoods.[68] Photographers were encouraged to join in this poring over the English countryside, to help conserve and perpetuate 'all that is beautiful in the natural view'.[69] Every segment of society that was culturally active had some specialism to offer, so that the power of the different groups combined to raise the level of interest in the past of England to the $n^{th}$ degree. Various types of scientific enquiry, and historical method were combined with philosophical theory, so that a society could be set up for the purpose of 'beauty' as in the Beautiful Oldham Society, the Beautiful Warrington Society, the Society for the Preservation of the Beauty of Hythe and neighbourhood, and the National Conference for the Cult of the Beautiful in Beautiful Centres.

This enthusiasm had real effects – seen most sharply in time of war. In 1915, for instance, photographs were used to put this full face of ancient England to modern patriotic purposes. Batsford published a book of 125 photographs entitled *The English countryside*, and in an afterword (dropped in the second edition of 1933) readers were given a gloss on the work:

It is the past which has made the England of today, and the present is but its continuation. Prehistoric trackway, ancient village, sleepy town, the farmhouse in the hollow, the sheepfold on the hill – all have rendered their share in the making of England, and in the building up of that race whose sons are emulating on the battlefield the deeds of their forefathers set forth in quaint inscriptions on the walls of many a village church or in the mouldering records of ancient boroughs.[70]

And the face in profile, the modern world, was immediately incorporated into the ancient scene: when the war was over, the dead were returned to the village greens, parks and promenades in the form of names upon a memorial. Their symbolic return matched perfectly the symbolism of the greens: dead men had become mythic heroes in a land of myth.

## Notes

1  See John Tagg, *The burden of representation, essays on photographies and histories* (Macmillan, 1988).
2  Charles Allen Ferneley, 'Landscape photography', *British Journal Photographic Almanac* (1874). pp. 131–3.

3  W. J. Reader, *Professional men, the rise of the professional classes in nineteenth-century England* (Weidenfeld & Nicolson, 1966), p. 202.

4  J. A. Randall, 'Co-operative photography', *British Journal of Photography* (5 June 1896), p. 361.

5  See J. A. R. Pimlott, *The Englishman's holiday* (Faber & Faber, 1947 and 1976).

6  E. R. Shipton, 'The wheel and the camera', *The Amateur Photographer* (4 March 1887), p. 108.

7  E. R. Shipton, 'The wheel and the camera', *The Amateur Photographer* (11 March 1887), p. 120.

8  H. H. Griffin, 'Cycling and the camera', *The Amateur Photographer* (2 January 1885), p. 201.

9  J. Dormer, 'The apotheosis of the hand camera', *British Journal Photographic Almanac* (1894), p. 758.

10  'Mr. Howell's *The Rise of Silas Lapham*', cited in Richardson Evans, *An account of the Scapa society* (Constable, 1926), pp. 8–9.

11  Richard Keene, 'Stray thoughts about home work', *British Journal Photographic Almanac* (1884), pp. 168–9.

12  Rev. B. Holland, 'Out-of-the-way villages', *British Journal Photographic Almanac* (1899), p. 795.

13  John G. Horsey, 'Photographs as records of the past', *British Journal Photographic Alamanc* (1885), p. 113.

14  G. W. Wilson, 'Photography in the field', *British Journal Photographic Almanac* (1866), p. 67.

15  *One hundred gems of English scenery, a collection of permanent photographs* (The Graphotone Company, 1902), n.p.

16  P. H. Emerson, 'Science and art', *British Journal of Photography* (19 April 1889), p. 269.

17  G. Millerson, *The qualifying associations, a study in professionalisation* (Routledge & Kegan Paul, 1964), pp. 246–50.

18  J. Macer Wright, 'On the present position of photography in England', *British Journal Photographic Almanac* (1882), p. 147.

19  P. H. Emerson, 'Photography a pictorial art', *The Amateur Photographer* (19 March 1886), p. 139.

20  N. Newhall, *P. H. Emerson: the fight for photography as a fine art* (Aperture, 1975), pp. 262–3.

21  H. P. Robinson, 'Naturalism and photography', *British Journal Photographic Almanac* (1887), p. 81.

22  See John Taylor, 'Henry Peach Robinson and Victorian theory', *History of Photography* (October 1979), pp. 295–303.

23  Emerson, 'Photography a pictorial art', p. 138.

24  Cyril Sheldon, *A history of poster advertising* (Chapman & Hall, 1936), p. 101.

25  A. Pringle, *Sun artists: Mr. H. P. Robinson*, no. 2 (January 1890), p. 13.

26  See Sarah Knights, 'Change and decay: Emerson's "social order" ', pp. 12–20, and John Taylor, 'Landscape and leisure', pp. 73–82, in Neil McWilliam and Veronica Sekules, ed., *Life and landscape: P. H. Emerson, art and photography in East Anglia 1885–1900* (University of East Anglia, 1986).

27  P. H. Emerson, 'The log of "The Lucy" ', supplement to *The Amateur Photographer* (10 December 1886), pp. 1–3.

28  F. M. Sutcliffe, 'Dr. P. H. Emerson's work at Russell Square', *The Amateur Photographer* (8 June 1900), p. 444.

29  F. E. Green, *A history of the English agricultural labourer* (P. S. King & Sons, 1920), p. 109.

30  Pamela Horn, *The changing countryside in Victorian and Edwardian England and Wales* (Athlone Press, 1984), p. 47.

31  T. Coan, 'Bloater land', *British Journal Photographic Almanac* (1889), pp. 403–6.

32  Cosmo I. Burton, 'The whole duty of the photographer I', *British Journal of Photography* (11 October 1889), p. 668.

33  *Ibid.*

34  Cosmo I. Burton, 'The whole duty of the photographer II', *British Journal of Photography* (18 October 1889), p. 682.

35  'The photographic survey of Warwickshire', *The Amateur Photographer* (30 May 1890), p. 397.

36  'Photographic survey and record of Surrey', *A Beautiful World, The Journal of the Society for*

*Checking the Abuses of Public Advertising*, no. X (September 1909), pp. 196–7.

37  'Revised proposals for the formation of a local amenities association under the title of the John Evelyn Club for Wimbledon', *A Beautiful World*, no. 9 (May 1903), pp. 65–77; and 'Some working examples of local associations', *A Beautiful World*, no. X (September 1909), pp. 180–96.

38  For an account of this group see *A Beautiful World*, No. 9 (May 1903), pp. 59–65.

39  SCAPA promoted the objectives and received the support of the following societies: The Commons and Footpaths Preservation Society; The Metropolitan Public Gardens Association; The Kyrle Society; The Selbourne Society; The Society for the Preservation of Ancient Buildings; The National Trust for Places of Historic Interest and Natural Beauty; The Thames Preservation League; The Cockburn Association, Edinburgh; The English Branch of the League for the Preservation of Swiss Scenery; and kindred Associations in the Colonies, the United States, France and Switzerland. It promoted the objective of The Coal Smoke Abatement Association; The Garden City Association; The Co-Partnership Tenants Housing Council; and Co-Partnership Tenants Ltd, and also assisted the efforts of the Association (later Society) for the Suppression of Street Noises. See *A Beautiful World*, no. X (September 1909), p. 204.

40  'Some working examples of local associations', *A Beautiful World*, no. 9 (May 1903), p. 180.

41  'A general account of Scapa: its reason, aim and methods', *A Beautiful World*, no. X (September 1909), p. 234.

42  *A Beautiful World*, no. 9 (May 1903), p. 96.

43  Ibid., p. 40.

44  Ibid., p. 121.

45  *A Beautiful World*, no. I (1893), p. 29.

46  Richardson Evans, 'A retrospect (1893–1922) and a forecast', *A Beautiful World*, no. XI (November 1922), p. 4.

47  *A Beautiful World*, no. X (September 1909), p. 43.

48  'An appeal to the editors of guide books', *A Beautiful World*, no. X (September 1909), p. 55.

49  'A general account of Scapa: its reasons, aims and methods', *A Beautiful World*, no. X (September 1909), p. 225.

50  'Landscape spoiling', *British Journal of Photography* (20 July 1894), p. 449.

51  'The moral paradox', *A Beautiful World*, no. X (September 1909), p. 66.

52  Cited in *A Beautiful World* (no. I) (1893), p. 12.

53  W. E. H. Lecky, *Democracy and liberty*, vol. I, p. 167, cited in *A Beautiful World*, no. 6 (December 1896), pp. 7–8.

54  *Advertisement disfigurement: the law*, SCAPA pamphlet no. 4 (1930).

55  'A new principle planted in jurisprudence', *A Beautiful World*, no. X (September 1909), p. 27.

56  'Advertisement Regulation Act, 1907, bye-laws for local associations', *A Beautiful World*, no. X (September 1909), p. 115.

57  '*Advertisement Regulation Act, 1925*', SCAPA pamphlet no. I (1926), p. 15.

58  *Advertisement disfigurement: the law*.

59  *The Advertisement Regulation Acts: their scope and limitations*, SCAPA pamphlet no. 5 (1929).

60  *A Beautiful World*, no. X (September 1909), p. 26.

61  *The Scapa Society annual report* for 1930, p. 4.

62  See *Advertisement disfigurement: the law* and *The Scapa Society annual report* for 1929, p. 5.

63  'A general account of Scapa: its reason, aim and methods', *A Beautiful World*, no. X (September 1909), p. 225.

64  Ibid., p. 224.

65  P. H. Ditchfield, *Our English villages, their story and their antiquities* (Methuen, 1889), p. 4.

66  P. H. Ditchfield, *The story of our English towns* (George Redway, 1897), p. 302.

67  Henry James, 'In Warwickshire (1877)', in *English hours*, 1st edn 1905 (Oxford University Press, 1981), pp. 113–27.

68 'A first list of Local Associations which have concern with some or more of the subjects indicated'. *A Beautiful World*, no. X (September 1909), pp. 198–9.

69 'Landscape spoiling', *British Journal of Photography* (20 July 1894), p. 450.

70 E. C. Pulbrook, *The English countryside* (Batsford, 1915), Afterword, n.p.

# 12

# Landscape as popular culture
## Fred Inglis

### I

The town-and-landscape is the predominant stuff of all popular art. On postcards, calendars, placemats, Christmas greetings, good and bad reproductions for the walls, in advertisements, photography and painting classes in the evenings, in colouring books and poster pictures for the infants, a whole society learns the crucial relation between the forms of its feelings and the forms of what is beautiful. But the learning and the loving do not stop there, in these small acts of self-expression (as they say) or decoration. A great communal act of public devotion also takes place on any sunny Sunday of a British summer, when the car-owning families of every city pile into the family automobile for a day in the country, at the seaside, at the wildlife park, going round the stately home, in the national park. Each member of those families, according to his or her lights, is joining in a messy, friendly, quite unritualised act of profane worship in the great church of Nature which the Romantic painters and poets set up something after 1776. Add to this the lifetime spent by so many British husbands and wives on the making of beautiful gardens, in National Trust houses at Petworth and Stourhead, no doubt, but much more importantly, behind, say, two houses of every five, and across as much of the English class system as possesses a garden. The landscape is, in England at least, largely a made, a man-created work – of art, and of the lack of it. It speaks for the immediate presence of art in everyone's lives. To find a way of speaking of that presence as the great Romantics did, to recapture the practical value and meaning townscape and landscape have for people, would be to come near that durable continuity and connectedness which make it possible to speak of both individual and national identity.

Romanticism, not in the least a swear-word, may be said to be the origin of all Anglophone culture. But any country, and overwhelmingly Britain, makes kitsch out of its popular art. By kitsch I mean the lying sentimentalities of over-decoration, false colour and cadence, surges of feeling and affect which may be ignored or indulged at will (mood mountains and golden sunsets), the magicking up of sudden, strong feeling in relation neither to an adequate object nor to a practical consequence (bosomy flamenco dancers with masses of tumbling curls, waif-like little girls with big tear-filled eyes). Kitsch is easy, slightly smelly magic, which is why we all like it occasionally. Anyway, kitsch for me may be worthwhile art to you (which is not to say that there is no objectivity in aesthetics, as we shall see).

Landscape in our society is counterposed to townscape much as leisure is counterposed to work. Landscape, we may say, is allocated to the realm of private feeling, townscape to the realm of public business. No doubt this is why the standard reproductions in department stores, or the busy trade in tiny little water-colours sold in tens of thousands along the tourist trails, are always idealised glimpses of the local countryside, and rarely townscapes. The only town buildings which appear are in mix-and-wash pictures of perfect Georgian terraces or dinky Victorian frame houses with the wooden veranda and barge boarding. This iconography includes the classical cityscapes of Impressionism – the grands boulevards and grands magasins, the rivers and celebrated churches of Paris, London, New York, Vienna, Amsterdam, Rome and so forth – but these exemplify the aesthetic taboo on politics which insists that the subject matter of art must be suitable for strictly personal reflection, and therefore town scenes can only be used for this purpose when one is a tourist, and in command of one's own time.

These categories are a present distortion in popular culture, even though they contain the human ingredients from which a greater urbanity can still grow. For both landscape and townscape were made by other people for other people, and made so across widely differing and extended historical eras. The purposes of buildings change with time; their surroundings do so as well and hugely. It is rare for any one of us to have much choice in the matter; the starkness of power, signifying freedom to do as you like with whatever other people want, is never clearer than in the architectural decisions which are embodied in city and country: the great buildings and the small, the copses and groves, the tiny arrangements of back and front gardens, of parks and playgrounds, are the results of the strenuous interplay of coercive power and freedom as they strain to make a place beautiful or useful, profitable or waste.

At this point, aesthetics becomes politics in some very inclusive sense which the least political person cannot escape. Because the organisation of the space through which we must move and in which we live shapes the nature of our encounters, gives scale to all our transactions, and marks off the ground with its meanings for us – public/private, work/leisure, cars/pedestrians, old/young, the list is endless; we can occasionally make of the space a thing of our own, but largely our townscape and landscape instruct us in their use and our social subordinations.

A useful point then to make is that in writing on this matter there need be no agonising about idealism and materialism. The facts *are* the values as you walk or drive through the English landscape. Faithfully to describe the experience of the street or the motorway, the life created or thwarted by a particular architecture, is to find the values or their absence in the facts of the matter. And then the only way to understand that formation is to dismantle the terms of its historical construction in as direct and straightforward a way as possible. That is, the experience and actuality of a British New Town like Telford or Peterlee derive from a historical mixture of sources whose uneasy compound of images of ideal cities, homes, and neighbourhoods has been blended with the exigencies of costs, labour, materials, the power of local and national governments, and the commands of capital, to make these places what they are. In the case of an old town, Tenterden, say, or Bury St Edmunds, an accurate historical eye and touch will tell you what forms of production and what sets of relations, as they say, issued from and are upheld in this varied, gregarious, private and polite High Street in Kent, or this stately, urbane and genteel concourse in Suffolk.

Such an eye must also be both sharp and wintry. For the tale told by the wildernesses of the old industrial estuaries of Tees, Mersey and Wear, or by the abandoned degradation of our old enemy, the high-rise block of flats and the blank estate slums, is every bit as much historical and political as the shaping of the tourists' way. The negligence and callousness are set in the same material circumstances and studiously distorted ways of seeing as the pictures of the picturesque.

Not surprisingly, Ruskin is our cue for reminding us that what we make of land-and-townscape is the experience upon which politics and aesthetics come together. Out of that naturally social, and naturally beauty-conscious life we make the theories which guide us into the future.

What is true of human polity seems to me not less so of the distinctively political art of Architecture. I have long felt convinced of the necessity, . . . of some determined effort to extricate from the confused mass of partial traditions and dogmata with which it has become encumbered during imperfect or restricted practice, those large principles of right which are applicable to every stage and style of it . . . There is no law, no principle, based on past practice, which may not be overthrown in a moment, by the arising of a new condition, or the invention of a new material; and the most rational, if not the only, mode of averting the danger of an utter dissolution of all that is systematic and consistent in our practice, or of ancient authority in our judgement, is to cease, for a little while, our endeavours to deal with the multiplying host of particular abuses, restraints, or requirements; and endeavour to determine, as the guides of every effort, some constant, general, and irrefragable laws of right – laws, which, based upon man's nature, not upon his knowledge, may possess so far the unchangeableness of the one, as that neither the increase nor imperfection of the other may be able to assault or invalidate them.[1]

Ruskin's grand project to tabulate the laws of architectural heritage sounds nowadays so dated that it can be revived by Quinlan Terry as exquisite pastiche. But his implicit appeal to what is continuous and reliable in human nature, however relative and historical we have rightly learned to think of that as being, still has a strong, moving force to it. It serves to recall for us that Ruskin, for all his oddity and his huffing and puffing about St George, was chosen as their hero by those British working men, women, and intellectuals who founded the first socialist party to win power without murder. I shall substitute the totem 'lived experience' for Ruskin's laws of human nature, and see how we turn landscape into art, and what good may come of it.

In John Fowles's novel *Daniel Martin*,[2] the novelist gives a favourite passage to his hero from Restif de la Bretonne's quasi-autobiography, *Monsieur Nicolas*. In it, while remembering his childhood in deepest Burgundy some decades before the Revolution, the Frenchman des-cribes shepherding his father's sheep into an unknown, rich, and beauti-ful combe – 'la bonne vaux' – where he finds unparalleled fecundity, rare (but not magical) birds and wildlife which he has never seen before, and what he senses as a perfect congruence of man and nature, a harmony of free, mutual life which properly belongs to Paradise. Momentarily, the ˈsacred valley, which he never found again, realises the dream of natural peace which was to haunt the Romantics and remains for us as their potent legacy.

## II

These sacred places and lost domains are scattered through the geo-graphy and bibliography of the next two centuries: from the ruined

Cistercian Abbeys via the Falls of Watendlath to Grasmere, Tintagel, the
Cotswolds, the Western Isles, the Orkneys and Caerleon in Britain; from
Le Grand Meaulnes's mysterious estate in Yonne down through la bonne vaux
in Burgundy to Provence, Westwards to the Languedoc in France, east to
the Côte d'Azur, the poets, painters and belles-lettristes (in the happy phrase)
marked the tourist trail with its shrines for the future. After 1918, as Paul
Fussell tells us,[3] the same drive expanded into the British literary dia-
spora, as the writers anticipated capital, seeking literal sanctuary in Asia
Minor, the Pacific Isles, Mexico, North Africa, and the Mediterranean
islands.

The books and pictures define the places reserved for a special but (I
contend) universal making of art-objects on the part of all of us. It begins
in everyday life – most memorably in childhood – but is then shifted to
holiday, more specifically tourist life.

All of us (this is an appeal) are familiar with a particular fondness for
this patch of townscape rather than that. We prefer to take this way home
because the walk (or drive) along a street, past a little field, over a solid
stone bridge and the mild river below, gives us special pleasure. The
other way there is a wide, rather blank road with a big, bullying electricity
sub-station whose odd, angular robotic figures look as though they
might suddenly move on us if we lingered too long.

But it is not necessarily a matter of the prettier run being the one we
prefer. The special route may have a snug corner where the pub fits the
angle of the street with engaging neatness, and its dark entrance leading
to the etched, opaque glass and heavy doors entices us with the promise
of magical encounters if only we get out of the car and step in. We never
do. The pleasure of waiting at that traffic light is given by the untested
daydream and the actual shape of narrow street, bay windows, stout pub
sign, hanging baskets (inevitably, the advertisers, best popular artists of
our time, are now irresistibly good at picking these images, and making
us loiter by them).

These little incidents hardly count as sacred places. But they are the
small token of the larger, much anticipated holiday moments, in which
the happiness of free time fits the picture we can make out of what we
have come to see. We feel at home in its deep familiarity, but home could
not provide the experience (unless we have been away from it for a
longish time) because its poignancy, the depth of the emotion it calls
forth, depends upon a certain intensity of longing and anticipation.

I am writing these paragraphs in just such a place. That is to say, it is a
place in which the harmless terms of my biography – the terms of a

fortunate, middle-aged intellectual and father, his teeth cut on Words-worth and the Romantic view of Shakespeare, his heart in the welfare state and a Trumptonish view of an England now under enemy occupa-tion – may blend with the given landscape in a moment of perfect happiness. How does this happen?

It is a low room, entered on either side of the base of its long 'L' by two decent plank doors with loudly clicking latches. Between the doors is a solid, old-fashioned, cast-iron and brass-railed range, well blackleaded and polished, with chased bread-oven doors and a wide, latticed hob. The floor is flagged (the house was an inn until 1920 or so). As you turn the corner of the 'L', the long upright corridor of the room, lined with a fine, silver-faced, longcase clock, a clasped and oilskin-bound trunk straight off the Orient Express, a walnut whatnot, culminates dramati-cally in what we well call a picture window, eight feet by five, the full space of the gable end.

Even more dramatically, the picture window (added, I guess, when the inn became a country cottage) gives straight onto a low dune of whin grasses at the end of a neat, short lawn, beyond which opens as abruptly as a blow the magnificent space of the Northumbria beach, curving flatly north and south in a huge and lovely arc.

The arc is filled by the sea. Just off the centre of the view (the picture) lies a low, rugged pair of islands, dolerite crags topped with thick turf and the white, stubby, reassuring shape of the Trinity House lighthouse on their cliff edge.

At first sight, the picture is complete: grass, dune, beach, sea, islands, and the big sky. As you come to know it, it changes; the window frames many pictures. The clouds move grandly across. The wind blows, and the whins wave furiously along the centre horizontal. The gulls wheel and glide and flap across its top half, glittering at times as the sun breaks through. A child trails a long seaweed down to the little waves at the sea edge.

The details of each picture depend upon the chance volitions of other people, or upon the weather and the natural life of the place. Their meaning is not that they are there to be watched. (The child and the gulls have their own errands.) There is no parade before the watcher at the window. Nor is the watcher a spectator in the sense we have been using it. He is more like an untaught painter – the person who says, as one often does, 'I wish I could paint that.' (Hence the importance of photography as popular art.) The watcher makes the varied life of the scene into his own work of art.

It is important that the scene does not have too much to fill it. I do not mean too many people: the picture window could as easily frame, say, a crowded promenade (the Jardin de Luxembourg, or Riverside Drive), though it is relevant that picture windows do generally frame landscapes. But too large an event would break into the short space between watcher and the other side of the window (between painter and canvas), and turn the watcher into the participant in spite of himself. Gazing upon such a scene, we try to fit the time we have (it may be no more than the time taken to drive that way home) to the area of the place. The fit of time to space depends on a particular mood, vacant but watchful (like Words-worth in *Daffodils*); when the time we have to fit the special pull of the place is not enough – as when the train hurtles too quickly past a pretty picnic spot – we are frustrated and disappointed. When the scene does not fill the time with enough small events, we become bored. (The events are small, like those of many Impressionist paintings: a young girl runs ahead of her mother into a poppy field, a man in a bowler hat sits on the river bank and looks at the Seine.) 'An experience of disinterested observation opens in its centre and gives birth to a happiness instantly recognisable as your own.'[4] At such moments, we successfully and selflessly shape our lives to the time and space in the picture we have made.

## III

These processes are surely common to most of us, though the contemp-lation they require is largely assigned to holiday time, or to the immobi-lised or elderly, or allowed to the raptness of small children. They are also some of the best expressions of our natural creativity, and under-stood by us all as our practical aesthetics. But, as one might put it, with an eye on Kierkegaard's famous distinction in *Either/Or* between morality and aesthetics, my practical (or popular) aesthetics does not denote what he criticised as a view of life disjoined into a series of beautiful tableaux, of separate but present moments. It is a remoralised aesthetics in which responsibilities in the future arise from past obligations, each holding the individual (and the nation) in continuous time, and conferring unity on the lives of that time.

The pictures we make, I have argued, shape our own lives to the time and space in front of us. Cultures provide forms for the containment and definition of the range of feelings considered socially permissible. The forms, such as landscape itself, and landscape-painting, must be flexible enough to accommodate different feelings and thoughts – feelings and thoughts as diverse as those of, say, John Sell Cotman, Thomas Girtin, Paul Nash, Fred Williams, Sidney Nolan, and Winslow Homer, as historically and geographically mixed a bunch of landscape painters as may exemplify my theme. On the other hand, when a form becomes too familiarly occupied, it becomes sentimental; so Turner's amazing triumph with the rendering of sublimity leads to a sharp and seventy-year decline in large-scale water-colour, just because grandeur became so trivially accessible in paint.

Our picture of the landscape, found in every corner of our homes, from the framed impasto souvenirs bought on the Costa del Sol to the delicate art of the picture postcard which now adorns so many noticeboards in scrubbed pine kitchens, quote to each of us that complicity of liberated man and woman with unspoiled but productive nature which is so unkillably a vision of perfect happiness, at least for all cultures cradled in the Mediterranean.

This system of imagery works by counterposing townscape to landscape. Architecture is then ungainsayably the political art. Landscape is its private complement, because even if (in Britain at least) the landowners prohibit our walking across most of it, when we can get a vantage point, we can make our imaginary pictures out of it. Of course, politics being what it is, architecture is often not to our taste, the scale too towering, the juxtapositions crude and arbitrary, the traffic hellishly noisy and dangerous, the town filthy everywhere, the dark streets dangerous. Adrian Stokes asked once:

What figure of today aesthetically best suits our streets, what figure aesthetically is best framed by our doorways? The answer is the man in a long overcoat with hand within pocket holding a revolver on which his fingers tighten. There is no gainsaying the aesthetic appropriateness of the thug in our streets and in our interiors. The idea of him saves our town environment from a suggestion of vacuum.[5]

He may have had too large a recent dose of Bogart and James Cagney. But those of us today, much more heavily dosed with *Miami Vice* and *The Sweeney*, are naturally and constantly *afraid* in a town of any size, afraid of dark, wet streets and car tyres squealing round their corners, afraid of groups of footloose lads, barging down the pavements yaddering bits of popsong, afraid of seedy, smelly heaps of rags and old coats, wheezing and reeking of rotgut cider.

Such images feature in every threnody on the loss of civic manners, whether sung by Left or Right. Only when the citizen gets home is he or she safe to reconstruct an image of the good town. In private houses and their gardens, the citizen builds a comity from the small spaces for pleased contemplation of dahlias and sweet peas, a little piazza of smoothly-mown turf which quotes in distant retrospect the urbane, polite plaza of the city. Stokes writes, 'When the objects of the senses compel in the percipient the profoundest emotions of the contemplative state, the soul is at peace', and 'Art is the symbol of human process.'[6] Without much of a wrench, we may pull Stokes's remarks out of aesthetics into politics. His aphorisms are at the heart of most Anglophone people when they speak of the founding arts of home-making and home-loving. By this token, in Lawrence's phrase, 'Art-speech is the only speech.' Or better, we all of us work out most easily what is going on in everyday life by recourse to such well-understood symbols as story-telling pictures and picture-creating stories. The dominant image in either will be the landscape.

Merleau-Ponty once wrote a precept of a properly human sociology – of art, or any other expressive form.

I am watching this man who is motionless in sleep . . . the moment the man wakes up in the sun and reaches for his hat, between the sun which burns me and makes my eyes squint and the gesture which from a distance over there brings relief to my fatigue, between this sweating forehead and the protective gesture which it calls forth on my part, a bond is tied without my needing to decide anything.

As long as it adheres to my body like the tunic of Nessus the world exists not only for me but for everyone in it who makes gestures towards it. There is a universality of feeling – and it is upon this that our identification rests, the generalisation of my body, the perception of the other. I perceive behaviour immersed in the same world as I because the world I perceive still trails with it my corporeality.[7]

The imaginary painter inside all of us, like the actual painter, tries to live through his images and bodily sympathy which Merleau-Ponty describes, a motion of both emotion and physical sensation which strains (in a trope) the limits of the Cartesian world; and splits it. The painter has to find an image which will hold that sympathetic movement in the form his conventions make available. A convention, however, is not fixed. To vivify the sympathy, as I so generally call it – it might be better named with Merleau-Ponty, the bond with the world – Giorgione must find the special, delicate luxuriance of colour with which Venetian convention tied bodies to the world; but Turner must find the innumerable golds and whites, indigo and obsidian which will juxtapose brilliance and death in the language of Romanticism.

In any case, the bond with the world is never direct. That is perhaps the mistake so intelligent a commentator as John Barrell makes[8] when he tells off Constable for painting the country folk deep in the middle distance, and commends Turner for joining the labourers rooting out the turnips on a bitter January morning. But the painter has to work with images which in turn become the conventions of his time – colour, drapery, anatomy, landscape, light, abstract form – but are in any case the marks of paint itself on board or tin or canvas or cartridge paper. This is only a platitude if we refuse to look at the deep, nameless obstructions between the painter's unenvisageable vision (he doesn't know what the painting will look like when it's finished) and the marks of paint in the picture. And in any case, his own experience with which he works, his truthfulness, are neither of them essences or substances which may be transferred directly to the canvas or the paper.

My contention is that somewhere in Merleau-Ponty's little tale of the man on the park bench, and in my clumsy account of what a painter does while 'matching and making' marks of baked squares of colour and water on stretched cartridge paper into a representation of his place in the place, we have the ground of being and the figure of thought. Landscape is popular culture because it standardly provides the images of non-con-suming, unself-regarding beauty out of which most people make their best thoughts and feelings. In The sovereignty of good, Iris Murdoch affirms that the best evidence we have that goodness exists is the scrupulous attention to the real world of the greatest artists. That truth-telling, she says, just is the practice of virtue. But it should not be necessary to have to repeat myself at any length in demonstrating that truth-telling can never be a matter of recording what is there, from nature. It is hardest of all to see this in that most natural of subject-matters for a painter since 1770, the landscape. There, too, of course, the painter, like the poet and thinker, has to find within his paints and their actualisation on paper the qualities which are equivalent both to what is in front of him and what he wishes were in front of him.

That represents another formulation of the practical and popular aesthetics for which this essay is a preliminary investigation. The specific claim is that such an aesthetics will find landscape painting an especially suitable topic because the topic itself matters so much to such an inter-national variety of people. In landscape (as in, say, sport), private and public meet; men and women contemplate what is common property and what is singular; they love what they can see for its own sake. Subject and object are in balance.

The political content of this frame of feeling and way of seeing was historically given, as must be the case. The content has been attenuated in its home in Britain, while it has filled up abroad, particularly in Australia. It begins with Romanticism, and I shall take, out of a vast selection, Cotman's several paintings of the junction of the rivers Greta and Tees, executed while he was the frequent guest of the Morritts at Rokeby Hall halfway from Barnard Castle to Richmond in North Yorkshire, and between July 1803 and the end of 1805, as my first examples. By 1803, the English water-colour tradition was fully established; I begin with Cotman for, as they say, personal reasons.

As Cholmeley told him, 'Every artist must . . . obey his master, the public . . . two-thirds of mankind . . . mind more what is represented than how it is done.' These paintings are of a place where as a child I spent innumerable hours of perfect happiness. Weekend after weekend for ten or more years, my parents used to bring my sisters and me to stay at a farm or a pub just down the road. At first, when I was only three or four, we came because the Tees estuary was being bombed, and later because it became one of the family's sacred places. I have visited it and loved it all my life. The water flows there in summer with a steady but safe current, and the huge limestone boulders afford marvellous climbing almost across the river; they have dangerous edges smoothed by aeons of winter floods. The water is strangely coloured a deep and dark brown by the deposits of iron it carries, but still is utterly unclouded and translucent. All about the slopes of the current the trees – ash, beech, oak, hazel – crowd, until the river turns and at the bend opens widely at each side into the gentle slopes of the cow-pastures, and the cows trundle amiably down to drink at the edge.

The stones are formed for a playground. They are thick and square, like the great coping-stones of a wharf. Walking on them, perching on the high ones, jumping over small gaps, is like walking along the quays of a busy harbour, the trees as masts, the further stones as moored barges. On a hot day the play of intensely contrasted light and shade is mildly busy with no more than a dozen picnicking families, and a couple of fishermen in the deeper water of the Cauldron, where the current boils a little as it breaks against their thighs.

I am not going in for fine writing. I am talking about all that Cotman's pictures remind me of. Behind and amongst the colour and line of the picture are those vivid memories. I think of Arthur Ransome's note added shortly before his death to a late Puffin edition of *Swallows and*

*Amazons:*

I have been often asked how I came to write *Swallows and Amazons*. The answer is that it had its beginning long, long ago when, as children, my brother, my sisters and I spent most of our holidays on a farm at the south end of Coniston. We played in or on the lake or on the hills above it, finding friends in the farmers and shepherds and charcoal-burners whose smoke rose from the coppice woods along the shore. We adored the place. Coming to it we used to run down to the lake, dip our hands in and wish, as if we had just seen the new moon. Going away from it we were half drowned in tears. While away from it, as children and as grown-ups, we dreamt about it. No matter where I was, wandering about the world, I used at night to look for the North Star and, in my mind's eye, could see the beloved skyline of great hills beneath it. *Swallows and Amazons* grew out of those old memories. I could not help writing it. It almost wrote itself.

The pressure of such feeling is peculiarly present for post-Romantic, urban men and women when looking at landscape-painting, although of course Ransome's love for his hills and mine for Cotman's paintings of the Greta are no different in kind to the love either of us may have for Mozart's A-Major Symphony or for *David Copperfield*. Indeed, Dickens's remarks in that novel about those who have retained 'a certain freshness, and gentleness, and capacity of being pleased, which are also an inheritance they have preserved from childhood' come vividly to mind. Well-loved works of art are useful for just this purpose, that for those who retain that childish disposition, those works can make them happy. They rejoin the spirit to nature. Walter Benjamin, in a passage hinted at earlier, wrote:

The liberating magic which the fairy tale has at its disposal does not bring nature into play in a mythical way, but points to its complicity with liberated man. A mature man feels this complicity only occasionally, that is, when he is happy; but the child first meets it in fairy tales, and it makes him happy.[9]

It is a restoration sought by many mature men and women; often enough, they find it, and their so finding it turns on the retention of that 'freshness' and 'capacity of being pleased' as well as the high spirits Dickens so unforgettably embodied.

## IV

Faced with any landscape-painting, we search it for a landscape it reminds us of, or perhaps, we look in it for a home which we can persuade ourselves we have always known. Even in the wildest Alpine disaster of Turner's we look for the place where we'd be safe. Looking at these Cotmans, each standing empty inviting the inhabitation of our eye and therefore our bodies, those to whom they are new seek to find some equivalence between those friendly, tranquil rocks and stones and trees, that wide water, and comparable places in their own lives. The discovery of such equivalence, after the hunting and discarding performed both by the memory and the imagination as we check the way the picture is against the way we want it to be, modifying each against the necessity of the other, dissolves at its heart into the sweetness and roundedness of understanding. This is the shape of all inquiry, its passage from restlessness to quiet.

Such great, domestic painting commemorates with its peers the Romantic creation of landscape as the icon of freedom: the validation of the individual's free feelings in the classless, commonly-owned space of the garden of Eden. These are the origins of calendars and picture postcards. Ruskin saw first, in *Modern painters*, what had actually changed in the frame of feeling and cognition which landscape-painting articulated. The opportunity of free movement in an open countryside unprohibited by landowners and their wardens is commemorated as an occasion for political exhilaration by the early nineteenth-century painters. Bonington's great panoramas have a dashing sweep and splendour far less reverential than Canaletto's. They are the work of a man in tune with Wordsworth's *Ode on Westminster Bridge*. He is unalienated by the city. He is its free citizen.

Such men painted the landscape as though it were ours. The peak of such painting lasted only as long as that national fulfilment remained a possibility, which is to say from the victorious French and American Revolutions to the Eighteenth Brumaire of Louis Napoleon. The deaths of Turner and Wordsworth, the demise of Chartism and the return of the Bourbons, are emblems of its end. Over that period, English painting, especially in water-colours, was at its best on its standard subject-matter, the landscape. New freedoms of ideas, ownership, consumption and mobility gave the form its lead. No doubt it had its essential ideologising from 1770 or so onwards. The man and woman of sensibility was born to the bourgeoisie out of Shaftesbury's philosophy and Burke's aesthetics: hardly a radical genesis. He and she learned from Gray and Cowper, Repton and Brown, Salvator Rosa and Gainsborough, that nature was the vast, solitary auditorium for serene, profound and objectlessly religious feeling. The nature in question is then organised into a hierarchical iconography with quite precise emotions assigned to it as suitable: sublime and beautiful certainly; but then cosy and holy;

domestic and solitary; pensive and passionate, and so on. This much was the institutionalisation of gentility. But at the same time, led always by Turner, the first businessman of art, the painters made their paintings speak for a representative freedom and independence – from patrons, from philistinism, from the filthy city, and for the transformation of nature into a common and equal homeland. For this brief period, this sedate, domestic, and genteel conjuncture gave rise to some of the most wonderful and vivid, passionate and beautiful of all European domestic painting.

But in voting fervently for Romanticism, I am anxious not to fall into the kind of art–historical incantation which Clark writes so elegantly and superciliously in *Landscape into art*. If we are to avoid the two-step art history which describes brush-strokes more or less formalistically, and then stands back to applaud, we will have to deploy analogy and metonymy. This requires more than a civilised vocabulary; it demands intelligence and daring. It is not a test I can pass, but perhaps I can suggest what better tropes *might* pass.

Faced by Girtin's *White House at Chelsea*, *Kirkstall Abbey*, the *Falls of Lodore in Watendlath Gorge*, the *View on the Wharfe*, *Above Bolton*, or the stunningly beautiful *Durham Cathedral*, we might say that the light and space of these pictures are open like the vases, or the perfect, expressionless *caritas* of the woman's face in Giorgione's *Tempesta*. Girtin, like Cotman, drew very broad washes of colour over the surface of the paper. Neither uses much body-colour or Chinese white. The paper itself, shining through the colour, is the source of light. They can only darken colours by letting the paper dry and then drawing another broad and sudden brush of colour over the top. In *Croyland Abbey* and *The Martpit*, Cotman's handling of mass in terms of colour is quite unexampled, even by Francis Towne. It is a too standard cliché these days to praise painters for their treatment of light. This seems to me a failure of thought. What painters as different as Constable (with his speckled whites), Pissarro (with his *pointilliste* effects) and Sidney Nolan (with his Turner-like transparencies of pink and gold over the white surface of the canvas) are all treating are mass and moisture or – the same subject in negation – waste and aridity. Cotman and the great water-colourists, particularly Turner, are painting moisture itself; their medium is well-named. He used water to paint water. But – to try for simile this time – he used water and unfilled space as Titian uses the bulk and age of the bodies in his paintings to provide a metonymy for what he valued in experience. Girtin, just as much a brilliant Romantic, painted without a vantage-point the panorama of the big English sky of which Ruskin wrote so incomparably in his essay on clouds in *Modern painters*. Cotman's moisture becomes, in Girtin, the space shaped only by an uncompromising horizon. The painter occupies the view from nowhere.[10] That is to say, as we move from one position to another in front of his best pictures, the vantage-point moves with us. It is an astonishing achievement. No lines of perspective are beamed towards us by the picture in order to tell us where to stand. The change becomes commonplace in Impressionism, but Girtin won it very early and completely. The unsituated painter declares for us all that the landscape he beholds is free for all. It is not his possession, nor his patron's. It is a free country. In *The Thames from Westminster* or *The White House*, unframed by coulisses, without refuge from which to command the prospect, Girtin celebrates the openness of a space from which Romanticism removed the evenness. Constable eponymously, Cotman and Girtin, and many fine but lesser painters after them: James Ward in *Gordale Scar* (1808), Francis Danby at the Avon Gorge in 1822, Copley Fielding at Rievaulx in 1839 – all spoke the authentic accents of Romanticism. They leave a sublime landscape perfectly unpeopled for the people to follow them and occupy, with plenty of room for everybody. In the inevitably uneven tide of cultural change, the same invitation could still be recovered by Rex Whistler in his painting of the Vale of Aylesbury in 1933. But by then his landscape is seen, so to speak, by a public school Claude Lorrain, from the railway compartment Eric Ravilious actually painted in 1940. The people have arrived, with exemplary delicacy, on an outing.

Cotman and Girtin, with the colossal eponyms of Constable and Turner overhead, mark the limits of the historical epoch at which the landscape could plausibly stand for common freedom balanced with private space: the dream of liberalism. Thereafter, the good painter led by Ruskin recoiled from the idea of the sublime enjoined upon them by the heirs of Burke and Kant, and settled down to paint, as Ruskin and Alfred William Hunt or the St Ives painters did, the rich details of a garden of wild flowers, the exact facets of a small rockface. Their last spokesman is Robin Tanner. The others took off into sentimental, indeed saccharine pictures of Victorian cottage-scape and its attendant roses and delphiniums, thatch and little, flounced seven-year-old Alices. According to this explanation, the honest painters were left with little choice but to concede victory to sentimentality and the camera, and paint increasingly formalist works of landscape-painting in the modes of Paul and John Nash, Rennie Mackintosh, or Keynes's friends Duncan Grant and David Bomberg.

## V

The danger with writing history as decline is that the present can only be a dead end. Nowadays, the contemporary profitability of landscape painting, its reassuring grip and stamina as the most popular of subjects for art, maintains itself in Britain only by recourse to the painting of glimpses. The modern mannerism is to catch landscape on the move and at a distance: the contemporary water-colour is quick, tachiste, caught as it were from a car window. Or following Nash, it reduces to the non-human formalism of geology. Humanity having blotted out the essential life of inorganic things, the painter cannot look too closely. For all its omnipresence, the image of landscape in Britain is now very hard put to it to keep any political promise except to the tourist.

(By my lights, the happiest successes in the present politics of land-scape-painting are in Australia, where democracy, economy and geography still combine to hold open the promises of freedom, fulfilment and self-awareness.)

The only way of breaking out of the dead end for which Larkin's grisly poem 'Going, going' is the epitaph is by an act of collective political will. In this essay, it can only sound like a brief, hopeful cadenza.

The commonplace of my tale is that popular aesthetics must work in the grain of the material of what is popular. Politics in the formal sense is mostly so awful and so boring; dismal, self-important people practise it, and give themselves such airs over us, who don't. Aesthetics in the formal sense is pretty grim as well; so much of its practice is comparably self-important. Both seem to stand at such a distance from the valuations of ordinary life. To celebrate local knowledge and ordinary feeling is not to set up shop as a plain man, blunt woman, or gross philistine. Nor is it to trust that entirely unreliable historical force, the people, to deliver us from evil. It is, however, to battle to make images of the good life out of the symbols and stories which give meaning and continuity to our life and times. Landscape painting is one of the few such systems of imagery which combines the value of non-utilitarian freedom with natural beauty. The politics of this oncoming epoch could start from there.

## Notes

1  John Ruskin, *The seven lamps of architecture, collected works*, eds. E. T. Cook and A. Wedderburn, vol. VII (George Allen, 1903), 'Introductory', p. 20.
2  Jonathan Cape, 1978.
3  See Paul Fussell, *Abroad: British literary travelling between the wars* (Oxford University Press, 1980).

4  See John Berger, 'Field', in *About looking* (Writers and Readers, 1980), a remarkable essay which I am trying to develop here.
5  Adrian Stokes, 'Colour and form', *Critical writings*, vol. II, 1937–1958 (Thames & Hudson, 1978).
6  *Ibid.*, pp. 111–12.
7  Maurice Merleau-Ponty, *The prose of the world* (Heinemann Educational Books, 1974), pp. 113, 136, but my analysis owes everything to Roger Poole, and his review–essay 'The bond of human embodiment', *New Universities Quarterly* (autumn 1974).
8  In *The dark side of the landscape* (Cambridge University Press, 1980), pp. 152–4.
9  Walter Benjamin, 'The storyteller', in *Illuminations*, ed. H. Arendt (Schocken Books, New York, 1969), p. 102.
10  The phrase provides the title – *The view from nowhere* – to Thomas Nagel's recent book (Oxford University Press, 1986). Nagel is balancing two moral traditions, one which seeks 'the view from nowhere' once taken by God but now empty, the other which lives incorrigibly in personal lives. His remarks bear strongly on what the landscape-painters tried to do. Nagel is clearly aware of this. The dust-cover of his book illustrates this point by reproducing Caspar David Friedrich's painting *The Large Enclosure near Dresden* of 1832.

# 13

# From Captain Cook to Neil Armstrong: colonial exploration and the structure of landscape
### Stephen Bann

I wish, here, to present a three-stage argument, based on the proposition that the West has seen three decisive 'ages of the navigators', the first of which can be identified with Columbus, the second with the voyages of Captain Cook, and the third with the myths, but also the realities of space travel in our own times. What interests me particularly is not the voyage of discovery in itself, but what might be called its 'semantic recoil'. However much we can document and thus to a certain extent objectify through cartography or other forms of exact measurement the tracks of exploration, we have to reckon at the same time with the cognitive apparatus through which such 'discoveries' were processed – and here I am assuming that not merely the navigators themselves, but their compatriots and colleagues in the new knowledge were exposed to such a processing. The privileged place occupied by the metaphor of exploration and discovery, as well as its reality in post-Renaissance Europe has meant that it is taken for granted as a central structuring element in any 'poetics' worthy of the name over that same period. And by poetics, I mean to suggest – and hope to show – is implied not simply the bundle of linguistic procedures and semantic effects which underlies the production of meaning in the literary arts at any one time, but also its correlative in that related and seemingly more down-to-earth domain, the practice of landscape-gardening.

A telling example (though it lies in the sphere of literary poetics) comes in a passage of dialogue from Gide's novel *Les Faux-monnayeurs*, published in 1926. Young Bernard remarks in a conversation about poetic method: 'When Columbus discovered America, did he know towards what he was sailing? His aim was to go ahead, straight on. His aim was himself, and it was himself that projected it in front of him'. To which his friend Edouard replies: 'I have often thought that in art, and in literature in particular, only those count who throw themselves towards the unknown. You do not discover a new land without consenting to lose sight, from the first and for a long time, of any shore.' Now Bernard and Edouard, despite their claim to be avant-garde, are actually adhering to a Romantic, or more precisely a Baudelairean, poetics of the voyage: 'Au fond de l'inconnu pour trouver du *nouveau*.' If we read a modern master of Russian Formalist poetics like Tzvetan Todorov, who has helpfully turned his attention to the semiotics of colonial exploration in *La conquête de l'Amérique*, we find that Columbus knew where he was going in the very precise sense that his unquestioned Catholic faith assured him of an ultimate landfall, and whatever he, so to speak, discovered had to be adapted to the framework of expectations derived from the texts of revealed religious truth. Not only this: Columbus had a convenient way of squaring the empirical evidence of his own eyes with received notions of the fabulous and exotic which he was not anxious to abandon. Columbus did not confess that he had not seen any mermaids on his voyages; he merely intimated that the mermaids he had seen were really not all they were cracked up to be, by the relevant authorities.

Whatever Captain Cook did, it was clearly more than was suggested by the Chilean poet Vicente Huidobro, who wrote in his poem Equatorial: 'Captain Cook / hunts the Aurora Borealis / at the South Pole.' Whereas Columbus had a classificatory system derived from the utterly fabulous authorities of medieval natural history, Cook arrived at a time when the heterogeneity of natural types was being steadily accommodated within the Latinate categories of the Linnaean system, and was able to offer as a long-term project the test, by reductio ad absurdum, of that all-accommodating system: that is, the naming of the legendary 500 and more varieties of eucalyptus native to the Australian sub-continent. Whereas Columbus named the shoreline of Central America according to the vouchsafed or withheld blessings of the Providence of God and all his Saints, mediated on earth by the beneficence of His Most Catholic Majesty the King of Spain, Cook names more eclectically, commemorating a patron at the Admiralty, a prominent financial backer, as well as the very discipline which allowed all those aberrant eucalyptuses to be classified. My proper subject though, is what I have called the semantic recoil of Cook's explorations. I am looking there for my most essential evidence, and particularly so, initially, in their recoil upon the poetics of the landscape garden. For, as is suggested by the contemporary landscape theorist Bernard Lassus whose practice will be discussed later, 'gardens have almost always foretold in advance the relationships

H

between man and nature, and between society and nature'.

Captain Cook died in the Sandwich Islands in February 1779. Yet, as Banks expressed it to Mrs Cook in 1784: 'His name will live for ever in the remembrance of a people grateful for the services his labours have afforded to mankind in general.' The suggestion that Cook's scientific, non-partisan achievement should stand on its own merits even at a time when the strategic importance of colonial exploration could not fail to be recognised, is nicely underlined by the epitaph provided by the French garden poet, the Abbé Delille, writing only three years after Cook's death in his long and influential poem, Les Jardins:

> L'ami du monde, hélas! meurt en proie aux sauvages
> (The world's friend, alas! dies a prey to savages)

It is a judgement that reminds us how little the recent memory of the Seven Years War, and the still internecine rivalry of Britain and France as colonial nations, interfered with the recognition of the global benefit which Cook conferred. And yet there is also, of course, the designedly asymptotic effect of that antithesis between 'the world' and the 'savages' of the Sandwich Islands. They are part of 'the world', of course, these 'savages'. Yet their action creates here perhaps the same sort of semantic frisson as a Greek of the classical period would have manifested in accommodating the barbaroi within the oikoumene.

If we can note the fulsome, but equivocal tribute to Cook in Delille's poem, we must also assume that such a tribute plays a structural role in the theory of gardening which Delille is advocating. After all, the paean to the navigator comes towards the end of a polemical defence of the poetic, philosophical and painterly garden against the 'mechanical' art of gardening which Delille associates with the architect. To help resolve this question, it is useful to bring into the account an actual garden (now unfortunately destroyed) which does not necessarily reflect Delille's ideals but at least shows a similar dedication to the memory of Captain Cook. The outstandingly interesting garden which the rich court banker Jean-Joseph de Laborde created at Méréville, near Etampes on the route from Paris to Orleans, in the early 1780s, contained at one of its most northerly limits a simple Doric Temple designed by Hubert Robert as a monument to Captain Cook. I should explain that the temple has long been removed from its original site; a simple wash drawing is one of the only surviving records. It shows the structure standing on its own small island, in the middle of a pond – reminiscent in this respect of the much smaller tomb which commemorates Rousseau at the Marquis de

Girardin's Ermenonville. There is a medallion of Cook under cover inside the open temple, and an inscription which tells how Cook 'crossed three times the immense extent of the Ocean' and visited 'the two poles in turn'. The relative inaccessibility of the Temple was offset by the provision of an inviting rustic seat placed opposite the little island, in front of a grove of trees.

Now there is a significant biographical detail which helps us to explain why M. de Laborde places a monument to Cook in his garden. Elsewhere at Méréville, there is a rostral column (perhaps modelled on the famous one at Stowe) which commemorates the two sons of the family who embarked with La Pérouse on his ill-fated expedition and perished off the Californian coast. This reference does not, however, in any way account for the role played by the Cook monument within the garden as a whole, or explain the special meaning of the different elements which have been assembled in this one particular feature. As a description by Alexandre de Laborde makes clear, the meaning does not stop at the evocative role of the neo-classical monument. He writes: 'The river flows slowly, natural rocks dominate the site, and a variety of trees covers it almost entirely. Everything that is there breathes recreation and reverie. A large number of foreign trees seem to reproduce there the savage and far-away countries which conceal the veritable tomb of this illustrious voyager.'

So the dual system arranges that we shall see the ideal monument, in the form of a temple, removed from us by a stretch of water that might signify the infinitely wider stretch between Europe and Cook's last resting place. But we are also surrounded by trees of exotic species which lend a different kind of access to the otherness of the foreign clime. Abbé Delille himself testifies in the Introduction to his poem Les Jardins that this use of the exotic tree as what, after Jakobson, we would call a *shifter* between one series and another, was well recognised in contemporary lore. The young inhabitant of Tahiti – Potaveri by name – who had been brought back to France by Bougainville impressed his attentive hosts by nothing so much as his affecting behaviour when confronted, at Versailles, with a species of tree from his native land. As Delille puts it: 'he embraced the tree which he recognised, which recalled to him his native land. It is *O-Taiti*, he said; and looking at the other trees, It is not *O-Taiti*. Thus these trees and his native land were identified in his mind.' Delille has, by his own admission, distorted this story slightly in the context of his poem by transplanting the scene from the royal garden at Versailles to the justly celebrated Botanical Garden, or Jardin Royal des Plantes, in

Paris. He is thus preparing the reader for the poetic expression of the same audacious metonymy as poor Potaveri, in the extremity of his disorientation, used to slide from Versailles to Tahiti:

Je voyage, entouré de leur foule choisie,
D'Amérique en Europe, et d'Affrique en Asie.
(I voyage, surrounded by the select crowd of trees
From America to Europe, and from Africa to Asia.)

Nevertheless, we may reasonably feel that the transport is weaker than in the case which authenticates it. And we may also feel that the example of the Botanical Garden, precisely a type of garden where the exotic tree is present *sub specie* – under its botanical name, is not conducive to the idea of a poetic transport.

This brings us back to the example of the Cook monument, and its attendant rocks and trees, at Méréville. For one might say that the contrasting case of Méréville shows up, in one crucial respect, the difference between a garden of this type, and a botanical garden. Where the botanical garden is in essence discontinuous with the surrounding world, demonstrating in the form of a paradigm the order of like and unlike species, the poetic or philosophical or painterly garden must enshrine metaphorically the definition of its own limits. Cook's Monument is therefore at the extreme edge of the garden at Méréville; here, where the garden ends, and adjoining hamlets would otherwise occupy the visual field, the imagination is captured by a kind of rhetorical demonstration of the breaking of limits, signified by Cook's unprecedented circumnavigations of the globe. The notional limitlessness that we cannot have in reality is achieved, in terms of the garden design, by the ingeniously exploited contemporary reference.

This marking of the limit by an evocation of the limitless, or (as it might be more precisely defined in an English context) the sublime, has specially convincing parallels with the practice of English gardeners of this epoch. I am thinking, for example, of the way in which the astonishing cascade at Bowood, added to Capability Brown's original scheme in the last quarter of the eighteenth century, causes the visitor to dip down, strangely enough, below the level of Brown's lake, and so forget in the proximity of the spectacular waterfall the close proximity of farming lands which even the Marquess of Lansdowne was unable to purchase. And this reminds me that Laborde's Méréville is also, in a real sense, a garden which looks towards the parallel achievements of the *jardin à l'anglaise*, rather than a mere additional to the French classical genre. As with Girardin's Ermenonville, the gesture is a political as much as aesthetic one. Laborde may not have harboured Rousseau, or defended his farming lands against the feudal encroachment of the Prince de Condé in hot pursuit, as Girardin did; but it comes as no surprise to find that he did not emigrate, as the royalist aristocrats predominantly did, and that he attempted to forestall his own eventual execution by the revolutionaries with the doubtless sincere argument that an exceedingly rich person was not, for that very reason, an enemy of the Revolution.

This reference to English and French garden types obliges me, however, to make a more explicit differentiation between the various national and historical modes, and to show their particular relevance to what I have called the 'semantic recoil' of voyages of discovery as it arises with the problem of limits. It is a necessary over-simplification if I establish a very sharp distinction between the English and French systems, maintaining for theoretical reasons a difference which is sometimes mediated, as in the case of Méréville. This being said, let me assert that the characteristic English practice is to establish limits through a pictorial, mythic or cultural framing.

Stourhead presents a series of perfectly composed vistas which borrow the compositional techniques of Claude; it also converts the otherness of a realised pictorial vista into a cultural otherness, through being displaced from the Wiltshire valley to the utopia of the Roman idylls. Even in the present century, a bastardised garden (now largely destroyed) like the Astors' garden at Hever depends first of all upon an enclosure – here a literal one – and secondly upon the stunning estrangement effect of authentic classical fragments cropping up among the climbing roses. Perhaps the defining mark of the English garden throughout the ages – from the medieval *Pearl* poem to Sissinghurst and Hidcote in the present century – is that we are either deeply inside it – 'well in', as Lewis Carroll might have said – or we are on the outside looking in. When Walter Pater describes 'park scenery' in his essay on the School of Giorgione, it is impossible to decide for a while if he is describing a picture by Giorgione or an English park. The point is, no doubt, that the very idea of the park is so rich with cultural mediation that no such distinction will hold, on the poetic level at least. What lies at the root of such an equivocal but passionate attachment to the garden is, as the Pre-Raphaelites and William Morris recognised, a mythic representation of the Earthly Paradise, which is always on the point of reversing itself into the Garden of Eden from which, in so far as we are knowledgeable, we have always already been expelled.

By contrast, the French garden is a minutely graded series of transitions, rather than a system of mythic rupture which creates an enclosed space and forces us to oscillate between the inside and the outside of it. The French system begins, as in Le Nôtre's garden at the Château de Champs, strictly at the constructed form of the house itself. Where the great houses of Stourhead and Hever are bizarrely dislocated from the space of the garden, Champs allows us to see how culture accommodates to nature through a series of exact moves. The château is both mineral and constructed; the garden of *broderie* immediately in front is mineral in composition, yet foliate in its rococo design when seen from the first floor salon of the château. The topiary and trained trees are vegetable in substance, yet trained to espouse the geometrical forms of the cultural system; elaborate urns, the statues of fauns and nymphs, continue this slow and systematic series, in which each term derives properties from those adjoining on other side, the 'natural' and the 'cultural' poles of opposition. When the gamut has been run from the château through all these intermediate and linked stages of mediation, we finally reach the untrained, undifferentiated limit of the surrounding forest. The forest, whose encroachment has been, as it were, successively deferred by the transitional system, can finally signify an unlimited wildness.

This brief and schematic account of oppositions has served its purpose. It was not designed in any way to exhaust the subject of English and French garden history. But it does identify a difference in procedure which could be equated with a fundamental difference in rhetorical options. Surely we have here that indispensable contemporary distinction between metonymic and metaphorical modes of discourse? The French system derives its closure from the seemingly inevitable accumulation of transitions between contiguous terms; when it has worked itself through, we are at an end. The English system depends upon a sudden break, a dislocation of physical continuities, and a metaphorical plunge into mythic, religious or cultural symbols which will serve to give meaning to the newly created space.

Let me leave out of account here the question of how far this opposition is a synchronic one, designed to explain the contrasting features of two systems of landscape design at any one time, and how far it has a diachronic dimension, referring to the gradual or sudden displacement of one system by the other. This is not my primary concern, since I shall in fact be locating the difference within the evolution of a single, contemporary career. Bernard Lassus, founder of the Centre de Recherche d'Ambiances in 1962 and Professor since 1969 at the Ecole des Beaux-Arts in Paris, seems to be virtually the only example today of an artist who has developed a poetics of landscape in the widest sense. That is to say, he not only reviews and criticises the historical development of landscape, extracting from his review particular theoretical principles which he sees as governing man's mediated relation with nature at different junctures, but he also applies his theory in an ever widening area of practice, which has taken him from kinetic works and environments in the 1960s, through an exhaustive documentation of popular garden forms in the early 1970s, to a formulation of garden schemes in the past ten years, largely in response to the challenge of special competitions within France. His garden schemes have tended to win prizes for their originality and then fail to be realised for the same reason. But, as I shall show, the recent results are encouraging, and some of Lassus's realised schemes, on a large scale, visibly overturn some of our firmest assumptions about contemporary man's relationship to landscape.

The first point I should make about Lassus, and the point which gives him relevance in this context, is that his work is rooted in a particular perception of the French classical tradition, as I have described it; but he has seen the need to assess the internal system of relations thus established against an overall view of the world which is, as it were, taken for granted in the internal system. We can take as his point of departure, reasonably enough, the Modern Classicism of Léger, in whose studio he worked during the mid-1950s. For Léger, the forms of nature are generalised, and as it were monumentalised; they receive the cultural seal of the industrial environment. His 'Walking Flower', from 1951, is the same kind of mid-term between nature and culture as the clipped topiary bush in the French classical garden, though its site is, of course, the ideal location of the gallery and not the real natural environment. When Lassus was asked to provide a sculpture for the new school being built at Guénange in Lorraine in 1969, he decided to break as far as he could with the protocol of the separate sculptural object on its podium, and to devise what he called 'Artificial Bushes' which both belonged to the prefabricated, contemporary environment of the new school, and yet also evoked the free form and colourful variety of natural foliage. Here was a medium term between the two extremes of the built form and the adjoining wood, which rendered the transition between them less abrupt and painful.

It is important to bear in mind that Lassus was not simply reviving an archaic system from the jardin à la française. His elaborate documentation

of the homes of what he was to call 'habitants–paysagistes' during the late
sixties and early seventies made him aware that, throughout France,
individuals quite unrelated to one another were transforming the small
open spaces available to them in ways which completely bypassed conventional good taste. Concrete walls would be broken up through
complex patterning which gave an illusory dimension to the surface;
mineral and vegetative elements would be combined in a plastic density
of effect, which might at first seem unsystematic, but gradually revealed
its principles of organisation. Lassus became particularly interested in
two mechanisms which he called the *retarded contrast* and the *common
denominator*. The retarded contrast was the transfer of one element in a
system to another system at their mutual limits: the common denominator was equally a dematerialisation, but through the treatment of all
juxtaposed elements according to the same colour code. Consequently,
when Lassus himself showed in sculpture salons in the early seventies,
he deliberately chose a mode of work which acknowledged the adjacent
parkland – which was, if you like, the minimal possible displacement
spatially and conceptually from the existing scene.

Yet Lassus's attempt to find a parallel practice, both to the French
classical garden and to the *habitants–paysagistes*, eventually came up against
a formidable problem, which was precisely the problem of limits.
Certain of the people whom he studied made a remarkable investment
in contemporary folklore, that is, the folklore of industrial man. M.
Pecqueur, a miner in a small village near Béthune in the Nord, covered
the internal walls of his small garden with painted scenes from the story
of Snow White and the Seven Dwarfs. The aim of this extraordinary
imaginative enterprise, as Lassus was finally to conclude, was precisely
that of making real on the symbolic level the notion of the Forest, as a
region of otherness against which garden space could be measured.
Snow White, realised as a statue with her hand on a small fawn, stood at
the very end of Pecqueur's garden, ecompassing with her glance the drab
industrial landscape of the Nord, and yet transforming it mythically into
the uncontaminated, natural paradise of which she became a kind of
honorary representative.

This kind of realisation was accompanied by a radical questioning of
the conditions of otherness, or wildness, for the French classical garden. Lassus's train of thought is epitomised in a delightful card which he
republished in 1981 under the title 'Arbres taillés', or 'Clipped trees'.
Here was, in miniature, a perfect example of a series of transitions, from a
land-based hotel, through a rock-based, permeable pavilion structure, to

an extraordinary rock-mounted ship. As the reference to clipped trees suggests, this was an analogous system to that of the classical garden, in which the final term – the otherness in terms of which all the transitions were relativised – was not the Forest but the Ocean. But the very irony implicit in this comparison makes us realise that Lassus was not in fact ratifying, but questioning, the basis of such transitional systems. Both Pecqueur's creation of the Forest, and the notion of the Ocean implicitly presumed by this Belle-Epoque extravaganza, have an air of straining to achieve the ultimate term which they can no longer merely take for granted. Why should it be so? At this point, it will be useful to consider a text written by Lassus in 1980. It will clarify a number of issues raised here:

What countryside, what horizons can be drawn into the garden? There are some who dare to give an answer. Like Charles Pecqueur, a modern alchemist who places a life-sized statue of Snow White, in painted concrete, at the end of his garden. From this point she can contemplate orchards, a railway line and a rubbish tip, all of which are changed into a deep forest peopled with birds and fawns . . .

Most frequently, it is through miniaturisation that these landscapes are created in the midst of the garden, since the miniaturisation is a means of warding off direct exploration by the touch. A few sailing boats, a light-house, a cement boat or a siren seated on the edge of a pond 'are the ocean', just as the stag and deer 'are the forest' which also no longer exists.

Is it not this same kind of nostalgia which impels others in increasing numbers to take to the ocean with a few square metres of sail, made of plastic admittedly, but without the support of a motor, which is the important thing?

The landscapes which took as their basis of articulation the great forest, and the ocean considered as limitless, exist no longer except in recurrent moments. The aeroplane may have transformed the sea into a lake, but the storm reminds us that it remains a domain beyond measurement.

It is the classical attitude to measurement – measurement which presumes a variable distance from an ultimate degree of wildness – which is now open for debate. Can we keep on making oppositions between the case of measurement by touch (the cottage whose every corner I know with my eyes shut) or by sight (the château with its gallery of mirrors) and the standard of immeasurability offered by the forest? Can we any longer attempt the traditional ways of progressively conquering wildness with constructed forms in the horizontal dimension, such as the topiary hedge, or in a more ironic vein, the 'artificial bush' formed from hundreds of balls of enamelled metal, in various colours, which is placed between an orthogonal, metal-framed building and a wood?

Numerous are the figures, from Christopher Columbus to Charcot, who have carried out this progressive exploration of the horizontal dimension, man's basic sphere of activity. It is no longer possible to have the same ambition as James

Cook – to go not only further on earth than any man had yet been, but as far as it was even possible to go.

I break off here in order to make a brief summary of the way in which Lassus's self-critical text dovetails with the argument I have been pursuing, as well as with what one might call the general evolution of French thought over the last quarter-century. Lassus's original perception of the classical system is also consistent with the moment of High Structuralism, with the acceptance of the opposition between Nature and Culture as unproblematic, and the poetic programme arising from this acceptance amounting to the creation of a range of intermediate terms. Yet Lassus locates the inevitable overturning of this problematic historically, as well as epistemologically. For the classical garden to have its plenitude of meaning, in his view, it is necessary not only for it to stop at the Forest, but for the undiscovered stretches of the Earth to be identified with the wildness of the Forest. In the limit which awaits us at the edge of the classical garden, we meet a dividing line which holds, and secures the system, only in so far as our knowledge of the Earth's surface is not complete. In the light of this perception, it becomes easily understandable that Cook's voyages should coincide with a decisive shift in the organisation of landscape; one which could be discussed in terms of the growing popularity of the English garden, and the relegation by contrast of the jardin à la française. The reason why Delille concludes his poem on gardens with a eulogy to Cook is that he is defending a concept of gardening which rejects the practice of mediating transitions, and opts instead for the poetic or philosophical plunge into an imagined space, in which a monument or a group of exotic trees can act as shifters to an immensity in the very process of being revealed, and exhausted. Cook's monument at Méréville is a decisive feature in a garden which swings, both ideologically and systematically, to the English pattern. But precisely because it reveals the connection between garden organisation and the contemporary state of exploration, it renders that connection problematic. How can the mythic values, the Edenic values, which support the enclosure effect of the English garden be successfully sustained?

A possible answer to this question, and a justification for asking it in the first place, comes again from Lassus:

A little more than 10 years ago, on 23 July 1969, Neil Armstrong walked on the Moon and saw the Earth.
As the Earth has grown smaller, losing the immeasurable dimension of its

landscapes which have submitted to the measurement of machines, techniques and apparatuses, it should have been transformed into a Garden of Delights or a Garden of Eden. But has it been?

The horizontal dimension is experienced at present as a continuum of manmade installations which man must live within. It is no longer possible to escape – no longer possible to leave everything and set out for the West, like the hero of a Western.

Exploration of the immeasurable in the horizontal dimension is succeeded by the approach to the immeasurable verticals: the conquest of space, of the depths of the sea, and the earth. The surface that we tread upon is also a depth – immeasurable, vertical and obscure.

Is it in fact mere rhetoric to cite the moon landing in this way, as effecting a qualitative change in the systems of measurement through which we adjust our relationship to the natural world? Certainly it would be so if such an intuition were unsupported by the evidence which comes from the prior history of garden forms and of voyages of exploration. But if Lassus has helped to show that the last three centuries have seen a gradual atrophy of the horizontal dimension as an intrinsic system, and if he has shown that this atrophy is linked to the physical exploration of the earth's crust – if he has shown that the new solutions to the gardener's problem have involved the poetic creation of depths (whether evoked, or in the case of the cascade at Bowood, physically constructed), then there is reason to suppose that this may be the imaginative correlate to an increasingly strong preoccupation with the vertical dimension.

Of course the problem remains: how is this to be done in such a way as to revitalise the contemporary garden, and the contemporary perception of landscape? It strikes me as fascinating that the very recent works shown by Hamish Fulton, the English Land artist, for the most part introduce the the moon metonymically, or metaphorically. 'Bamboo Moon Shadows' cast themselves across the image which indicates a walk in Japan, while his stunning record of a 'Seven Day Walk in North Eastern California on the night of the October Full Moon' preserves the silver shadow of moonlight on intricately decorated wood, within a vignette shape that itself recalls the Moon. Even 'An Eleven Day Wandering in Central Australia', dating from 1982, includes in its full title the word 'July Moon Eclipse'. It is as if the severe combinatory of elements and epithets required this index of an intermittent and occluded moonlight to create a space for its deployment.

Lassus, of course, goes about things in an entirely different way. He takes for granted not only the social, interactive nature of a landscape practice in the strict sense of the term, but also the need to achieve an image of height, or depth, which is contrived by human artifice. His project, 'The Well', dating from 1972, was an initial demonstration of the structures involved. Taking the common lore of throwing a pebble into a well as his pretext, he arranges the so-called well in such a way that the expected splash, after a brief interval, never in fact comes; what comes instead is one of a number of randomly triggered stimuli, producing screaming sounds, or blood-coloured jets of water, or perhaps most strangely no sound at all. In this case, as Lassus suggests: 'The pebble can then wound the Loch Ness monster, pass through the Earth or rejoin the thousands of pebbles which rain in Eternity . . ..' In other words, the human contrivance which disrupts causation also makes the depth imaginatively available as an infinite dimension – and so restores the sense of limit and unlimitedness which has been lost in the horizontal domain. And for Lassus, this vertical dimension can also take on a historical character. His project for a park in the new town of L'Isle d'Abeau

**9** Bernard Lassus, sketch plan for the Garden of the Anterior.

grapples with the difficult question of how to confer a dimension of depth upon a community which has no historical roots in the location. His solution to the problem is to make the extensive park not a visually accessible domain, which the eye can cover and exhaust at a glance, but by contrast an area 'with no walks and pathways', where 'you will discover – as the ground becomes more and more wild – the occasional field scattered with groups of trees, a few domestic animals, almost abandoned fields which retain parcels of earlier cultivation, fallow land, woods, bushes, thickets or briar surroundings practically inaccessible ponds, fringes of the forest where the dead branches are no longer gathered up . . .'.

Dotted throughout this area, however, are the micro-landscapes which illustrate the legends and tales of the region:

At sunset you will be able to hear, close to the banks of the pond, the strange tolling of the submerged bells of the Lac du Bar; and a little further on, the image of a submerged village will emerge, in a halo of light, from the depth of the water.

To aid the discovery of these secret places and to allow the pedestrian to find his way, columns will be installed beside each of the microlandscapes. At the top of each of them, which you reach by a few steps, there will be a peephole through which one or more of the other columns can be seen: they mark the spot of the Tour de la Belle Allemande, the Grotte de la Bonne Femme, the Enchanted Tree, The Wolf of Virieu.

Lassus's 'Garden of the Anterior' for L'Isle d'Abeau (Fig. 9) is organised around micro-landscapes of which one could appropriately use Alexandre de Laborde's phrase: 'Everything that is there breathes recreation and reverie'. Through disrupting the visual continuum, making the going difficult, and singling out the individual feature with its viewing column, he breaks completely with the French classical garden; instead, he opts for the prolongation in depth, in the real and imaginative profundity, of a recreative image of the mythic and historical place. There are no longer the exotic species, conjoined to Cook's temple, which encourage the sense of being transported across to the other side of the globe. But there is perhaps the hovering, potential presence of the cosmonaut, whom Lassus is to celebrate in a remarkable text called 'The monument', written in 1979. Here he tells a kind of fable of the discovery of a monument, in the form of three large spheres which two travellers come across after an arduous journey across a slope 'bristling with rocks'. The three large spheres tell of the journey and return of Apollo XI, and recall that the monument has been erected to commemorate the bicentenary of man's first step on the Moon. But the text itself is adorned with two roundels which display the Utopian and the Distopian version of land-scape: a section of Milton's *Paradise lost* taken from Delille's *Les Jardins* and a wonderful description of the 'sublime horror' of Chinese landscape as described by Chambers in a book published in Paris in 1776.

The third, absent roundel is no doubt the one which signifies our own contemporary choice – neither Utopia (for the Earth has not become a 'Garden of Delights') nor Distopia (though the point of the fable is precisely to warn against that). In Lassus's case, this third choice is perhaps most fully represented in his most ambitious garden scheme so far, the 'Garden of the Planets' which he submitted in 1980 in the competition for the Parc de la Villette (Fig. 10). Here, in planning the large and splendid site around the new Science Museum of the French State, he chooses to leave the external face of the land extraordinarily simple, with meadow grasses, wild flowers and the butterfly as a super-numerary flower which will populate this area so utterly different from the French formal garden, maintained as a fetish by contemporary muni-cipal planners. But the design acquires its interest particularly because of the underground 'Path of Abysses', which opens up behind a fountain's curtain of water:

And so, under the ground, visitors would come upon the celestial, immaterial vault of a planetarium, with its suggestions of infinity, a measureless vertical, taking the place of our measureless horizontals, the new forest of the classical garden. Then further on, in a descending gallery, there would be a reconstruction of the visual field of Armstrong, walking on the Moon, set around one of the stones which he brought back: the first flower of this new botanical garden.

At the lowest point, with a dull growling, there would be section models of volcanoes, both active and extinct, bordering on a bottomless pit, in homage to Jules Verne's *Journey to the Centre of the Earth*; another measureless vertical which is still beyond our apprehension: the depths of the Earth.

What I have tried to do here is to bring together, both historically and theoretically, certain basic ideas about the relation to the unexplored which is taken for granted in the garden, or man-made landscape, and to suggest that Lassus is a contemporary theorist and practitioner of land-scape design who makes us think about the relation of our human systems of measurement to the independent and cumulative achieve-ment of circumnavigators and cosmonauts. If I am bound to say that this last design, for the 'Garden of the Planets', very narrowly missed being chosen in a competition which attracted far more attention in France than any comparable one in modern times, then I can also draw a historical moral from its lack of success. The Abbé Delille, in 1782, stigmatised the tendency to leave garden design to architects, suggesting that we should banish from the garden 'all this confused mass of diverse edifices, lavished by fashion'. He might indeed have been describing the winning entry for the La Villette competition, by Bernard Tschumi. It is still valid to pit against the imperialist architect's architectural garden design that syntagm of terms which Delille chooses to express his positive endorsement. Let us be attentive to the gardens of the philosopher, the painter and the poet.

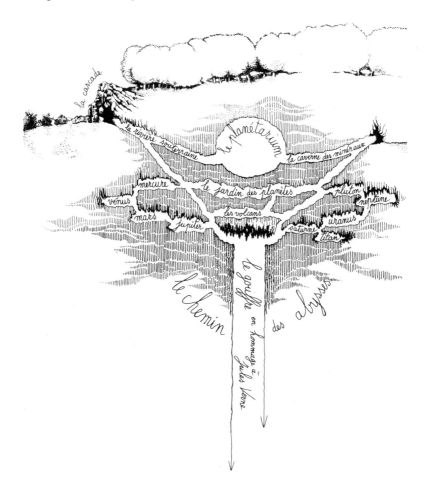

**10** Bernard Lassus, sketch plan for the Garden of the Planets.

# Notes

First published in J. C. Eade (ed.), *Projecting the landscape* (Canberra, 1987).

Extracts from the Abbé Jacques Delille's poem, *Les Jardins*, are taken from the first edition (Paris, 1782), and from the new edition, with introduction (Paris, 1801).

The best brief introductory article on M. de Laborde's garden at Méréville is Oliver Choppin de Janvry, 'Méréville', in *L'Oeil*, no. 180 (December 1969), pp. 30–5 *et seq.*

Extracts from the writings of Bernard Lassus are taken from 'The landscape approach of Bernard Lassus', texts translated and introduced by Stephen Bann, *Journal of Garden History*, vol. 3, no. 2 (April–June 1983), pp. 79–107.

# 14

# The greening of capitalism: the political economy of the Tory garden festivals
### John Roberts

The integration of the public spectacle or festival into the economic programme of capitalism can be dated back, in any coherent fashion, to the formation of various Societies for the Encouragement of Arts, Manufacture and Commerce in Europe between the middle of the eighteenth century and the beginning of the nineteenth. However, it is not until the passing of a number of museums acts in the leading industrial countries that we get any direct concern on the part of the European ruling classes to establish a wider public culture for the consumption and regulation of capitalist interests. The Great Exhibition in Britain in 1851 is of course one of the first major examples of this legislation in action and the obvious forerunner of so many commercial festivals and events today. However, with the advent of the second and third technological revolutions and the expansion of communications in general in this century, we have witnessed a far greater reliance on the cultural event to secure the ideological reproduction of capitalism than was available or conceivable to the organisers of the Great Exhibition. The post-war literature on this process is now enormous, and certainly does not need to be rehearsed here. Nevertheless, for the sake of clarity we might say that what distinguishes late capitalism from competitive capitalism is its extended capacity to rule through ideological inclusion.[1] Late capitalism is the attentuation of the disguise of capitalism as a mode of production through the cultural extension and seeming enhancement of the extra-economic sphere. Thus along with the media *et alia*, the cultural event or spectacle – be it theme-park, stately home, open-air museum – have become explicit points for the affective transmission of capitalist relations. Even so, as a number of recent commentators on the expansion of the leisure/museum economy have stated, this process of ideological manufacture is as much about leaving things unsaid as any aggressive form of bourgeois myth-making. History as the neutral unfolding of technological development is canonically preferred to any model that might touch on history in any way as a process in which human agents play conflicting parts.[2]

It is no surprise therefore that the Tories, through the current recession, should turn to various culturalist strategies to ameliorate or distract the full impact of Britain's place within the economic world crisis. However, such strategies, in the shape of the recent spate of garden festivals in the North of England and Scotland, are more than simply ideological distractions. For they are responses to, and products of, massive qualitative changes in the global economic order. The so-called 'de-industrialisation' of the British and other Western economies is no more or less the break-up of the old capital bases in the smokestack industries as part of a new cycle of capital accumulation. In fact what is happening under the development of new technology is not so much 'de-industrialisation' but re-industrialisation. Britain, however, because of its particular economic history and conditions of decline, has suffered more at the hands of these global structural changes than most other Western economies. The anomalies of the situation are revealed graphically at the time of writing by the fact that despite the credit boom we have the worst balance of trade ever. That is a consequence of the historical weakness of Britain's manufacturing base and the Tories' over-optimistic belief in an expanded (and non-unionised) service industry. The Tories have gone for short-term entrepeneuralism under the shield of the new technology, leaving the prospect of long-term 'recovery' even more of a hopeless illusion. This is why one of the main structural problems facing capitalism in recent years has been the over-accumulation of capital in the absence of its investment in production. (Hence the large amounts of capital slushing about in the City chasing short-term profit.) Which in turn is a product, under the effects of recession, of wage-levels and conditions fought for and maintained by the working class. Because the ruling class cannot raise the level of exploitation in certain industries in order to be competitive, it will simply not invest. This is one of the reasons why a large percentage of the manufacturing output of the West has been taken up by the Newly Industrialising Countries (South Korea, Taiwan, Hong Kong, Singapore), and why the West, particularly Britain, has looked to the new technologies to create new forms of competitive advantage. 'De-industrialisation' or re-industrialisation thus covers a more general process: the decline of monopoly production in the West and the rise of the increased specialisation of economies on a global basis.[3]

In looking at the phenomenon of the garden festival, then, we need to address three main areas: the changing nature of the global economy, changing patterns of collective consumption in Britain, and the politics of British national culture. It is at their intersection that we can begin to get a clearer picture of how much festivals are both a symptom and response to capitalist crisis.

As I have said, the ideological function of the festival is not new. When the Festival of Britain was organised in 1951 it was self-consciously imitating the nationalist confidence-building of the Great Exhibition. Both sought in clear national–populist terms to galvanise the self-understanding of the British people as a race and political community. The recent garden festivals at Liverpool (1984) Stoke (1986) and Glasgow (1988) operate very much within this tradition. Taking as their general themes reclamation and renewal, all three seek to present the people of the North of England and Scotland with a message from the 'new economic frontier'; that we have entered a brave new entrepeneurial world. In this we see one of the main functions of such festivals: the codification, under the impact of changes in the forces and relations of production, of a new relationship between work, leisure and the public sphere. Such festivals on this scale address visitors in a sense as new kinds of citizens. This is why it is particularly instructive to compare the garden festivals with the Festival of Britain. For if the Festival of Britain is a product of the Keynesian welfare state and *étatiste* thinking generally, the garden festivals are pedagogically and formally anti-statist. The imagined relationship between the new citizen and the public sphere is consequently very different indeed.

The Festival of Britain was organised under conditions of low productivity and an austerity economy. 1951 was pre-boom. The economic optimism and environmental modernism of the Festival then attempted to cut a swathe through the general sense of British dereliction. Britain might have won the war, but had emerged to find itself a net debtor to the rest of the world. The profits of empire, which had protected Britain through the crisis of the thirties, had been used extensively to pay for the war. The Festival of Britain therefore became the focal point of British renewal; the site of a whole range of modernising aims, directives and plans. In this respect one of the main functions of the Festival was to *visualise* a new Britain, a Britain that could now throw off the fusty remnants of Victorian and Edwardian culture and take its place within a modern capitalist Europe. Thus central to the Festival was not just an emphasis upon new and more rational forms of production, but the need for Britain to integrate and advance the lessons and experience of European modernism. Environmental planning and design were emphasised as principal factors in the emergence of a new Britain. Good design and efficacious planning would create new forms of social space and interaction that would be equal to the demands of a new social democracy.[4] Slums, urban decay and the general desuetude of pre-war industrialisation would give way to a clean and predominatly suburbanised environment. All those things that 'created' social division – poor housing, poor amenities, urban fragmentation – would disappear. In essence the Festival of Britain invited the visitor to view social democracy in state-led terms as a form of controlled and benign social engineering. State-led planning and design, through an expanded public sector, would create the new Britain. Which is why the overriding form of the symbolisation adopted by the Festival was regeneration and growth through a kind of 'social holism'. Design, planning and technology were to be welded together in the pursuit of a harmonious, stable environment.

Thirty-eight years on, of course, and this optimism has been swept aside as state-led economies in Britain and elsewhere have collapsed under the impact of the new slump. Moreover, the environmental modernism we associate with expanded public sectors of the post-war Western economies has proven to be an aesthetic and ecological disaster. Experiments in integrated design and the suburbanisation of Modernism have led to Ronan Point and mock-Georgian semis. Economically in Britain this period has also been a disaster. Contrary to the technological projections of the Festival of Britain, manufacturing production dropped from 25 per cent in 1950 to 9 per cent in 1975,[5] which was of course the period when the social–democratic state went into sharp economic crisis. For it was in 1976–77 under Labour that public spending cuts were introduced. The great vision of an environmental modernism marching hand in hand with a social evolutionism (enshrined in many ways in Tony Crosland's reformism) had come to a pathetic end, dashed on the rocks of Labourism. It is no surprise therefore that Thatcher's more strident form of capitalist 'crisis-management' has retained so much political support, for she had her way paved for her. The failures of Labourist social evolutionism have been used as a convenient sop by the Tories to attack state interventionism and to defend the 'free market'.

However, irrespective of whether the Labour Party or the Tories are in government the formats of representation of bourgeois rule remain essentially nationalist ones. It has been of particular interest then to see how the Tories in the wake of the crisis of social evolutionism, and in the face of the current slump, have attempted to represent their would-be national recovery. For whatever the economic and cultural failings of statism, Labour-led post-war social democracy managed to project with a considerable degree of success the vision of a multi-class-based demo-cratic community. This is what the ameliorative planning strategies of the Festival of Britain were all about. Thatcherism has not been so successful, despite all the hectoring and unction about a return to traditional British values. And this is why the garden festivals are so revealing, because they reflect the general inability of the Tories under the present economic crisis to re-establish the bourgeois national project in any confidently expansive way. The festivals may speak of national realities, but as political strategies they are principally regionalist in context and audi-ence. In short they are not so much generalised responses to national recovery and growth, but to the lag that the North has experienced behind the South through the current restructuring of the economy. The garden festivals are only able to apply the formats of bourgeois nationalist representation in a partial way.

It is worth noting at this stage then, how little national media attention they have received. For what the festivals reflect is not the amelioration of social division bound to populist consensus, but a series of palliatives *thrown at* social division. As such, what has happened under the Tories' crisis management of poor economic performance and high unem-ployment is the increasing inability of the ruling class to incorporate those aspects of cross-class conviviality that were so successful in the festival of Britain. The contradictions of late capitalism are getting harder to 'green' over.

Broadly speaking, the recent garden festivals were organised by the Tories in order to attract business to 'de-industrialised' areas in the North and Scotland. Advertisements for urban regeneration amongst the fallen social fabric of the old industrial centres, the festivals are in themselves ingenious acts of reclamation (albeit impermanent). The Stoke festival was built on the site of a disused steel mill, Liverpool and Glasgow on the site of old oil-storage depots. The symbolism of reclamation, then, remains important in establishing the future commercial possibilities of the areas. By landscaping sites of dereliction into areas that combine the qualities of parkland, the open-air museum and the trade fair, the image of the pastoral secures a vision of the North as a potential future competi-tor in the new cultural/services industries. One of the organisers of the

Glasgow festival is quite frank about this: 'to be thought of as the best cultural city in 1990 gives one the belief that many such events could follow in sequence. Some people are now discussing what happens in 1992 and whether we can have the Olympics.'[6] Furthermore the image of 'greening' extends the bourgeois dream of collective suburbanisation to the most recalcitrant of urban areas: the Northern inner city. It is interesting to note that one of the accompanying conferences to the Liverpool Garden Festival was entitled 'Green Towns and Cities, UK/USA: Can we Do it?' Suburbanization has been an essential part of capitalist crisis management. The move to the suburbs in the fifties and sixties by the inner-city working class was both a way of stimulating industrial capital – tax concessions to the building industry – and maintaining social stability – cheap mortgages. Moreover, it was a way of offloading the financial pressure of social consumption within the inner cities. The suburbs are subsidised by social capital at the expense of the inner cities, which remain a 'drain' on the state. This of course has been the logic of Thatcherism as it tries to stabilise the fiscal crisis of capitalism by reducing already depleted levels of social consumption even more; and the logic behind the garden festivals. In this respect the garden festivals revivify the suburban–pastoral dream as the basis for an individualist solution to social consumption. Which is why their mobilisation of the suburban–pastoral may accord with the Festival of Britain's use of the pastoral to ameliorate the realities of industrial decline and class conflict, but the economic framework within which it finds its expression is radically opposed. For we have to be clear: the garden festivals are coded attacks on collective consumption; the crisis of British capitalism is now of a qualitatively different order.

Far from promising the possibility of a progressive and integrated unfolding of the economic and the cultural as in the Festival of Britain, the garden festivals in Stoke, Liverpool and Glasgow invoke the virtues of the self-sufficient and *ad hoc*. In fact their commemoration of the passing away of the great smokestack industries of the North (at Stoke, in the form of the presentation of industrial 'remains') celebrates the passing away of industrialism as such. The festivals' revivification of the bourgeois pastoral myth is essentially the product of a 'post-industrial' perspective; anti-modernist and anti-planning in ideology, the festivals symbolise the would-be demise of the state-led industrialised economy as a new era of industrial democracy. New technology is ushering us into a world where the suburban ideal can become a reality, where home and work are located within the same non-urban area. The old large-scale industries based on class and union solidarity are giving way to small high-tech 'family' firms and individual entrepeneuralism, in which the merits of individual choice over collective identification will become the admired norm. This in reality is the Tories' view of their 'clean' service economy. 'Grow with Computers', says one of the company stands at Liverpool, echoing the organicism of its surroundings.

The Tories' use of the garden festivals to promote a new multi-class political community through the auspices of 'post-industrialism' employs, then, one of the central formats of bourgeois national representation: the idea of technology as ideologically neutral. The geographical mobility of the new high-tech industries will continue to release workers from the inner city into the suburbs and the countryside, goes the argument. However, as I have said, there are real limits to the consensual powers of such a format. For the garden festivals are not just celebrations of the new technology but responses to its divisive effects. The idea of new technology being the harbinger of a new cross-class communal conviviality in the North of England when new technology has obviously contributed to unemployment amongst the working class is clearly a category mistake of some size. Thus there is a fundamental contradiction in trying to represent new technology as the bearer of social conviviality today: the new technology under neo-liberal market conditions in fact stands to *destroy* human conviviality as it re-routinises the labour process and creates unemployment. Moreover, the Tories' ideological conflation between 'post-industrialism' and the end of collective social identities is a complete fantasy. Contrary to popular bourgeois myth, the level of trade union membership over the last ten years has remained relatively the same, which is remarkable considering that the real level of unemployment remains at around four million. Furthermore, although the proportion of workers employed in manufacturing in Britain has dropped from 34 per cent in 1964 to around 25 per cent today, the percentage remains higher than in the United states, and is comparable with Italy and France.[7] The politics of uneven development aside, Britain as the oldest industrialised country still remains relatively powerful industrially; it also contains a numerically powerful working class. Consequently we need to see the break-up of the inefficient and unprofitable capital bases in the North of England and Scotland not as further evidence of the demise of the working class but its continuing recomposition. The Tories have used therefore what has seemed like an inevitable process of industrial senescence as ideological cover for their neo-liberal economics.

In all this the garden festivals, like the Festival of Britain, have attempted to secure a new self-understanding on the part of the British citizen by attempting to link up economic change with cultural change. This is why the garden festival's attack on planning and the state-led economy has also been a direct attack on the deleterious effects of environmental modernism. In fact it could be said that the order of these points should be reversed. As Habermas has reminded us, one of the characteristics of bourgeois formats of representation is the conflation of cause with effect.[8] Thus in many respects it is because of the disastrous effects of environmental modernism under étatiste bourgeois economics that the Tories have had the success that they have in attacking social planning. The received image of the festivals is of a pastoralised commercial culture in which the eyesores of environmental modernism have been banished. Consequently one can understand why the festivals have taken the form they have in the North of England and Scotland. Up until the fifties Stoke had the largest amount of derelict land in the country. Both Liverpool and Glasgow had terrible records in housing and health as a result of the brutalising effects of environmental modernism. The 'canniness' of the garden festivals there lie in their direct appeal to popular memory, in so far as they can say: this is what Labour does: it uglifies. Moreover it can say it in terms which directs attention back to what Martin Wiener has called the dominance of the 'southern metaphor'[9] in the history of the bourgeois English pastoral myth. As an area which escaped the worst ravages of industrialisation, the image of the South as predominantly green is implanted in the North as a collective vision of what the whole of Britain might attain. The use of the English suburban pastoral myth of communal unity, then, is not to be seen as peripheral or fanciful, but as actually central – given its place within a deeper ruling-class cultural reflex – to the ideological functioning of the festivals. For what is being attempted here is the abolition of the North–South divide itself.

Political geographers talk about the question of territorial justice. Who gets what, where, how and why?[10] Such issues have of course been particularly conspicuous on the political agenda under Thatcherism; the discrepancies in public services and collective consumption generally have become markedly geographical ones. The old industrialised centres of the North as the home of municipal socialism have been high on the Tories' rate-capping hit-list. Thus the historical divisions between city and country, inner city and suburbs, have been exacerbated by an increasing division between North and South. This division has to a great extent always been in place under British capitalism, but because of the Tories' attack on the political bases of social capital, it has grown wider and deeper. The risks involved in this for the Tories have been considerable; faced with Scotland and the North depressed by unemployment and public spending cuts, the Tories have been unable to play their 'one nation' card. In fact some commentators talk about Thatcherism as an explicit rejection of 'one nation' conservatism.[11] However, even if the Tories are prepared to create and live with a demoralised under-class in the inner cities both North and South, bourgeois politicians are never happy about losing their grip on the myth of national unity. Contrary to various currents on the Left, the Tories have not let the North and Scotland 'go'. They're actually worried; which is why the garden festivals have attempted to re-situate the image of national unity through the format of a Southern/English-centred pastoralism. It is one of the basic ideological functions of all pastoral traditions to deflect or cover opposed class interests through the collective experience or memory of nature and the landscape. This is as much a factor of seventeenth-century English landscape poetry, with its oppositions between the pleasing perspectives of the Estate and its loyal peasantry and the violence and unpredictability of the social world,[12] as it is the rural literature of England earlier this century with its denigration of the industrialised North as a bastardised Englishness (read middle-class values). When W. V. Morton said in In Search of England (1927): 'The only consolation is that these monster towns and cities of the north of England are a mere speck in the amazing greeness of England',[13] we are clearly being shown what is at stake in the celebration of Englishness as essentially a Southern experience; the need for an integrative symbol of Englishness that will retain the link between national unity and an image and experience of the landscape as expressly class-free. This is why in many respects the pastoral tradition remains such a powerful tradition within British ruling-class ideologies from the seventeenth century onwards. Because of Britain's early political unification, the spread of the market economy into the countryside and the destruction of the peasantry, the countryside in England, in contrast to the Continent, was relatively free of strong class associations. The South then became an increasing focus for rural mythologising and site of national beauty as the North underwent heavy industrialisation. One only has to look at the extensive amount of literature produced during the last century and through the first half of this century (Alfred Austin, Morton, Robert Blatchford, J. B. Priestley, Sir John Betjeman) to realise how much of an obsessive political problem the divide between country and city has been for the ruling class.

The garden festivals fall very much within this long history of conservative 'green thought'. However, the ideological parameters of such thought have changed considerably since the days of Morton and Austin. Although conservative ruralism still secures an aspect of bourgeois nationalist representation, the basis of such mythologising is no longer available for mobilisation in the way that it was at the nostalgic height of the pastoral tradition in the thirties, forties and fifties. The argument is no longer one of simply idealising the values of the countryside in *contrast* to industrialisation and urban living, in a sense of celebrating that which remains untouched by capital, but of actually defending those values *against* the encroachments of capital. Without a check on pollution and deforestation, without a check on the proliferation of the nuclear industries, there will be no environment worth protecting. The Tories' use of the garden festivals, therefore, as an ideological extension of the English pastoral tradition, has had to make concessions, as the tradition has generally, to ecological analyses. Clearly there are structural limits to such concessions, but nonetheless conservative pastoralism's extension into 'ecological awareness' is a constituent part now of how the ruling class seeks to present the bourgeois nationalist myth. Mrs Thatcher's recent 'greening' is particularly illuminating in this respect. In a speech to the Royal Society in September 1988 she declared, 'protection of the environment is one of the greatest challenges of this century'. If we might be sceptical of what this means practically, nevertheless it is further evidence of what I mean by the conventional formats of bourgeois nationalist representation being unable to secure a convincing image of cross-class conviviality. The production of new technology and the ecological crisis of late capitalism has meant a search on the part of the ruling class to find new ways of foreclosing the gap between the crisis of capitalist futurity and human flourishing. Which is why the garden festivals not only celebrate anti-planning and an individualist entrepreneurial culture but lay claim to the self-sufficient and small-scale. In fact what the garden festivals attempt to do is denigrate the feasibility of a planned *socialist* economy through an explicit link-up between the anti-productivism of the English pastoral tradition and a consumerist environmentalism. In all the festivals the images and results of reclamation and conservation abound as essentially *individualistic* responses to the crisis of capitalist futurity. Thus if the Festival of Britain symbolised the future as an unfolding and collective partnership between the British people and state-led economic and cultural development, the garden

festivals, built as they are on the direct results on modernist environmentalism, are at pains to distance themselves from any collective
political–technological 'narrative'. In fact if we can talk about the Festival
of Britain constructing a new environment for social democracy based
on the rational integration of technology, science, architecture and art,
the garden festivals offer a radically heterogeneous response to the social
world. This is reflected in the environmental individualism of the layout
of the festivals themselves. At Stoke there were displays devoted to
environmental issues, a pavilion housing a video presentation on land
reclamation, a camera obscura, a small farm containing chickens, calves
and sheep, innumerable garden displays (classical and modern), and the
hut of a woodcarver with the woodcarver at work, as well as over a
hundred sculptures dotted around the landscaped grounds amongst the
company stands. In Liverpool there were forty sponsored theme gardens and twenty international gardens amongst the sculpture and company stands, all laid out in a way that Brian Hatton has described as
Paxtonian: meandering paths, serendipitous views and artificial mounds
are used in order to create a maximalisation of visual variety in a confined
space.[14] Glasgow likewise, through the themes of water and the mari-
time, recreation and sport, health and well-being, plants and food,
science and technology, land and scenery, presented a vision of variety in
confinement along the banks of the Clyde.

Now of course these nineteenth-century techniques of adapting
picturesque techniques to confined urban spaces are not peculiar to the
environmental design and architecture of the eighties. Something similar
was espoused in the Festival of Britain. Then it was called *sharawaggi*
(Chinese for 'graceful disorder'). 'Adaptability to site and sympathetic
tolerance to extension and addition were desirable attributes at a time of
contingency building and economies of space.'[15] *Sharawaggi*, in short, was
picturesqueness adapted to utility. The *sharawaggi* of the garden festivals,
though, is of a very different character. Where the Festival of Britain, and
the cultural and economic Keynesianism of the fifties and sixties
generally sought to adapt modernism to the picturesque within the
realm of an integrated social environmentalism, the politics of the garden festivals use the picturesque to undermine the public sphere as a
place of shared cultural values and provision. As Hatton says, the heterogeneity of the Liverpool Garden Festival is 'merely the eclectic universality of countless individual, private consumer selections; the public
realm is implicitly, simply, a neutral infrastructure, like a set of ground
rules for athletics'. In a sense all the value systems that capitalism has

split apart and that the Festival of Britain sought to integrate through 'good design' – nature and production, the aesthetic and the moral, the public and private, economics and politics – are presented as reconcilable only through personal life-style and consumer choice; hence the integrative emphasis on *gardens* as traditional sources of personal retreat. Which is why the overriding feature of all the festivals, particularly Stoke, is a sense of mourning: that the rational projections of the modern past are not just myths but violent and degrading impositions, and that all there remains by way of progress is a defence of the integrity of one's own back garden, so to speak.

In these terms the festivals work on two levels in tension. On the one hand they serve quite obviously as economic palliatives as part of the Tories' reconstitution of the bourgeois nationalist project, but on the other, in the face of the crisis of environmental modernism, they genuinely serve to engage with a set of values and aspirations that stand to re-enchant a massively routinised everyday capitalist lifeworld. There is a strong sense that in the plural reality of fragmentation and heterogeneity there is an expression of values that go towards critiquing the instrumentalities of capitalist production as such. Thus we might speak of a certain kind of 'corrective vision' in the festivals' images and words. Although the environmental displays at Stoke failed to mention the high unemployment in the area and the fallen social fabric of the North itself, there was a general feeling of sanguinity that the environmental problems of industrialisation that affected Stoke so badly from the eighteenth century to the beginning of this century – life expectancy in the pottery industry was around forty-five – was over. One man interviewed for the land reclamation video said things had definitely improved: his flowers no longer suffered from black spots because there were no longer excessive amounts of sulphur in the air. The 'other', 'progressive' side of the garden festivals lies, therefore, in their regenerative aspects; in the way the aesthetic, the moral and social are linked to a critique of environmental modernism's brutalisation of nature. Thus the themes of ecology and environmentalism may be framed and regulated within spaces of display that are conservative, but the meanings people re-create from such events cannot be assumed in advance. As Patrick Wright has said in *On living in an old country*, which looks at the integration of the cultural spectacle into the formation of the British national past, such public events also provide 'positive energies, which certainly can't be written off as ideology'.[16]

Nevertheless we should not make out the festivals to be innocent in spirit. On the contrary they represent the continuing denigration of the public sphere under late capitalism as a place where we might encounter history on an active basis. The garden festivals' mixture of parkland, open-air museum and trade fair fits comfortably into the burgeoning area of consumerist 'ethnohistory' or the Heritage Industry.

One of the most striking developments within the museum/leisure sector in the West over the last twenty years or so is the extension of notions of 'tradition' to include the artefacts of working-class and peasant culture as of value in themselves. This has developed in the form of numerous museums and theme-parks that deal with 'ways of life'. As Philippe Hoyau has pointed out, this 'open history' tends to cohere around three major models: the family (the dwelling, customs, domestic production), human conviviality (community life, festivals, production) and the spirit of a place (language, architecture, cultural identity).[17] What is involved in this process though, he says, is not simply an older bourgeois pastoralist dream of the 'good society', but an 'opportunity to renew the public's commitment to the political sphere and give fresh stimulus to local and regional allegiances; the leaders of a certain "soft" socialism are already working towards this goal, as are the uncritical advocates of a decentralized, self-governing 'ecological' society, which will somehow take over "from below" at the end of the "crisis".'[18]

If this is an apt description of the green consumerism of the garden festivals it also hints at why the formats of bourgeois nationalist representation have of necessity had to change over the last twenty years. It is perhaps worth reminding ourselves that by 1939 only a small number of the advanced capitalist countries had a democratic government. Things changed dramatically with the war. Both defeated and victorious bourgeoisies rallied to democracy following the experience of fascism. Democracy became something to be defended rather than attacked as inviting social anarchy. Thus it is with the post-war advance of the European working class that we see developing – in a hegemonic fashion – a bourgeois-led notion of a new democratic community. The Festival of Britain is perhaps the first major cultural expression of this new 'open history' in Britain. The changing agendas of the new museums therefore need to be seen in terms of how bourgeois nationalist representation continually adapts to class struggle through the severance of notions of community from collective and political life. Consequently the garden festivals may be opposed to the Keynesian dictates of the Festival of Britain, but their political logic within the framework of bourgeois nationalist representation remains the same.

'Decentralisation', 'ecological self-governance', 'post-industrialism' are the new bourgeois myths of community and democracy.

The garden festivals are perfect illustrations of the native forces of late capitalism: the control and displacement of economic crisis through forms of affective cultural identification. By symbolising the transformation of Stoke, Liverpool and Glasgow from dark and ugly manufacturing centres into 'truly' green and pleasant landscapes – to quote one of the commercial brochures – the privatised form of this process is given a stable and evolutionary character. However, the equitableness of this 'greening' couldn't be further from the truth given the ferociously competitive nature of international capital today. The garden festivals may be elaborate shop-windows for local governments to attract private capital to their areas, but the net effect is that the local governments of Stoke, Liverpool and Glasgow are competing with one another to attract a relatively small number of mobile firms. Moreover, these firms as part of the new cultural/leisure service industries are incapable of promoting industrial regeneration in economies now dominated by multinational enterprises; most services anyway are not internationally tradeable.[19] The garden festivals then may temporally 'enhance and humanise'[20] the local environment, but their economic projections do not touch the structural realities of British capitalism's crisis of profitability. They can only mask them.

# Notes

1  See for example Göran Therborn, *What does the ruling class do when it rules?* (NLB, 1978).
2  See in particular Donald Horne, *The great museum* (Pluto, 1984).
3  Nigel Harris, *The end of the Third World, newly industrializing countries and the decline of an ideology* (Penguin, 1987).
4  See Owen Gavin and Andy Lowe, 'Designing desire – planning, power and the festival of Britain', *Block* 11 (winter 1985/86).
5  See Pete Green, 'British capitalism and the Thatcher years', *International Socialism*, 35 (summer 1987).
6  Richard Cork, 'Interview with George Mulvagh', in *Art in the garden: installations, Glasgow Garden Festival* (Graeme Murray, 1988), p. 12.
7  Green, 'British capitalism'.
8  'Modernity – an incomplete project', in Hal Foster, ed., *The anti-aesthetic: essays on postmodern culture* (Bay Press, 1983).
9  *English culture and the decline of the industrial spirit 1850–1980* (Cambridge University Press, 1981).
10  For an overview of the recent literature see Steven Pinch, *Cities and services: the geography of collective consumption* (Routledge & Kegan Paul, 1985).
11  See Bob Jessop, Kevin Bonnett, Simon Bromley and Tom Ling, 'Authoritarian populism, two nations, and Thatcherism', *New Left Review*, 147: 'We believe that Thatcherism can fruitfully be seen as a 'two nations' project' (p. 50).

12  See James Turner, *The politics of landscape* (Basil Blackwell, 1979).

13  Methuen, 1927, p. 181.

14  'Blooms from the blackstuff', *Building Design* (August 1984).

15  Barry Curtis, 'One continuous interwoven story (The Festival of Britain)', *Block 11* (winter 1985/86), p. 52.

16  *On living in an old country* (Verso, 1985), p. 78.

17  'Heritage and "the conserver society"; the French case', in Robert Lumley, ed., *The museum time-machine* (Comedia/Routledge, 1988).

18  *Ibid.*, p. 32.

19  Green, 'British capitalism'.

20  Isabel Vasseur, 'Preface' to *Art in the garden*, p. 8.